Discord, Dialogue,
and Concord

Discord, Dialogue, and Concord

Studies in the Lutheran Reformation's Formula of Concord

edited by Lewis W. Spitz and Wenzel Lohff

with contributions by

Lewis W. Spitz
Ekkehard Muehlenberg
Robert C. Schultz
Ralph W. Quere
Oliver K. Olson
Robert D. Preus
Robert P. Scharlemann

Manfred P. Fleischer
Trygve R. Skarsten
W. Brown Patterson
W. Robert Godfrey
Jill Raitt
James J. Megivern

FORTRESS PRESS Philadelphia

This publication is made possible by a grant from The Center for Reformation Research, St. Louis, Missouri.

Library of Congress Cataloging in Publication Data
Main entry under title:

Discord, dialogue, and concord.

    1.   Lutheran Church.   Formula of concord—Addresses, essays, lectures. I. Spitz, Lewis William, 1922–
II. Lohff, Wenzel.
BX8069.4.D57   238′.4′1   77-78644
ISBN 0–8006–0511–X

6443E77   Printed in the United States of America   1–511

Contents

I. THEOLOGICAL ESSAYS
Key Issues for the Life of the Church

Contents

II. HISTORICAL ESSAYS
The Response to the Formula of Concord

CONTENTS OF THE GERMAN COMPANION VOLUME

Contents

CONTRIBUTORS

Lewis W. Spitz, Stanford University, Stanford, California

Ekkehard Muehlenberg, School of Theology at Claremont, California

Robert C. Schultz, Lutheran Theological Southern Seminary, Columbia, South Carolina

Ralph W. Quere, Wartburg Theological Seminary, Dubuque, Iowa

Oliver K. Olson, The Lutheran Theological Seminary at Philadelphia

Robert D. Preus, Concordia Theological Seminary, Fort Wayne, Indiana

Robert P. Scharlemann, School of Religion, The University of Iowa, Iowa City

Manfred P. Fleischer, University of California, Davis

Trygve R. Skarsten, Lutheran Theological Seminary, Columbus, Ohio

W. Brown Patterson, Davidson College, Davidson, North Carolina

W. Robert Godfrey, Westminster Theological Seminary, Glenside, Pennsylvania

Jill Raitt, The Divinity School, Duke University, Durham, North Carolina

James J. Megivern, University of North Carolina, Wilmington

ACKNOWLEDGMENTS

A word of appreciation is in order to a number of people whose good will and assistance have made the publication of this work possible. Dr. Robert Kolb, director of the Center for Reformation Research, St. Louis, first conceived the plan for a two-volume *Festschrift* commemorating the four hundredth anniversary of the Formula of Concord and has continued to encourage the editors in this undertaking. The Evangelical Church in Germany, through a substantial subvention to the Center, made possible the publication of both the English and the German volumes. The arrangements were made through the good offices of Dr. Franklin Littell of Temple University. Mrs. Elaine Rosin and Ms. Bonnie Payne assisted with the correspondence and in preparing the typescript. Dr. Edna Spitz eased the burdens of reading proof on the manuscript and galleys. A word of thanks is also due to Dean Halsey Royden of Stanford University, for relieving me of administrative duties for a semester in order to facilitate the editorial work on this volume. My colleague Prof. Wenzel Lohff, who has assumed primary responsibility for the German counterpart of this volume, has been most helpful and cooperative in planning both volumes and seeing them through to publication.

Stanford University LEWIS W. SPITZ
Spring 1977

Foreword

For generations the interest in pursuing the theological terrain opened up by the reformers has overshadowed interest in the Formula of Concord. One has only to survey the published technical literature dealing with this area of study to substantiate this observation. Most Lutheran clergymen subscribe to the Lutheran confessions, but apart from Luther's catechisms and the Augsburg Confession, the confessional books are neglected.

From the very outset the Formula of Concord was concerned with the theological controversy and was not "received" by the churches in every area and territory. But by its clarification of doctrine the Formula of Concord created a new consensus, and, at the same time, also occasioned further points of delineation and disputes.

There can be no doubt that it was the Formula of Concord which first gave shape and form to the churches of the Lutheran Reformation and thereby won for itself a place in history. The remark about one of the Formula's major contributors, Martin Chemnitz, demonstrates that it was in this way that the Formula was regarded in its own day: *"Si Martinus* (Chemnitz) *non fuisset, Martinus* (Luther) *vix stetisset* (If it had not been for Chemnitz, Luther's work would scarcely have stood)."

So then, we rejoice that the four hundredth anniversary of the Formula of Concord has given occasion for a significant number of scholars in the United States and in the Federal Republic of Germany to join forces in publishing special studies on the origin, significance, and effect of the process of formulating confessions and the resolution of doctrinal questions, particularly with respect to the Formula of Concord. For this reason we have deemed it appropriate to publish the collected American and German studies in two separate but simultaneous volumes. The American studies are being published by Fortress Press in

Philadelphia under the title *Discord, Dialogue, and Concord,* and the contents of that volume are included in the Table of Contents to the German companion volume. The German studies are being published by Calwer Verlag in Stuttgart under the title *Widerspruch, Dialog und Einigung,* and the contents of that volume are included in the Tables of Contents to the American companion volume.

The development of the ecclesiastical forms taken on by the Reformation churches and the Formula of Concord which was written in the midst of that development confront us with such a complicated, multisided process that it is admittedly very difficult to grasp even the earliest stages of the Formula discernible in a wide range of proposals and objections proposed by the various regions and schools of that day. We are quite aware that our studies in the area of the development and ultimately the confessional determination of Reformation doctrine can only point out a variety of details and aspects. These studies clearly show that in the Reformation churches confession of the faith represented not a collecting of and commenting on doctrinal points and statements, but an all-embracing life event (Apology to the Augsburg Confession, 4).

We are grateful to the church bodies which made possible the publication of this volume. We are also grateful to colleagues who teach in various institutions of learning or function in positions of church administration. Through their contributions to these volumes they have given testimony to the living significance of confession and concord. In an age in which Christians yearn for a fellowship which extends beyond denominational lines, the Lutheran Formula of Concord with its strengths and weaknesses may possibly be helpful in our quest for that which unites and holds us in faith.

WENZEL LOHFF
LEWIS W. SPITZ

ABBREVIATIONS

BC   *The Book of Concord, The Confessions of the Evangelical Lutheran Church,* trans. and ed. Theodore G. Tappert (Philadelphia: Fortress Press, 1959).

      AC   Augsburg Confession
      Apol.   Apology of the Augsburg Confession
      SA   Smalcald Articles
      LC   Large Catechism
      FC   Formula of Concord
           Epit.   Epitome
           SD   Solid Declaration

BK   *Die Bekenntnisschriften der evangelisch-lutherischen Kirche,* 4th ed. rev. (Göttingen: Vandenhoeck & Ruprecht, 1959).

CR   *Corpus Reformatorum* (Brunsvigae: C. A. Schwetschke et Filium, 1834–60).

CORR.   Theodore Beza, *Correspondance de Theodore de Beza,* ed. M. Meylan, A. Dufour, C. Chimelli, and M. Turchetti (Geneva: Libraire Droz, 1973).

LW   *Luther's Works,* American edition, ed. Helmut T. Lehmann and Jaroslav Pelikan (Philadelphia: Fortress Press; St. Louis: Concordia Publishing House, 1951–).

M 55   *Melanchthon on Christian Doctrine: Loci Communes, 1955,* trans. Clyde L. Manschreck (New York: Oxford University Press, 1965).

MW   *Melanchthons Werke in Auswahl,* ed. Robert Stupperich (Gütersloh: C. Bertelsmann Verlag/Gütersloher Verlagshaus Gerd Mohn, 1951–75).

Reg.   *Registres de la Compagnie des Pasteurs de Genève, 1565–74,* ed. Fatio and Labarthe (Geneva: Libraire Droz, 1969).

WA   *D. Martin Luthers Werke.* Kritische Gesamtausgabe (Weimar, 1883–).

Introduction:

The Formula of Concord Then and Now

Lewis W. Spitz

Four centuries have passed since the first signatures were affixed to the Formula of Concord of 1577, the last of the classic confessions in the heroic age of Lutheranism. "Taking heed to the doctrine" (1 Tim. 4:16), Protestants have routinely commemorated ecclesiastical confessions, sometimes in a sentimental, partisan, or monumental way, but increasingly in a reflective analytical mood. Students of historical theology have described and summarized the theology of the Lutheran confessions with such thoroughness that yet another volume of that kind on this occasion would be a work of supererogation.[1] The celebration of the *Book of Concord* in 1980 would in any event seem to be a more appropriate time for such a holistic treatment. The present volume will take a different and independent approach.

Christianity has lived by confession of faith, for "many that believed came, and confessed, and showed their deeds" (Acts 19:18). From Luther's brave stand at Worms, which the English historian Froude described as the finest scene in human history, the evangelical move-

---

1. The bibliography on the confessions, extending from Leonard Hutter's *Libri Christianae Concordiae: Symboli ecclesiarum Gnesios Lutheranarum* (Wittenberg, 1609) to the present, is enormous. An introduction to the literature is provided in Edmund Schlink, *Theology of the Lutheran Confessions* (Philadelphia: Fortress Press, 1961), pp. 318–44. Holsten Fagerberg, *A New Look at the Lutheran Confessions (1529–1537)* (St. Louis: Concordia Publishing House, 1972), is limited to the earlier documents written by Luther and Melanchthon. Just as it is difficult to understand the Apology without a knowledge of the Catholic *Confutatio Augustanae Confessionis*, so it is impossible to comprehend the asymmetrical thrusts of the Formula of Concord without a knowledge of the controversial developments between 1537 and 1577 within Lutheranism, a reason for paying special attention to the Formula of Concord. An admirable recent *Festschrift* for a confession is Joachim Staedtke, ed., *Glauben und Bekennen. Vierhundert Jahre Confessio Helveticus posterior. Beiträge zu ihrer Geschichte und Theologie* (Zurich: Zwingli Verlag, 1966).

ment intensified the confessional aspect of Christian life, linking profession of allegiance to the person of Christ with a biblical understanding of that relationship. Profession of faith and confession of the creed were joined historically in the Lutheran movement. The Formula of Concord, too, couples teaching of truth with defense against error (*Lehre und Wehre*), offering thetical statements introduced with a ritualistic "we believe, teach, and confess" and antithetical statements introduced by a formalistic "we reject and condemn."[2] This concern of the Formula of Concord with controverted points of doctrine underlines the wisdom of its incorporation into the *Book of Concord* which included the ancient ecumenical creeds and the *Augustana*.

There is a strange phenomenon operative in church history with respect to the relation of credal statements or dogmatic earnestness and the reality of ecclesiastical control. Where hierarchical governance or domination is relatively secure and effective, wide latitude of religious experience and theological speculation is allowed. When ecclesiastical governance is weak, authority decentralized or congregationalized, and cohesion depends upon voluntary association, church bodies have tended toward strong credal statements and doctrinal conformity. Witness the Catholic Church, the latitude of opinion allowed in the secure medieval period, and the narrowness of Trent once papal power was shaken. Contrast the clerical strength of the Episcopal or Methodist churches with concomitant doctrinal permissiveness and the loose association of Southern Baptists with their strong emphasis on credal fundamentals. Or compare the power of the ministerium in eastern nineteenth century American Lutheranism which tolerated Samuel S. Schmucker's *Definite Platform*. In this the president of the General Synod's Seminary called for a revision of central articles of the Augsburg Confession, and the dispersed authority of the Evangelical Lutheran Synod of Missouri, Ohio, and other states, guaranteeing congregational supremacy in its famous constitutional article seven, but with a powerful emphasis under the leadership of C. F. W. Walther upon loyalty to the Lutheran confessions *quia* rather than merely *quatenus*. One can doubtless cite exceptions to this general rule, especially in American Lutheran church history, which, for example, has seen Congregationalism suffer nearly complete doctrinal disintegra-

---

2. Cf. Hans-Werner Gensichen, *We Condemn: How Luther and 16th-Century Lutheranism Condemned False Doctrine* (St. Louis: Concordia Publishing House, 1967).

tion. But that, one might argue, was the price paid for an intimate involvement in the process of Americanization; most ethnic church bodies have not experienced comparable involvement until recent times. In the sixteenth century the confessions provided a focal point for allegiance and supplied a cohesive force which spared Protestantism from complete ideological disintegration.

Emperor Charles V, who had observed the controversies within Lutheranism as well as the debacle of his own Roman Catholic Church, commented sardonically, "How absurd to try to make two men think alike on matters of religion, when I cannot make two timepieces agree!" The problem of authority has quite rightly been called the Achilles heel of Protestantism. Luther's personal appeal to conscience and to *ratio evidens* at Worms, before the diet and again later in the presence of the mediating archbishop of Trier, posed the problem of subjectivity. Through the years he asked himself, *"Nam tu solus sapis?"* He found comfort in the thought that he was not alone, but in the company of prophets, evangelists, apostles, and of fathers and brothers, from Augustine and Bernard to Johannes Tauler and Philipp Melanchthon. His conscience was "captive to the Word of God," and his teaching corresponded to a sound tradition within the church.

Given his volcanic temperament and his personal religious struggle, Luther was not cut out to be a systematician, as his uninspired commentary on the Nicene Creed suggests. Yet his personal contributions to the confessional canon, the catechisms, and the Smalcald Articles were simple, forceful, and unambiguous statements of evangelical essentials. Still within his own lifetime, beginning already in his Wartburg months, deviationism set in even among his Wittenberg brethren.[3] Père Daniel Olivier, distinguished ecumenical Catholic Reformation scholar, argues that Luther's formula of justification by faith was basically unstable and could be held together only by a man of his unusual intelligence, religious experience, and theological background. Already during his own lifetime the formula of justification by faith was distorted in three directions: legalism, the intrusion of synergism, and antinomianism. After Luther's death heresies sprang up as though from dragon's teeth; some of them were even expounded in his name. Of course, St. Paul and St. Augustine had suffered the same fate with their theological formulations, so in this respect Luther was not alone.

3. See the perceptive account by Mark U. Edwards, *Luther and the False Brethren* (Stanford: Stanford University Press, 1975).

In part there was the usual problem with epigoni who lack the master's brilliance. One can only feel bemused at human limitations when one observes Amsdorf's exaggeration about good works being harmful to salvation, Osiander's strutting as he rejected the forensic sense of justification, or the hero of the Gnesio-Lutherans, Flacius Illyricus, declaring man's very substance to be sin (although he distinguished *substantia materialis* and *substantia formalis,* and really meant the latter, but refused to clarify his statement). Was it then already a case of the German tendency to exaggerate? "Hoeschel," Julius Caesar Scaliger once commented, "though a Lutheran, is a learned man." The urbane French historian Michelet once defined theology as the art of befuddling oneself systematically. Historians have found the theological wrangling of the decades following the death of Luther, the trauma of the Interims, and the Peace of Augsburg, 1555, such a dismal scene that they quite mistakenly created the historical myth that Lutheranism had lost its vigor, with the torch snatched and carried forward by the Calvinists.

Lutheranism continued to be rigorous and expansive during the second half of the sixteenth century. Although most Lutheran lands were Lutheran in name prior to the Peace of Augsburg, the Reformation had been an urban phenomenon. Only with the education of thousands of ministers in the Lutheran theological schools could the country parishes in so vast an area be recast in an evangelical mode. Several of the largest states such as Prussia and Sweden were satisfactorily reorganized only in the latter half of the century. The Lutherans were consolidating their territories up until the outbreak of the Thirty Years' War. As late as 1598 the city of Strasbourg became Lutheran and accepted the Formula of Concord. The Palatinate itself, which had Calvinist presbyteries from 1570 on and became the center of the Reformed churches in Germany, became Lutheran for the seven years after 1576. The tumult and the shouting, vehemence and acrimony, the abuse and heated emotions of the doctrinal controversies bore negative witness to the fact that Lutherans cared and were very much alive and energetic.

Protestantism has always carried with it a potential for total organizational disintegration. With the proliferation of sects in the sixteenth, as in the nineteenth and twentieth centuries, Protestantism has resembled nothing so much as a banyan tree. Yet the fact that 90 percent of Protestantism's adherents are members of a relatively few major church bodies is phenomenal. Such cohesion in lieu of a supreme ecclesiastical authority insuring unity can be explained historically by three factors: the domination of the church by the political powers which insisted upon religious uniformity for the good of the state; the fact that while ideas make for change in history, institutions make for stability, which gives long-term advantage to organization over individualism; and, finally, by the general adherence to the major confessions. Among these major confessions the Formula of Concord holds an honored place.

As its name suggests, the Formula of Concord grew out of sincere desire for peace and unity. It sought to be faithful to the ecumenical creeds, to Luther's evangel, and to the normative Augsburg Confession of 1530. It undertook to define doctrine on the basis of the Scriptures as the only rule and norm in order to correct error and end controversy. Lutheranism was satiated with the doctrinal controversies which had raged so long between the two camps of the Gnesio-Lutherans and the Philippists. "Religious contention is the devil's harvest," observed La Fontaine. "The itch of disputing is the scab of the churches," wrote Sir Henry Wotton in *A Panegyric to King Charles*. Lutherans, too, had endured enough, and support for a centrist position grew stronger. Princes and theologians took steps to bridge the chasm that had become even wider and was revealed to all at the Colloquy of Worms in 1557. That such high matters were not for secular princes to resolve became evident at the meetings of the princes at Frankfurt on the Main, 1558, and Naumburg, 1561. It was time for constructive and pacific theologians, with the moral and financial support of Christian princes, to undertake the blessed task of peacemakers.

The story of the origin of the Formula of Concord has been told so often and so well that only a brief summary is needed here for the uninitiated.[4] Two men of quite different background were the progenitors and principal authors of the Formula, Jacob Andreae and Martin

---

4. On the origins of the Formula of Concord, see the excellent new popular introduction by Eugene F. Klug and Otto F. Stahlke, *Getting into the Formula of Concord. A History and Digest of the Formula* (St. Louis: Concordia Publishing House, 1977), with a translation of the Epitome; *Die Bekenntnisschriften der evangelisch-lutherischen Kirche herausgegeben im Gedenkjahr der Augsburgischen Konfession 1930*, 5th edition (Göttingen: Vandenhoeck & Ruprecht, 1963), *Einleitung*, pp. xxxii–xliv; *The Book of Concord, The Confessions of the Evangelical Lutheran Church*, trans. and ed. Theodore G. Tappert (Philadelphia: Fortress Press, 1959), pp. 463–64; F. Bente, *Historical Introductions to the Book of Concord* (St. Louis: Concordia Publishing House, 1965), based on the 1921 edition of the *Concordia Triglotta;* Willard Dow Allbeck, *Studies in the Lutheran Confessions* (Philadelphia: Fortress Press, 1952), pp. 239–53.

Chemnitz, "the second Martin." All six signators were members of the center party, but a homogeneous group they were not, either in personality or in terms of their early theological backgrounds and influences. Andreae had come under the formative influence of Johannes Brenz and Württemberg Lutheranism. Chemnitz, Nicholas Selnecker, the third member of the original triumvirate, and David Chytraeus had Melanchthon as their teacher. Andreas Musculus and Christopher Koerner were of a lesser influence on the Formula. But they were all united in their loyalty to the authentic Reformation tradition and sought to be true to Luther's evangelical message and to the Melanchthon of the Augsburg Confession and Apology.[5] Despite striking differences in their personalities, and even a deep personal dislike for the mercurial Andreae, they worked together for the common cause.[6]

Jacob Andreae, for whom the cause of Lutheran unity became his life's vocation, in 1568 proposed a "Confession and Brief Explanation of Certain Disputed Articles," and in 1573 he enlarged upon these five articles in his *Six Christian Sermons, on the Divisions . . . among the Theologians of the Augsburg Confession. . . . How a Simple Pastor and a Common Christian Layman Should Deal with Them on the Basis of His Catechism.*[7] These sermons on the righteousness of faith in God's sight, on good works, on original sin and free will, on church usages and adiaphora, on the proper distinction of law and gospel and the third use of the law for the regenerate, and on the person and majesty of Christ became the nucleus of a number of confessional statements leading up to the Formula of Concord, the Swabian Concord of 1573,

5. On the importance of Luther also for the Formula of Concord, see the chapter by Arthur Carl Piepkorn, "The Lutheran Symbolical Books and Luther," in Carl S. Meyer, ed., *Luther for an Ecumenical Age* (St. Louis: Concordia Publishing House, 1967), pp. 242–70. The attempt to pit vital reformers against dead creeds is a popular parlor game these days especially among existential theologians; cf., for example, Holmes Rolston III, *John Calvin versus the Westminster Confession* (Richmond, Virginia: John Knox Press, 1972).

6. Theodore R. Jungkuntz, *Formulators of the Formula of Concord. Four Architects of Lutheran Unity* (St. Louis: Concordia Publishing House, 1977), provides striking portraits of the four key authors of the Formula, combining perceptive psychological insights with religious and intellectual analysis. Of special human interest is the section "Selnecker's Diary on Andreae's Behavior," pp. 146–54. On Chemnitz, see also E. F. Klug, *From Luther to Chemnitz on Scripture and the Word* (Grand Rapids, Mich.: William B. Eerdmans Publishing Company, 1971), pp. 115–42.

7. See the translation of the *Sermons* and the excellent scholarly introduction and notes by Robert Kolb, *Andreae and the Formula of Concord. Six Sermons on the Way to Lutheran Unity* (St. Louis: Concordia Publishing House, 1977).

6

the Swabian-Saxon Concord of 1575, and the Maulbronn Formula. When the crypto-Calvinists in Wittenberg were exposed due to the discovery of the indiscreet Peucer letter, Elector Augustus of Saxony dropped his support of the Philippists and joined the unification movement. Late in the spring of 1576 he convoked a conference of theologians in Torgau. They combined the Swabian-Saxon Concord and the Maulbronn Formula into the Torgau Book, which Andreae then summarized in the Epitome, which made up the first part of the Formula of Concord. The triumvirate, as Chytraeus called them in 1581, Andreae, Chemnitz, and Selnecker, on the elector's order, met on March 1, 1577, at the Monastery of Bergen, near Magdeburg, to consider all the briefs and criticisms received from all over Lutheran Germany, and to edit the new confession. They finished on March 14, and later a final revision took place in May with all six signators present. On May 28, 1577, the revised form of the confession was presented to the elector. It was known as the Bergic Book, or the Solid Declaration, or the Formula of Concord, or the Book of Concord, a title later reserved for the complete collection of Lutheran confessions publicly presented on June 25, 1580, exactly fifty years after the presentation of the Augsburg Confession before the Emperor Charles V and the diet in 1530. Andreae and Chemnitz added as an appendix a *Catalog of Testimonies* to support by citations from the Fathers the correctness of Article VII on the communication of attributes and the majesty of Christ's human nature. The Solid Declaration was subscribed to by the electors of Saxony, Brandenburg, and the Palatinate, by 20 dukes and princes, 24 counts, 4 barons, 35 imperial cities, and 8,188 theologians, ministers, and teachers. Two-thirds of all the Lutheran territories of Germany adopted the Formula of Concord as a reaffirmation of genuine Lutheranism, for as the Preface to the Formula put it: "We . . . have wished, in this work of concord, in no way to devise anything new."

The confessions of the Christian church have never sought to exhaust divine truth and infinite wisdom through the agency of human language. They have sought to state as clearly as is humanly possible propositions which would, by affirmation or rejection, rule out certain human doctrinal abbreviations which were not compatible with what can be known of divine truth from the Scriptures, also given in human language. Every article in the Formula of Concord is concerned with the issues of a major controversy within Lutheranism. Article I on Original Sin responds to the Flacian controversy; Article II on Free

Will to the synergistic controversy; Article III on Righteousness of Faith before God to the Osiandrian and Stancarian controversy; Article IV on Good Works to the Majoristic controversy; Article V on Law and Gospel to the Antinomian controversy; Article VI on the Third Use of the Law to the Antinomian controversy; Article VII on the Lord's Supper and Article VIII on the Person of Christ to the crypto-Calvinistic controversy; Article IX on the Descent of Christ to Hell to the Aepinus debate; Article X on Church Rites to the adiaphoristic controversy growing out of the Interim situation; Article XI on God's Eternal Foreknowledge and Election to the Marbach-Zanchi dispute; and Article XII on Other Heresies and Sects in response to the Anabaptists, Schwenkfelder, and other sectaries. But despite the polemical and apologetic purposes, the Formula remained evangelical and confessional in the positive sense and breathes a pacific spirit. The great nineteenth century church historian Philip Schaff paid the Formula this tribute: "It sums up the results of the theological controversies of a whole generation with great learning, ability, discrimination, acumen, and, we may add, with comparative moderation."[8]

Certainly a confession of such interior strength, which has had such an impact upon the history of the church, merits more than a bland or innocuous monument to piety. It deserves to be taken more seriously as a challenge to contemporaries, some sympathetic, others in a critical position or in a tradition outside Lutheranism. For balance, six of the essays in this volume are theological in nature, dealing with key issues for the life of the church, and six are historical essays, recording the response to the Formula in Silesia and Scandinavia and the Anglican, Dutch Calvinist, French Reformed, and Catholic reactions to it. With the first four theological essays dealing with the issues of specific articles this volume reverts to the very oldest presentation of

8. Philip Schaff, *The Creeds of Christendom* (New York: Harper and Brothers, 1899), 1:338; Allbeck, *Studies,* pp. 291, 242–44; Klug and Stahlke, *Getting into the Formula of Concord,* pp. 14–15. In recent years we have been favored with excellent English editions of major writings by the authors of the Formula of Concord, many bearing on doctrinal issues covered in the confession, notably Martin Chemnitz, *The Two Natures of Christ* (St. Louis: Concordia Publishing House, 1971), trans. J. A. O. Preus; Martin Chemnitz, *Examination of the Council of Trent,* part I (St. Louis: Concordia Publishing House, 1971), trans. Fred Kramer; David Chytraeus, *On Sacrifice* (St. Louis: Concordia Publishing House, 1962), trans. John Warwick Montgomery; *The Doctrine of Man in Classical Lutheran Theology,* trans. from the works of Martin Chemnitz and John Gerhard, ed. Herman A. Preus and Edmund Smits (Minneapolis: Augsburg Publishing House, 1962).

the theology of the confessions when scholars undertook the analyses of the confessions article by article. Thus J. B. Carpzov, the "father of symbolics," went through the whole Formula of Concord in a rigidly schematic manner in his *Isagoge in libros ecclesiarum lutheranum symbolicos* (1665, 1675). The results from the thought and pens of our present authors are quite far removed from those of Carpzov.

Professor Muehlenberg, whose chapter on *"Synergia* and Justification by Faith" focuses on Article II and indirectly on Article I, has great difficulty coping with the paradox of the monergysm of divine grace in human conversion as presented in the Formula and finds "not just paradoxes of faith but contradictions in the Formula's logic." "I will not conceal my intention," he writes, "of showing that the rejection of synergism as well as the consequences implied by it is one-sided." Contrary to the traditional view that the Formula did not mark a posthumous triumph of Flacius and indeed condemned Flacius's view of man's substance and original sin, Muehlenberg sees a subordination of the grace/faith issue to the predominant importance of original sin. It hardly behooves the editor to debate the issue with the contributor, but the reader may well enjoy a round with him.

After surveying the changing modalities in views of original sin, Professor Schultz, whose chapter centers on Article I, makes the rather bold proposal that the church consciously and deliberately choose the path of pluralism in its theological formulations and invite polymorphous approaches to the doctrine of original sin. One might wonder how an open-systems approach to theology can avoid an all-engulfing relativism, but in wondering the reader will be led to reflect more deeply on the affirmations of the first article.

Professor Quere offers a revisionist view of the traditional explanation of the eucharistic controversy which eventuated in Articles VII and VIII. The consensus has been that the Formula represented Luther's position against that of Melanchthon as a proto- or crypto-Calvinist, Quere contends, and that Melanchthonism was put down in the Formula. Quere argues, however, that numerous Melanchthonian motifs made their way into the Formula also in the controverted eucharistic doctrines, a subtle thesis.

Professor Olson, a Flacius expert keenly interested in liturgical questions, directs his attention to Article X, and sees its political importance in the fact that it makes a decisive judgment on the rival arguments of Wittenberg and Magdeburg on the question of resistance to tyranny. The Wittenbergers held that resistance was optional, a matter of Christian liberty, whereas the Magdeburgers insisted that resistance was obligatory, and the decision was in favor of Magdeburg. The Formula of Concord in this article favored political action and liturgical order, Olson concludes, and today Lutherans must pay a good deal more attention to the specific basis of human government.

Professor Preus, the author of a solid and important work on the theology of post-Reformation Lutheranism, offers a surprising discovery which revises one of the old assumptions about the Formula's place in Protestant thought.[9] It did not serve as a confessional halfway house between Luther and Melanchthon and the so-called scholastic orthodox theologians. On the contrary, Preus reports, the orthodox theologians related directly to the Augsburg Confession and virtually ignored the Formula of Concord.

The most radical questioning of the role of an ecclesiastical confession, be it the Formula of Concord then or the Barmen declaration now, is that of Professor Scharlemann, who asks whether a confessional theology can ever be *true* or whether, on the contrary, truth can be attained only from the standpoint of *scientia*. He wrestles with the problem in the context of the question of truth and certainty over against the question of truth and distinction. Assertions made as a matter of confession seem incapable of surviving a critical scrutiny of whether they are true, he asserts, and he traces the development from Scripture-based orthodoxy through idealism, Schleiermacher, Barth, and Daub. *Confessio* is a living act, without truth; *scientia* has truth, without life. Moreover, the author charges, making a confession may solidify one group but it separates itself from other groups who declare the same faith. Confession accordingly produces a difference between two sides, but it loses the identity that might enable it to be true because the issuance of the confession divides one faith into two distinct beliefs. These challenging theses certainly will not remain unchallenged, particularly by confessionalists who believe in the power of language as the best available tool for expressing truth and who

---

9. Robert D. Preus, *The Theology of Post-Reformation Lutheranism,* 2 vols. (St. Louis: Concordia Publishing House, 1970, 1972). A caricature of the old cliché is to be found in the essay of the Marxist historian Leo Stern, "Probleme der Reformation im Spiegel ihrer Jubiläen," in *450 Jahre Reformation,* ed. Leo Stern and Max Steinmetz (Berlin: VEB Deutscher Verlag der Wissenschaften, 1967), p. 25: "The rigidity of Lutheran Orthodoxy, which found its first expression in the *Formula Concordiae* of 1577 and was later deepened dogmatically by John Gerhard, Martin Chemnitz, and Leonhard Hutter, arose out of the determined protest against Rome. . . ."

view a confession as a clarifying first step toward a unity based on mutual understanding. Scharlemann's essay is calculated to stimulate a lively debate about basic theological assumptions.

The six historians offer a lively dialogue between the past and the present, then and now. Professor Fleischer recounts the reception of the Formula of Concord in Silesia, an area which led Germany in literature and philosophy between the Reformation and the Enlightenment. He brings to bear his own intense research in that area, which was the only Hapsburg land to preserve the faith of the majority of its people. Professor Skarsten relates the story of the reaction in Scandinavia, where Frederick of Denmark is said to have cast the two elegantly bound copies of the Formula sent to him by his sister, the wife of Elector Augustus of Saxony, into the fireplace. Later, even the Danes came to esteem the Formula.

The final four essays written by non-Lutherans, Professors Patterson, Godfrey, Raitt, and Megivern, present the reaction of the non-Lutherans of that time to the Formula of Concord. The gift of these essays qualify the donors for the Robert Burns award:

> Oh wad some Power the giftie gie us
> To see oursels as ithers see us!
> It wad frae monie a blunder free us,
>   An' foolish notion. . . .
>   —"To a Louse," 1786

Written with sympathy and candor, their essays constitute a valuable contribution to our knowledge of that time and have important implications for our own.

The Formula of Concord was a confession of great historical significance. It ended the major doctrinal controversies within Lutheranism. It was widely accepted as an expression of convictions as well as a doctrinal guide. It showed how the second generation of Lutheran theologians understood Reformation truths. It restored harmony within Lutheranism in the empire, thereby assuring that the privileges gained politically in the Peace of Augsburg could not with right be challenged.[10]

Moreover, the study of the theological content and the history of the Formula of Concord can be most instructive for Christendom now. Churchmen can learn from it the meaning of concern for religious truth, the importance of integrity, and the value of the theological

10. Allbeck, *Studies,* pp. 250–53.

enterprise. They can learn from the heroic efforts made to transcend personality differences in the interest of a common cause. They can cherish the concern for the *una sancta* there evident in the placement of the evangelical creeds in the *Book of Concord* after the Ecumenical Creeds which were declared to have the "very highest kind of authority" (*summae auctoritatis*). They should conclude that just as the Formula addressed the problems of its day, so doctrinal concerns should be directed toward the real problems of our times: relativism, skepticism, secularism, totalitarianism, cynicism, nihilism. In the harmonizers of that day they can sense the spirit of charity accompanying the concern for truth. Rejoicing over the Torgau agreement Andreae wrote: "Truly, this is the change of the right hand of the Most High, which ought also to remind us that since the truth no longer suffers, we should do everything that may contribute to the restoration of good feeling."[11] Those peacemakers had learned something from Luther regarding the study of theology, for, he said, *"it [theology] calls for a certain modesty."* When it comes to theology, a certain modesty is indeed called for!

11. Bente, *Historical Introductions,* p. 246.

I

THEOLOGICAL ESSAYS

Key Issues for the Life of the Church

1

Synergia and Justification by Faith

Ekkehard Muehlenberg

The Formula of Concord rejects the teachings of the synergists in the Solid Declaration, Article II. The preceding union formulae had arrived at the same judgment, even though there were different degrees of rejection of the Philippists' position on free will and on the powers of man in the process of conversion. The majority of the Protestant representatives saw in the synergist teachings a return to the Pelagianism of which the medieval papal church had been accused. Thus, the very substance of the Lutheran Reformation was at stake. Apart from the eucharistic controversy, it was the synergism doctrine that caused the greatest concern. Because of his humanistic tendencies, Melanchthon was suspected of having sacrificed to the Papists Luther's doctrine of justification by faith alone. The Leipzig Interim (1548)[1] was seen as proof for this charge. Erasmus, the humanist par excellence, was considered the father of the synergists "in our age."[2] Melanchthon did not deny his rapprochement with Erasmus concerning the question of free will; moreover, he stressed (*CR* 9:769) that Luther himself had changed his mind since the writing of *The Bondage of the Will.*

The Roman Catholic tradition does not know of a synergism heresy although it has recently admitted that the Protestant rejection of synergism may merit some further consideration. The Eastern churches do not know nor do they understand the rejection of the term *synergia;* for this term occurs rather often in the writings of the Greek Church Fathers, especially in Gregory of Nyssa, and, there, it is

---

1. Cf. Melanchthon, *Corpus Reformatorum* (Brunsvigae: C. A. Schwetschke et Filium, 1834–60), 7:260.51; hereafter cited as *CR.*
2. See *Die Bekenntnisschriften der evangelisch-lutherischen Kirche,* 4th edition revised (Göttingen: Vandenhoeck & Ruprecht, 1959), p. 903 n. 4; hereafter cited as *BK.*

not intended to limit grace and, I think, does not do so.[3] How, then, does the Formula of Concord justify its rejecting of the term *synergia* and the teachings indicated by it?

It is true that Melanchthon's Reformation doctrine and, more generally, humanism are repudiated by the condemnation of the synergism teachings.[4] When the role and validity of the Lutheran confessions within the church were discussed in the last century, the rejection of synergism received renewed attention; for it appeared that the moral and ethical character of Protestant faith was at stake, as Luthardt for instance argued.[5] In our century the most explicit confrontation on the problem underlying the synergism controversy occurred when Karl Barth replied to Emil Brunner with a booklet entitled *No*.[6] "No" was to the assertion of an anthropological point of contact or starting point for Christian preaching; the idea of an *Anknüpfungspunkt* ("point of contact") was already at the bottom of Luthardt's argument.[7]

I propose to discuss, in the form of theses, a number of questions raised by Article II of the Formula of Concord, and I will not conceal my intention of showing that the rejection of synergism as well as the consequences implied by it is one-sided.

1. The way in which the Formula of Concord formulates the issue of the synergism controversy does not do justice to the range of questions raised by the proponents of synergism. Rather, the Formula of Concord from the beginning adopts the perspective of the Flacians and says: "The chief issue is solely and alone what the unregenerated man's intellect and will can do in his conversion and regeneration, by those powers of his own that have remained after the Fall, when the Word of God is preached and the grace of God is offered to him. Can man prepare himself for such grace, accept it and give his assent to it?" (2; *BK* 871.11–20).[8] The Flacians contended that the doctrine of the

---

3. See below, note 35.

4. Cf., e.g., Robert D. Preus, *The Theology of Post-Reformation Lutheranism: A Study of Theological Prolegomena* (St. Louis: Concordia Publishing House, 1970–72), 1:82.

5. Christoph Ernst Luthardt, *Die Lehre vom freien Willen und seinem Verhältnis zur Gnade in ihrer geschichtlichen Entwicklung dargestellt* (Leipzig: Dörffling und Francke, 1863), pp. 191–278.

6. Karl Barth, *Nein! Antwort an Emil Brunner, Theologische Existenz heute,* no. 14 (Munich: Chr. Kaiser, 1934).

7. See, e.g., Luthardt, *Die Lehre,* p. 267.

8. I cite the translation by Theodore G. Tappert, *The Book of Concord: The Confessions of the Evangelical Lutheran Church* (Philadelphia: Fortress Press,

so-called synergists is nothing else but the revivification of scholastic theology which attributes to man the power of preparing himself for the acceptance of grace by his own strength. There was no question, not even among the Philippists, that such a formulation of the controversial issue denies the idea of *sola gratia,* that is, limits the sole efficacy and operation of grace in justification. However, the question which had been asked concerned the process of conversion and what took place in this process in which the human self is certainly a participant.[9] But the Formula of Concord does not enter into a discussion of the nature of human involvement in the process of conversion; rather, it prefers to put the synergism question into the framework of Article I on original sin and to make synergism an appendix of the article. Thus, the Formula of Concord adopts the viewpoint of Flacius for the presentation of the issue, for the so-called synergists asserted that man has to be a participant in the process of conversion. However, their assertion is excluded from any further consideration by the fact that the analysis, by virtue of its initial statement about the issue of the controversy, focuses on the human powers prior to conversion.

For additional clarity it should be noted that the Formula of Concord understands conversion as a point of change rather than a process. Viktor Strigel was right, from his point of view, when he refused to acknowledge the distinction between "before conversion" and "after conversion" and refused to answer questions on the basis of such a distinction; he insisted that his thesis was correct with respect to "in conversion." Had Strigel admitted the validity of Flacius's distinction, he would have been caught between two abstract extremes whereas his sole concern was the selfsameness of man in a gliding transition.[10] For Strigel, *synergia* or cooperation is not the doing of sinful man since, by definition, the sinner resists God and fights against God; nor, for Strigel, is *synergia* the doing of the regenerated person since, again by definition, the regenerate man fights against sin. There was no clear winner of the debate between Strigel and Flacius, and, therefore, the political issue involved was not solved by it. Rather, after the disputation in Weimar (1560) had been published, it should have been ob-

1959) according to the paragraphs of Article II of the Solid Declaration (SD) of the Formula of Concord (FC). After a semicolon I add the reference to the edition of the original German text in *Die Bekenntnisschriften der evangelisch-lutherischen Kirche,* with the abbreviation *BK* plus page and line(s).

9. Cf. Luthardt, *Die Lehre,* pp. 193–96.

10. Ibid., pp. 213–14.

vious that the issue of the controversy was a definition of man's selfsameness, and it was a mistake to avoid this question by a withdrawal into the old tracks of raising the charge of Pelagianism. To be sure, the charge of Pelagianism was only possible after the controversial issue had been reduced to a question of the powers of sinful man before conversion. For in this perspective—namely, what are the powers of sinful man?—any reference to human cooperation sounded like a contribution of the sinners to their regeneration and that was not only a contradiction against Scripture but also against logic. One has, however, to mention that in the Weimar disputation Strigel acted like a good chess player; he knew what mistakes he had to avoid, but confronted his opponent Flacius with constructive counter-moves only in a stammering way, with hesitation, and in clumsy and ambiguous formulations. That the outcome was not a total disaster for Strigel but rather favorable for him is due more to the fact that Flacius scored a number of self-goals, especially by his assertion that sin is the substance of man, than to Strigel's clarity in the formulation of his ideas.

2. The narrow formulation of the controversy's main issue is responsible for the contradictions present in Article II.

Before I proceed any further I must clarify the objection that contradictions in Article II are not only unavoidable but also intentional, as the Formula of Concord declares: "It is true that they [our replies to the questions] are contrary to proud reason and philosophy, but we also know that the 'wisdom of this perverse world is folly with God' [1 Cor. 3:19] and that it is only from the Word of God that judgments on articles of faith are to be pronounced" (8; BK 874.27–34). For revelation may be deemed to contradict reason, and, therefore, a theological statement may appear as a paradox in the light of philosophical thinking. The Flacians argued against the Philippists that philosophy causes their deviation from Scripture, be it because of philosophy's autonomous procedure or its framework for questions, or be it because of its terminology;[11] the Formula of Concord hardly suppresses the Flacians' charge. However, the issue of revelation versus reason is not my issue. I want to lay open contradictions within the line of argument that the Formula of Concord itself pursues. The contradictions I want to point out do not consist in the incompatibility of statements of the Formula of Concord with positions which philosophy—historically Aristotelian philosophy—has developed on its own,

11. Ibid., p. 231.

but with statements and implications presented by the Formula of Concord itself.

a. First, the Formula of Concord teaches the responsibility of sinful man for rejecting God's grace, but it also implies individual predestination.

Article II affirms that sinful man can contribute nothing in any way whatsoever to his conversion (7; *BK* 873.19). When conversion or regeneration occurs, it is solely and alone the work of the Holy Spirit. The Flacians had made use of the expression *ubi et quando visum est Deo* (where and when it pleases God) in Article V of the Augsburg Confession. But this doctrine of particular predestination was generally seen in the Lutheran camp as a Calvinist aberration. For the Formula of Concord wants to affirm God's will for universal salvation, be it only out of a pragmatic concern for the church's life. Therefore it asserts: "It is not God's will that anyone should be damned but that all men should turn themselves to him and be saved forever" (49; *BK* 891.18–21). The Formula of Concord takes account of God's will for the salvation of all mankind by stressing the external means through which the Holy Spirit effects conversion. It is the public preaching of God's Word addressing all men by its very publicity. "And it is God's will to call men to eternal salvation, to draw them to himself, convert them, beget them anew, and sanctify them through this means and in no other way—namely, through his holy Word (when one hears it preached or reads it) and the sacraments (when they are used according to his Word)" (50; *BK* 891.40–892.1).

The Holy Spirit, then, works through the external means of preaching. However, not everyone who listens to or reads God's Word is automatically seized by the Holy Spirit. There are two possible explanations for the absence of automatic conversion. The Formula of Concord rejects particular predestination and chooses the following explanation: the person who scorns the Word as the Spirit's vehicle of operation is not converted and not saved; it is, therefore, man's fault if the Spirit cannot accomplish its work through the Word (57–58; *BK* 894.10–34).

The Formula of Concord has thereby assumed exactly that position of Melanchthon, which underlies the assertion of *synergia* or cooperation (see below, section 4); for the synergism thesis is nothing other than the reversion of this statement about man's responsibility and guilt. Moreover, the Formula of Concord cannot help but use the reversion itself when it begins the section under consideration with these words: "All who would be saved must hear this preaching . . ." (52; *BK* 892.19–20). A more accurate translation would read: ". . . who desire to be saved. . . ."

But how can, prior to conversion and prior to any operation of the Spirit, a wish and desire for salvation be attributed to man? For a few paragraphs earlier the Formula of Concord says, in an effort to make any turning to God already the work of the Holy Spirit: "[The Holy Spirit] opens the intellect and the heart to understand the Scriptures and to hear the Word. . . ." John 6:44, for instance, is quoted for confirmation: "No one can come to Christ unless the Father draws him" (26; *BK* 882.46–883.39). There can be no doubt that individual, that is, particular predestination, is taught here. I do not see how one can reconcile this statement with the earlier one on man's responsibility. And it is of no use to claim that the dogmatic approach shifts to a more practical or polemical approach.[12] It is simply a contradiction.

This contradiction is caused by the perspective the Formula of Concord has adopted at the beginning. The framework for the ensuing argument is set in a fundamental way and, one might say, in a whole-sale manner by these words: "We believe that in spiritual and divine things the intellect, heart, and will of unregenerated man cannot by any native or natural powers in any way understand, believe, accept, imagine, will, begin, accomplish, do, effect, or cooperate but that man is entirely and completely dead and corrupted as far as anything good is concerned" (7; *BK* 873.16–874.2). Hence, with inner consistency, it is repeated against the synergists: "Therefore men teach wrongly when they pretend that unregenerated man still has enough powers to want to accept the Gospel . . ." (45; *BK* 889.42–890.3).

Whether or not one tries to explain it as a practical approach versus a dogmatic approach, after such affirmations one cannot reintroduce man's responsibility by saying that unregenerated man refuses to listen to the Word or, while listening, refuses to believe in the instrumental presence of the Spirit (55–56; *BK* 893.20–30). For unregenerated man does not know what he refuses; he cannot understand that salvation might come through the Word, and, thus, he has no reason whatsoever to come to church or open the Scriptures. To be sure, we speak no longer of the situation of the original Fall, but of man's situation

12. Ibid., pp. 184, 224.

20

after the Fall and in the state of sin. It is impossible as well to count the capability of going to church among the powers of the free will in external matters; for the spiritual and divine things of God's Word, even in their external instrumentality, have no relation to civic virtues, since one has a consciousness of the merit of civic virtues, whereas a consciousness of matters spiritual is denied.

b. Second, there is a self-contradiction in that the Formula of Concord rejects the notion of a forceful conversion explicitly but, in effect, teaches it more or less directly.

The first section of the body of the article affirms that, prior to conversion, man is dead; and as nobody is able to give life to his own body once it is dead, neither can anybody resurrect himself from spiritual death (11; *BK* 875.43–876.3). The second section enhances the same argument and goes a step further by saying that sinful man actively resists God prior to conversion and is hostile to God (17–23; *BK* 878.1–882.5). It is only in the conversion that the Holy Spirit ends unregenerated man's enmity and hostility toward God, or as the article expresses it: "breaks our hearts" (54; *BK* 892.38). If the relation of unregenerated man to his own conversion is to be described, then not only is unregenerated man "a stone, a block, or a lump of clay" (24; *BK* 882.16–17) but worse, his heart is like a "wild, unbroken animal" (19; *BK* 879.24–25), refusing and repudiating the grace offered in the preached Word.

Nevertheless, we are assured in the same context that unregenerated man is free to decide whether or not he wants to go to church and listen to the preaching. If there is such thoroughgoing resistance, it is hard to understand why anyone should want to go to church. But even so, let us assume that somebody has come to church or has opened the Bible; there is no relenting of the resistance against God. Of course, the Philippists raised the question of how a resister can be converted any way other than by force so that the resisting will is broken. Flacius and his followers had occasionally insisted on the provocative thesis: The Holy Spirit is given to resisters.[13] The Philippists drew the conclusion that their opponents imagined conversion to be like a mark forcefully impressed upon unregenerated man and like something newly engraved into him, against his will. They

---

13. See Kurt Dietrich Schmidt, "Der Göttinger Bekehrungsstreit 1566–1570," *Zeitschrift der Gesellschaft für niedersächsische Kirchengeschichte* 34–35 (1929–30): 83–95; see also 103–5.

used metaphors like the impressing of a seal into wax or the carving of God's image into man like into a stone.[14]

The Formula of Concord sides with Flacius and reflects his vocabulary on this point (59; *BK* 894.35–896.7); the mediating paragraphs of the Torgau Book (see *BK* 895), the immediate predecessor of the Formula of Concord, are rejected. The Flacians were not very impressed by the illustrations just mentioned. However, with a few exceptions they did not want to admit that God acts with man as he acts with brutes.[15] Strigel had forced the distinction between God's way of acting with man as a rational creature and God's way of acting with brutes as irrational creatures and wrung it from Flacius, his opponent. The Formula of Concord joins Strigel and says at first: "Nevertheless, the Lord God draws the person whom he wills to convert, and draws him in such a way that man's darkened reason becomes an enlightened one and his resisting will becomes an obedient will" (60; *BK* 896.14–19). Later on, the antitheses acknowledge explicitly that a change of man must take place in conversion: "For conversion is that kind of change through the Holy Spirit's activity in the intellect, will, and heart of man whereby man through such working of the Holy Spirit is able to accept the offered grace" (83; *BK* 906.13–19). Extreme Flacianism is not accepted; rather the Philippists' charge that the Flacians teach a wooden repentance (*Klotzbuss*) is duly integrated.[16]

The further explication of the last quote adopts the whole Philippist argument, and, thus, there are implications much broader than the Formula is otherwise willing to admit. For it says: "All who stubbornly and perseveringly resist the Holy Spirit's activities and impulses, which take place through the Word, do not receive the Holy Spirit but grieve and lose him" (83; *BK* 906.19–24). Were one to take the Formula at its words as expressed in this citation, then there is the concession that unregenerated man has the capacity of refusing grace when it begins its work through the Word. Nevertheless, the Formula of Concord denies vigorously that, by the same token, an assent which is indispensable takes place where the power of refusal is not exercised. If resistance must not be, there is some form of assent. For either the Holy Spirit effects and accomplishes an initial turn and change of sinful

14. See Luthardt, *Die Lehre,* pp. 235, 245–46.
15. Ibid., pp. 211–13.
16. Cf. the recommendation by Martin Chemnitz in 1570 (reproduced by Schmidt, "Der Göttinger Bekehrungsstreit," pp. 96–98).

man against the thoroughly sinful will of man, or unregenerated man is capable of responding to the offer of grace. In other words, either the Spirit accomplishes a forceful change of the resisting will, or the unregenerated will voluntarily accepts grace in the process of conversion, if only for the possibility that the process may start at all. The Formula of Concord wants it both ways, that is, it rejects forceful conversion but does not admit the Philippist alternative either. Therefore, there is a self-contradiction.

I see two possible objections to my analysis. First, one could say that the Formula of Concord does not intend anything other than the rejection of two extremist positions, namely, the Flacian position of a forceful conversion and the Philippist position of *synergia* of fallen man. My reply is the following. The Formula of Concord presents in Article II its own affirmative theses and claims that these theses are the middle course between two extremes; but it cannot provide a middle course between forceful conversion and voluntary assent of the unregenerated will. I might add that this dilemma has not been solved since then. Second, one could say that the Formula of Concord offers a solution in that it allows for the human freedom of rejecting or accepting the means of grace, that is, the preached Word, a freedom unregenerated man has, and classifies this type of assent under freedom in external matters. I reply that according to the Formula's own position unregenerated man cannot want to expose himself to these means of grace since unregenerated man hates God, resists God, and is hostile toward God. One could, of course, imagine that going to church were one of the civic virtues, and even unregenerated man is capable of performing such virtues. But in case this were a valid objection, it is assumed that the virtue of going to church is a prerequisite action performed by unregenerated man as a preparatory step so that grace may start its work. The desire for salvation, be it even in the perverted form of a desire to earn salvation, would be a point of contact or starting point for the Spirit's work. In effect, however, the Formula of Concord denies any such point of contact.

c. Third, there is a self-contradiction in that the Formula of Concord teaches a transformation of the human will but teaches at the same time that the sinful will of unregenerated man continues to fight against the Spirit even after conversion.

The Formula affirms that the Spirit creates a new will but denies that it is an alien implanted will; the Formula affirms that the sinful will is transformed but allows the sinful will to continue after conversion. The Flacians heavily exploited the argument that man is not yet

23

perfect after the act of conversion but rather involved in a fight against his own sinfulness. But it was an open question whether this argument would not suit the Philippists better. Scripture makes it sufficiently clear that such an inner conflict exists in man; in Pauline terminology it is the conflict between the old and the new man. Neither of the parties wanted to deny the existence of the conflict between Spirit and sin in the process of conversion. Hence, how the inner conflict in man was described was decisive. Two extremes had to be avoided: on the one hand, a duplication in man by grafting a new will into man, on the other hand, a denial of the Spirit's efficacy. Duplication results from the thesis that man receives a new will besides his sinful will and that then the new will fights against the old will.[17] The opposite thesis, namely, the assertion that the natural human will becomes a collaborator of the Spirit in the fight against sin, seemed to limit the sole efficacy of grace. One would even have to consider the monstrosity that natural will, which is by definition sinful and hostile toward God, fights against itself. Or, if sinful will is transformed, there is no will left to fight against. The Formula of Concord knows well that neither the extreme of the Flacians' position nor the extreme of the Philippists' synergism was acceptable within the framework of Christian faith. Nevertheless, the Formula limits one evil by the other and, so to speak, unleashes one devil against the other.

The Formula summarizes its own position in the following words: "Hence according to its perverse disposition and nature the natural free will is mighty and active only in the direction of that which is displeasing and contrary to God" (7; BK 874.19–22). This means that man commits sin in and by his very faculty and powers which are called comprehensively the natural free will. Moreover, sin itself consists in hostility toward God, and nothing in man is capable of hostile movements other than the will. The Formula refers to experience, pointing out that even after conversion or regeneration man's hostility toward God continues to persist in some degree. Such hostility persisting even after conversion is effected by "natural or carnal free will" as the Formula asserts (see 18; BK 878.37–38). Natural free will, therefore, is the subject, bearer, and origin of sin not only in the state of sin but also after regeneration. We must remember that it is the same free will which had the capability of accomplishing God's will before the Fall in the state of creation!

17. See Strigel in Luthardt, *Die Lehre,* p. 225.

24

In a glorious inconsequence Martin Luther is quoted to the effect that human will—and only one human will is meant—was originally created for freedom, lost its freedom in the Fall, and is liberated again from the bondage of sin by the power of the Holy Spirit (see 23; *BK* 880.29–882.3). Exactly this line is pursued further when Strigel's "mode of acting," that is, a formal sameness of operation in the unregenerated and regenerated man is condemned; for natural free will is dead in matters concerning the good, it is even hostile toward them (see 61; *BK* 896.22–32). It should be added that Strigel himself is not able to carry through the pure formality of a "mode of acting."[18] Consistent with the idea that there is only one will, the Formula affirms that *synergia* or cooperation is possible and actually occurs after regeneration insofar as the liberated will is a force empowered by the Holy Spirit and, thus, cooperating with the Spirit (63–66; *BK* 897.6–898.20). The last step in this train of thought is, of course, the explicit rejection of the synergists' doctrine because they teach a *synergia* or cooperation of natural free will (see 77–78; *BK* 903.23–904.25). It is obvious that the Formula of Concord remains consistent with its own position to a great extent and means it when it says that creation of a new will in regeneration is transformation of the old will (see 81; *BK* 905.12–39). In this way it has largely avoided introducing a duplication of wills, a charge the Philippists leveled at the Flacians.

However, the Formula of Concord has thus achieved a self-contradiction; for it can no longer identify and name the force which effects and performs the hostility toward God remaining in man after conversion. There is an awareness of this much-debated trap because it is said: "But the regenerated man delights in the law of God according to the inmost self, although he also sees in his members the law of sin at war with the law of his mind" (85; *BK* 907.11–15). This formulation is admittedly cautious, does not identify the warring forces, and takes refuge in the biblical terminology of Romans 7.

There were two possibilities for an identification of the opposite powers. One could speak of a new will created by the Spirit; it would be a second will which is implanted in man alongside the old sinful will, that is, natural free will. This is one possibility, and it is the Flacian position that is most strongly advocated. The natural free will before conversion is hostile toward God because this same natural free

18. Cf. Luthardt, *Die Lehre,* p. 219.

will is still hostile toward God after conversion. Another argument occurs in the positive explanation that cooperation after conversion is rightly understood, because we are told of "new powers and gifts" (65; *BK* 898.1–2) in addition to natural carnal powers. So much on the first possibility, the Flacian option.

The other possibilities include not the Philippists' position but the middle course which the Formula steers as well as all the preceding formulae, including the Swabian Concord. They all prefer to speak of a renewal and transformation of natural free will even if they are, at a number of crucial passages, not consistent with the position of one will to be transformed. Basically, it is a Philippist position without the consequences the Philippists drew from it. Hence, the Formula of Concord maneuvers itself into the disadvantage that it is unable clearly to separate itself from the implication of forceful conversion. One could say that the Formula prefers the implication of a forceful or magical transformation of the will to the option of a duplication of wills. This was inevitable after the concession had been made that conversion takes place only as a true change which man does feel. Nevertheless, having taken one big step in the direction of the Philippists, the issue of *synergia* forces a contradiction; and so we hear of "new activities and emotions in the intellect, will, and heart" (70; *BK* 901.3–5) alongside resisting older ones.

The same contradiction runs through the Torgau Book. We find in it the same affirmation that speaking of conversion is speaking of a real change in man, a change man feels or is aware of so that man is a participant in conversion. This position is further explicated in a statement about the issue of the three causes. Melanchthon had said that in conversion three causes come together, and that the coincidence of these three causes constitutes the act as well as the process of conversion. The three causes are God, the Spirit working through the Word, and human will. Which human will, unregenerated or regenerated? The Torgau Book goes so far as to allow the dangerous terminology of "three causes" and gives it its own orthodox interpretation. A regenerated will participates and cooperates in the process of salvation. "The third cause is man's reason and will—man's reason insofar as it is enlightened by the Holy Spirit and enabled to contemplate and understand God's command; man's will insofar as it is renewed, governed by the Holy Spirit and now desiring voluntarily, though still in great weakness, to be obedient to God's Word and will." It is clearly articulated that one and the same reason had been blind and is now enlightened and that one and the same will had resisted and is now cooperating. But the text continues, spelling out a very different assumption: "Nevertheless, great weakness, disobedience, and resistance of the old natural free will against God's law and will remain even in the regenerate and converted . . ." (*BK* 900). Natural free will, as I read the implication, is renewed only initially and to a small degree, perhaps a part of it; the rest is still sinful. Let us assume that the text means something like this: Man's self is to hold fast the renewed part of the will like holding fast an enkindled spark, and man's self is to rely on the power of grace efficacious in this spark. Well, I ask, what is such a self? The Torgau Book says that the old natural free will is reason, heart, and will and that the Spirit has changed and renewed reason, heart, and will. I do not see how one can assume an additional self and where it is to be located. By the way, the Swabian-Saxon Formula is here the immediate prototype of the Torgau Book.[19] The Swabian Concord does not hesitate to state a duplication of wills and says explicitly that two wills fight with each other.[20]

3. The contradictions described in the preceding section have only one cause, namely, the presupposition that man in his totality can be sufficiently grasped by the notion of "free will."

The formal reason for my assertion is very simple. If man in his totality is described by one single term and only considered as an overall oneness, any anthropological process is denied, and only points of change can be indicated. The Formula of Concord claims indeed that questions concerning man can be adequately dealt with under the presupposition that man is a single unity; however, since the Formula declines to deal with any factors or elements constituting the unity of a human being, there are no alternatives to the contradictions previously indicated. It is, hence, not accidental that the Formula of Concord does not find a middle course. For both extreme positions of the Flacians and of the Philippists contained a partial truth, as the Formula, despite its leaning toward the Flacians, acknowledges. Such a concession made, it becomes impossible to extract the heretical extremes from either side, articulate them, and reject them; it was not necessary for the Formula of Concord to delineate its own position.

19. Cf. Heinrich Heppe, *Geschichte des deutschen Protestantismus in den Jahren 1555–1581,* 4 vols. (Marburg: Elwert, 1852–59), 3: Appendix, 210–11.
20. Cf. H. Hachfeld, "Die schwäbische Confession nach einer Wolfenbüttler Handschrift," *Zeitschrift für historische Theologie,* n.s. 30 (1866): 245.

I shall take a major issue of the synergists to illustrate my point. It was evident that man does not effect his own renewal. Yet, once this was said, the synergists were by no means defeated because they had never taught self-justification. So the synergists returned with a piercing argument. It was undeniable that man participates in his conversion. For if nothing happened with man or changed in him of which there was some form of awareness, a conversion simply had not taken place. Moreover, conversion was the renewal and regeneration of fallen sinful man. The Flacians, therefore, had to admit that conversion is transformation of sinful man, not a substitution or a totally new creation because sinful man remains God's creature and is not a creation by the devil (see FC, SD I, 41; *BK* 856.46–857.31). Hence, regeneration was not a new creation either. Most decisive was the argument involving the resurrection of the dead. The one who has died and not someone else receives life in the resurrection. In a similar way awakening from spiritual death is to be imagined inasmuch as the sinner is liberated from bondage, and an enemy of God is transformed into a believer. It is the sameness which had to be preserved and could not be violated whatever explanation for this sameness might be given. Once the necessity of some sameness between unregenerated and regenerated man received attention, the synergists pushed further and raised the question of how the transforming regeneration takes place if sameness must be preserved. The synergists asserted that a point of contact had to be identified in order to spell out the sameness, and I have attempted to show that the Flacians, despite their efforts, were unable to avoid the alternative of a forceful conversion (see above, 2.b).

I do not want to pursue any further the questions and alternatives within this controversy; all I want to indicate is that the synergism doctrine could not be taken care of through a wholesale rejection. The Formula of Concord entered the road toward self-contradiction in the very moment when it defined the main issue of the controversy in the way the Flacians saw it. To follow the Flacians in the articulation of the main issue and then to concede some truth to the Philippists was a fatal mistake.

The Flacians considered man as a unity and oneness in different states. The idea of these states originated in medieval scholastic theology (Peter Lombard),[21] and the distinctions are as follows: orig-

---

21. It should be noted that Augustine's scheme—before the law, under the law, etc.—is different because it describes man under various conditions and does not absolutize the conditions themselves.

inal creation, sin, sanctification, and resurrection. The synergism controversy concerned the second state, the state of sin. And the one single total unity of man was to be characterized within the state of sin. It is certainly not impossible to make a theological or dogmatic statement about man in the state of sin. Exactly this was intended in order to end the controversy. But the Flacians did not realize that one cannot deal with the synergism doctrine within the framework of the four states, since the synergism doctrine is a statement about the process of conversion itself. Through the focus on man's powers in the state of sin, that is, man as a sinner, more than half of the synergists' theses escaped rejection because they were not about the state of sin at all but about conversion, that is, the unaccounted area between the state of sin and the state of sanctification. Some of the unrejected theses of the synergists contained some truth and were accepted. All in all, the one-sidedness in which the contrast was set up produced a distortion of the Formula's own position.

The main thesis of synergism did not refer to man in the state of sin but rather referred to the process of conversion. The Formula of Concord and its antecedents suppress the process character of conversion and ask only what man is capable of doing in the state of sin.

The formal mistake of the Formula of Concord consists in that it understands man as an undifferentiated unity. It is almost a standard argument that any theological or dogmatic approach necessarily comes to the conclusion that man is an undifferentiated unity in the face of God, namely, a total sinner. The argument is not valid. Article I had dealt with it and adopted the conclusion that sin is not identical with the substance or nature of man, for man remains a creature of God in his substance (see FC, SD I, 41; *BK* 856.46–857.31). So we have a differentiation from a theological or dogmatic perspective. Strangely enough, Article II ignores this conclusion. And this is all the more strange since the controversy about original sin originated from the controversy about *synergia* in conversion. For Flacius thought that if he could win the argument on original sin he had won the battle against synergism and its proponents. The authors of the concord formulae defeated Flacius's argument on original sin, but were convinced, nevertheless, they could win the battle. I think they were mistaken.

It is my assertion that the Formula of Concord becomes entrapped in self-contradictions because Article II in contrast to Article I views man as an undifferentiated unity in the state of sin and then tries to answer a question about the conversion process of differentiated man.

29

The dilemma I mean is most obvious in the contradiction between sameness and reasonableness of man that I have described above in section 2.b. I want to repeat my point in another formulation. The sameness of man before conversion and after conversion had to find an adequate expression, just as Article I acknowledged the sameness between the original creature of God and the sinner. Sinful man is converted, not another substituted for him. But man is a rational creature and not a brute; hence, conversion cannot be a forceful change. Sameness excluded the alternative of duplication—the Formula of Concord is caught for no other reason than its assumption that man even as a sinner can be taken as a lump-total. A differentiation within man, whatever its concrete elements may be, would have permitted facing conversion as a process without losing the sameness of man in the process itself.

4. Melanchthon and his "synergist" followers, with various degrees of clarity, presupposed a differentiation among reason, will, and drives. This differentiation is ignored in the preparation for a formula of concord.

In this section, I want to answer two questions: first, how Melanchthon understood this differentiation, and, second, whether or not there is an intelligible reason for its suppression. I start with the second question.

a. It is obvious that the union formulae all understand free will as the total powers of sinful man. Andreae deals with the subject in the third of his six sermons. There, he presents the conflict between the parties in such a way that it is clear how important a differentiation in man is for a grasp of the issue. For, according to Andreae, the Philippists appeal to natural knowledge of God which sinful man has not lost altogether, whereas the Flacians try to defuse this argument by qualifying knowledge of God.[22] When Andreae proceeds to the presentation of the right doctrine he adopts the Flacian position and formulates summarily: "If all this is the work of the Holy Spirit, it is not the work of our reason nor of our will."[23] Reason is understood as a human power in the same way that will is. Consequently, conversion is an act and not a process; for the enlightening of reason, the recreating of the will, and the converting of the heart happen all at the

---

22. See Heppe, *Geschichte des deutschen Protestantismus,* 3: Appendix, 32–33.
23. Ibid., p. 34.

same time and are essentially identical.[24]   The Swabian Concord follows Andreae's lead and states explicitly that free will covers reason and will in one word; hence, conversion is a single act with enlightenment of reason and change of will happening in one undifferentiated act.[25]   The Swabian-Saxon Formula betrays its Philippist leanings by its insistence that sinful man has a certain knowledge of God and, thus, is capable of civic virtues.[26]   Furthermore, this formula makes an attempt to stick to the question of the will's power[27] but fails to grasp the importance of any distinction between will and knowledge so that, in the end, enlightenment of reason and renewal of the will coincide.[28] I need not present any further evidence.   We find that reason and will are taken together as one, and the same occurs in the description of sinful man and in the description of conversion as well; the Formula of Concord has even increased this trend (cf. 9; *BK* 874.34–875.6).

It is not very difficult to find the cause which brought about the identification of reason and will.   Andreae had given a correct presentation of the Flacians' position and said that man in the state of sin before conversion has no *true* knowledge of God, but Andreae dropped this qualification in the course of his reply.   The Torgau Book, however, consistently gives this qualification and denies that sinful man has true knowledge of God, but allows for natural knowledge of God. Nevertheless, the Formula of Concord gives heed to the Maulbronn Memorandum and eliminates the qualification throughout the text because it could not be denied that the distinction between knowledge of God and true knowledge of God was an argument favoring the synergists.[29]   The Maulbronn Memorandum[30] even suggests the elimination of the expression "meditate on the Word of God" because this argument was more grist for the synergists' mill as well, and the Formula of Concord accepts the advice.

Martin Chemnitz reveals why these arguments supported the synergists and how they were to be countered; he writes in his *Examination of the Council of Trent:*

24. Ibid., p. 35.
25. See Hachfeld, "Die schwäbische Confession," pp. 246–47.
26. See Heppe, *Geschichte des deutschen Protestantismus,* 3: Appendix, 192–95.
27. Ibid., pp. 206–12.
28. Ibid., p. 201.
29. Ibid., p. 357.
30. Ibid., pp. 361–62; also *BK* 893 n. 2.

It is certain that the beginning must be made from the Word, which according to the command of God man must and also can in a measure hear, read, and ponder. This also is certain, that conversion and renewal do not occur without some movement and activity of the mind, the will, and the heart, as we have said above. But the question is whence man has and receives the ability, powers, or faculties for beginning and effecting such movements and actions. This question is understood more correctly through a comparison. In matters which are subject to the senses and to reason man has natural powers in his mind and will, that is, faculties in his nature, inherent and implanted from his first birth; through these man can, when objects are placed before him and brought to him, conceive impulses and call forth actions in harmony with the peculiar nature of his mind and will. The question therefore is whether in the same manner the mind and the will have implanted in them, from the moment of birth, such power, such forces and faculties that when he reads, hears, or meditates on the Word God, he can, without the Holy Spirit, through purely natural powers (as the Scholastics say) conceive such impulses and elicit such actions in the mind, will, and heart as the Scripture demands for contrition, faith, and the new obedience.[31]

The impulses of contrition and faith, Chemnitz tells us, emerge during or through the reading and hearing of God's Word, and the actions of new obedience spring forth. According to true doctrine, says Chemnitz, it is the Holy Spirit who awakens and begets and enkindles such impulses whereas the Council of Trent—and he could have included the synergists as well—teaches that such impulses are effected and created by man's natural powers, and that is a Pelagian heresy. Chemnitz is familiar enough with Melanchthon to give a clear description of the actual process, but Chemnitz is mistaken about the heretical deviation of the synergists.

b. Melanchthon, in the *Loci Communes* of 1535 (see *CR* 21:373–75), makes the following distinction: Reason is the power of judgment evaluating the quality and desirability of objects and objectives. Will is the locomotive or moving power which either follows the judgment of reason or disregards it. Underlying will as locomotion are the affects or affections which by themselves strive toward an object in love and desire or which by themselves avoid an object in hatred, hostility, and fear. On the basis of this differentiation Melanchthon describes man's sinful condition as well as the demanded righteousness. He admits a weakening of the power of judgment but not

31. Martin Chemnitz, *Examination of the Council of Trent,* trans. Fred Kramer (St. Louis: Concordia Publishing House, 1971), p. 425.

the complete extinction of reason. Furthermore, he thinks that the devil has created and implanted evil affections in man. Will is in between these two poles; will has retained its power to join reason and assert itself against evil affections although the devil may prevent it to some extent. If will follows the judgment of reason against evil affections, the result is virtue, civic virtue. Essentially, virtue is a negative phenomenon since it consists in the suppression of an evil affection and is thus the prevention of an evil action. Melanchthon fails to make clear why will sometimes does not follow the judgment of reason. Within the framework of his theory the occasion can only be a combination of very powerful evil affections together with a weakness and fuzziness of reason's judgment. Hence, will as locomotive power has no judgmental faculty but would be totally dependent on the clarity of the power of judgment. But this analysis apparently does not cover all of Melanchthon's concept; for he can also say that will follows the judgment of reason or rejects it. It is not possible to exhaust the meaning of this formulation by relating it to the combination of unclear judgment with strong evil affections, but there seems to be an additional judgmental faculty in will itself.

In any case, the righteousness God demands consists in the right affections like fear of God, love of God, and trust in God. Melanchthon says about these affections: "Human will without the Holy Spirit cannot effect the spiritual affections demanded by God" (*CR* 21:375). A sentence like this must have been in the mind of Chemnitz when he formulated his statement on right and wrong doctrine of the free will. The Council's error, for Chemnitz, is the reversion of Melanchthon's sentence, reading as follows: Human will can effect or generate spiritual affections. Just this is Chemnitz's very consequential mistake. For in light of the differentiation Melanchthon presupposes man cannot effect or generate any affections, be it with the support of the Holy Spirit or be it without the support of the Holy Spirit; all human will can do is to curb, check, and govern affections once they have been generated. It is basic to realize that affections are generated or evoked from outside man; affections are always reactions to something.

Melanchthon's description of conversion flows naturally from what has been said, and the often quoted phrase from his *Loci Communes* of 1543 reads: "When we begin with the word, the three causes of a good action come together, namely, the Word of God, the Holy Spirit, and the human will assenting to God's Word and not resisting it" (*CR*

21:658). Anthropologically this means: The Holy Spirit effects and generates the new spiritual affections through the reading or hearing of the Word of God, that is, the preaching of God's demands evokes fear of God, and the proclaiming of God's mercy in the righteousness of Christ generates love of God. To be precise, faith consists first of all in the knowledge of God's demand and God's mercy. Reason does not have such knowledge by itself; it has to learn it, or rather, this knowledge has to be communicated to reason, which then is enlighten-ment in a different terminology (cf. CR 13:426–27). The affections like fear of God and love of God are also effects and results of the Spirit's work through the Word, for they are the affective reaction to it without any doing of reason or will.[32] In addition, the role of will consists in the appropriation of the objective content of God's Word in the attitude of trust and confidence. Conversion, then, occurs when the human will follows the knowledge of God's mercy and the affection of love of God. Human will does not materially add anything to the process, because object and objective are given in reason's knowledge and the movement or locomotion in the affection. Nevertheless, human will has to turn to the new affection and has to follow it against other affections in man. In other words, the human self must recog-nize itself in the new knowledge and in the new affection and not in other affections. Human will participates and cooperates in the process of conversion insofar as it identifies itself with the new affection and, for instance, prays that it may be sustained and strengthened. The word synergism, taken in this context, has only one misleading con-notation, namely, that *synergia* in Greek can mean that the will is a contributing actuality and power. Strigel has clarified the ambiguity and declared that the will's assent is a formal mode of acting, although all his illustrations were mistaken.[33]

Melanchthon has consciously and decisively changed his position on the nature of human will. In his *Loci Communes* of 1521 he demon-strated the total bondage of man by claiming that there is no will besides affections and that the scholastic theologians were mistaken when they assumed a will in distinction from affections; will and affections are one and the same thing (see CR 21:90–93). Later on

---

32. Cf. my article "Humanistiches Bildungsprogramm und reformatorische Lehre beim jungen Melanchthon," *Zeitschrift für Theologie und Kirche* 65 (1968): 431–44.

33. See Luthardt, *Die Lehre,* pp. 233–34.

Melanchthon realized the dangerous consequences of predestinarianism and mechanical conversion but also recognized the experience of virtue, that is, checking affections. Turning again to Aristotle's ethics he learned to differentiate the human self into three elements. Luther and the Formula of Concord follow Melanchthon in that they admit a distinction between will and affections; for external righteousness, even if called a pharisaic virtue (cf. 24; *BK* 882.21), is the curbing and governing of affections; it is not the generation of affections.

c. Has the Formula of Concord misunderstood the synergism doctrine as I presented it in its Melanchthonian form, or has the Formula of Concord explicit reasons for rejecting it? Both, I would reply.

The Formula claims that human will is a power capable of producing affections. This assumption is wrong. For the movement or locomotive force rests in the affections and the will does nothing other than release or suppress it. The error is the consequence of an undifferentiated understanding of man and of human powers. The Formula gave up any distinctions among reason, will, and affections and assumed that "reason, will, and heart" are the one human power of free will. Consequently, the Formula assumes that will is a power capable of effecting or generating something. Such an assumption misrepresents the synergism doctrine. Let us focus on the word "assent." Melanchthon says: "assenting and not resisting." The Formula takes account of this human act. When one agrees to listen externally to God's Word, the Formula says, one has given one's assent; since this is an act concerning external matters human will has the power for it before conversion.

Nevertheless, the Formula is correct when it assumes that the synergists as well as Melanchthon refer to the very process of conversion and that they speak of the assent to the affection of love for God generated by the Holy Spirit. Melanchthon and the synergists mean "accept acceptance," to use a modern idiom, and not simply "accept the invitation to come to church." No doubt, the Formula of Concord does not allow "accept acceptance." Melanchthon and the synergists do not differ on this point. But Melanchthon has committed a sin of omission, and his students, as far as I can see, have not discovered what the mistake was.[34] For he has to assume that human

---

34. Cf. Otto Ritschl, *Dogmengeschichte des Protestantismus,* 4 vols. (Leipzig: J. C. Hinrichs'sche Buchhandlung, 1908–27), 2:299; on Strigel see Luthardt, *Die Lehre,* p. 218.

will possesses a cognitive and evaluative power which makes it possible to give assent to the new affection of love of God and to refuse assent to the affections which react with hostility toward God's Word. Conversion is not automatic or mechanic, and therefore a cognitive or evaluative power tips the will toward the affection in the process of conversion. Moreover, such a cognitive power of human will is different from reason. Melanchthon has not sufficiently reflected on this implication.

5. Melanchthon has identified the Latin-Augustinian will (*voluntas*) with the Greek-Aristotelian will (*prohairesis*) and introduced it into the Aristotelian anthropology.

Two things have escaped his attention. First, *prohairesis* is not a third force alongside reason and affection but is the affection governed by reason or the affection confirmed and released by reason; in other words, will as *prohairesis* is the result of the relationship of reason and affection, and it is by no means a separate third force which could actively mediate between reason and affection. Second, will as *voluntas* in Augustine is devoid of any cognitive powers and is pure willing in itself without being identical with affection. Will in the Augustinian understanding is not bound by an object nor is it evaluated by its relation to an object; rather, it is judged by the quality of its movement.[35]

These two traditions are different, and Melanchthon does not integrate one into the other; he confuses the two. Therefore he is mistaken when he appeals to the Greek Fathers for his synergism doctrine. He senses support but does not know exactly what it is.

The Formula of Concord takes its ammunition against the synergism doctrine from Luther's Augustinianism. Within this perspective, any synergism doctrine appears to be a Pelagian revival and merits only condemnation. For how is it possible that sinful will, hostile toward God, and sin by definition, can assent to its own liquidation by grace?

However, the Formula of Concord is also wrong because the Augustinian understanding of will is one-sided. When the Formula enters into an anthropological discussion, it is equipped with the wrong tools; for the Augustinian understanding of will excludes all differentiation in man and therefore foils any anthropological concepts (e.g., it cannot deal with a concept like conversion as a real change) and

---

35. See my article "Synergism in Gregory of Nyssa," *Zeitschrift für die neutestamentliche Wissenschaft* 68 (1977).

prevents the development of an anthropology which can describe an inner process. Article I holds out a hand which Article II rejects.

Within the scope of this paper I cannot offer a solution to the question which gave rise to Article II of the Formula of Concord. I do think that the idea of perversion provides a concept on which a theological anthropology can be based. For it is not possible to reject the concept of an *Anknüpfungspunkt* ("point of contact") altogether.[36] The "mode of acting" to which the synergists pointed was not an auxiliary argument for something else; it was at the center of their interests.

36. Cf. Traugott Koch, "Natur und Gnade: Zur neueren Diskussion," *Kerygma und Dogma* 16 (1970): 171–87.

2

Original Sin: Accident or Substance: The Paradoxical Significance of FC I, 53-62 in Historical Context

Robert C. Schultz

The doctrine of sin fulfills important functions in any system of Christian theology. This essay proposes to examine the first article of the Formula of Concord in terms of two basic functions. The first and most obvious function is to describe those factors in the human situation that make salvation necessary. Such a description also identifies the data of human experience that are relevant to our understanding of this need. Data of human existence that are excluded from consideration in this doctrine are also excluded from the process of salvation.

This function is the basis of a larger, more generalized function. The doctrine of original sin is the point at which a system of theology describes the kind of data of human experience that have religious significance. The narrower the content of this doctrine, the narrower the range of religiously significant data. This doctrine thereby becomes the point at which the scope and focus of the system are defined. Original sin may, for example, be described as a boundary problem; but the boundary may be variously located—within the structure of the soul, between the soul and the body, between the person and reality or the law, between persons, and between man and God, or some combination of these. Experience will determine the choice; the doctrine will describe it.

The actual doctrinal decisions made by Article I are of limited significance. On the one hand, this article may be seen as a repetitive reaffirmation of the doctrine of original sin in the second article of the Augsburg Confession and the Apology and in Part III, Article I of the

Smalcald Articles. As a summary of those earlier confessions, the Formula makes no particular contribution either in terms of content or of clarity.

On the other hand, Article I may be viewed as a response to the controversy between Viktor Strigel and Matthias Flacius Illyricus. That controversy and the Formula's response revolved around matters of terminology. Insofar as substantive issues were involved, they were identified neither by the participants in the controversy nor by the authors of Article I.

Analysts of the controversy, such as Wilhelm Preger and Lauri Haikola, have struggled to identify the real issue of the controversy without satisfying results.[1] Each asks and tries to answer the question: What would the participants have had to consider in order to determine the underlying point at issue, if any? This essay builds on the work of Preger and Haikola by assuming that this question cannot by fully answered from an analysis of the controversy itself. Rather, the controversy can be understood only if we do what the participants did not do: consider the controversy in the context of the larger historical development of the doctrine of original sin. The results of that investigation may assist us in understanding the significance of assumptions shared by all participants in the controversy and the effect of the decisions of Article I on the later development of Lutheran theology and its capacity to respond to its constantly changing contemporary world.

A thorough consideration of the history of the doctrine of original sin and even an adequate analysis of the controversy between Flacius and Strigel would require more space than is available in this essay. I have therefore chosen to limit the following sketch to the alternative definitions of original sin as the substance or an accident of human nature and the relevance of the larger historical context to an understanding of Article I. The footnotes refer the reader to more detailed discussion of various questions but make no claim to completeness.

The controversy between Flacius and Strigel and even Article I of the Formula of Concord are minor incidents in the development of the doctrine of original sin in the Western church. This development was

1. Wilhelm Preger, *Matthias Flacius Illyricus und seine Zeit* (Erlangen: Theodor Blaesing, 1861), 2:310–412, see esp. p. 411. Lauri Haikola, *Gesetz und Evangelium bei Matthias Flacius Illyricus. Eine Untersuchung zur lutherischen Theologie vor der Konkordienformel* (Lund: C. W. K. Gleerup, 1952), pp. 48–164, see esp. p. 164.

basically determined by the controversy between Augustine and Pelagius. For Pelagius, all sin is actual sin. Augustine's doctrine asserts that original sin is a condition of human existence after the Fall: all men are born without the supernatural relationship to God which enabled human nature to do works deserving of salvation; and even that nature itself was weakened.

This disagreement resulted in the Pelagian controversy. Augustine's position was affirmed by the Western church. His influence was so great that another possibility was overlooked: the developmental approach to the doctrine of original sin that was common in the Eastern church and most clearly formulated by Irenaeus. This approach describes original sin in far less tragic terms than Augustinian theology does and views man as being in a very immature and primitive stage of development. There is nothing to fall from. Sin and the Fall are rather seen as a minor misfortune, as a stumbling along the way to maturity.[2] This view is quite distinct from the Pelagian view that every man fully possesses the goodness of creation. Yet both the Pelagian and the more common Eastern view were, as a result of the Pelagian controversy, simultaneously rejected as available options in the Western church.

Augustine's position set the limits for almost all subsequent development of the doctrine of sin in the Western church until the eighteenth century—with the exception of a brief period in the sixteenth century. Even Thomas Aquinas would only gingerly question Augustine's description of the effect of sin on human nature. And Augustine's doctrine reflects his personal experience of sin which was dominated by a sense of shame and guilt.[3]

Medieval theologians attempted to reconcile and combine Augustine's various statements.[4] The typical solution describes original sin in terms of the structure of the soul. After creating human nature

2. For a discussion of and a modern restatement of this view, see John Hick, *Evil and the God of Love* (New York: Harper, 1966).

3. See the instructive series of articles, "St. Augustine's Confessions: Perspectives and Inquiries," ed. Paul Pruyser, in *Journal for the Scientific Study of Religion,* 5:1 (Fall 1965): 130–52 and 5:2 (Spring 1966): 273–89.

4. In addition to the standard works on the history of doctrine, see J. N. Espenberger, *Die Elemente der Erbsünde nach Augustin und der Frühscholastik* (Mainz: Kirchheim & Co., 1905); Odon Lottin, *Psychologie et Moralé aux XIIe et XIIIe siècles,* vol. 4 (Louvain: Abbaye du Mont César, 1954); Artur Michael Landgraf, *Dogmengeschichte der Frühscholastik,* vol. 4, 1 (Regensburg: Friedrich Pustet, 1955).

God gave man an additional, supernatural gift of original righteousness which enabled man to achieve a relationship to God. Man now can be described in terms of nature and supernature. Original sin affects both. The supernatural capacity for achieving a relationship to God is lost. That loss is a given reality of human existence and man is guilty as a result of this loss only insofar as he participated in the act of Adam's sin that resulted in the loss. Human nature itself is God's good creation. However, it is weakened as a result of original sin: the human intellect is darkened, the human will weakened, and the human appetites or desires are in rebellion. As a result of this weakness of human nature, man commits sins and becomes guilty of breaking the law of God. This guilt becomes a positive barrier to any relationship with God. The weakness of human nature and the loss of the supernatural gift are carefully distinguished so that the continuing goodness of human nature as God's creation can be affirmed.

Theologians found it difficult to describe the relationship between the loss of supernature and the weakness of nature in a way that did not threaten to deny the goodness of God's creation. There were two typical solutions: Peter Lombard defined original sin as a "morbid quality" of the soul. This means that human nature even as God's creation contains some sort of incendiary material that could result in sin. This position runs the danger of making God the cause or the creator of the cause of sin. Anselm of Canterbury defined original sin in terms of the loss of original righteousness. Man is guilty of not having what he should have. Thomas Aquinas combined the two positions. This combination, like Lombard's doctrine, seems to make concupiscence a necessary part of human nature. Aquinas believes that is not the case. He asks: Is original sin concupiscence? Aquinas answers that the loss of original righteousness, the original relationship to God lost in original sin (*aversio a deo*), is the formal cause, whereas concupiscence (*conversio ad creaturam*) is the material cause of original sin.[5]

Aquinas's view of concupiscence is based on his understanding of the human soul. The human soul has four powers or faculties: reason, will, the irascible appetites, and the concupiscible appetites. The latter two are roughly comparable to anger and love in dual drive personality theory.[6] If man were unspoiled by original sin, each of

---

5. *Summa theologica,* I, II, quest. 82, art. 3.
6. Karl Menninger et al., *The Vital Balance: The Life Process in Mental Health and Illness* (New York: Viking Press, 1963), pp. 114–23.

these powers would manifest itself in one of the four cardinal virtues: reason in prudence, will in justice, the irascible appetites in fortitude, and the concupiscible appetites in temperance. As a result of original sin, however, four corresponding vices have appeared. Reason is not perfectly oriented to truth and ignorance results. Will is not perfectly oriented to the good and malice appears. The irascible appetites have been weakened; and the concupiscent appetites are directed toward improper objects. As a result, human life is characterized by a mixture of prudence and ignorance, justice and malice, fortitude and weakness, and temperance and concupiscence.[7]

For our purposes, it is important to note that sin was experienced as a problem in the human soul or person that appeared at every point in its structure, in reason, in will, and in appetites. The experience of sin might be focused in one power more than the others, but the participation of all was necessary to an act of sin. Concupiscence, the rebellion of the appetites by itself, could not result in sin unless reason and will were also involved in a conscious and deliberate act. As a result, a person before the age of reason was burdened by original sin but could not commit an act of sin. In this way, medieval theology asserted the doctrine of original sin without denying that people are God's good creation.

Thomas's position is of particular importance not only because of its coherence but because it is the theology most likely to be encountered in dialogue with Roman Catholics. Thomas, however, was not the dominant theologian in the fifteenth and sixteenth centuries. Fifteenth century theologians developed alternative options that determined the context within which the Lutheran reformers defined their doctrine. Thus Gabriel Biel seems to prefer the approach of Anselm of Canterbury and of Thomas Aquinas.[8] People have lost the original righteousness which they ought to have, and this is the guilt of original sin. It is then sufficient to describe concupiscence as actually being present without deciding whether it is the guilt or only the punishment of original sin. Biel concludes, however, that all three basic approaches

7. *Summa theologica,* I, II, quest. 85, art. 3.

8. Recent investigations provide considerable information on the development of the doctrine of sin during the period immediately preceding the Reformation. See Heiko A. Oberman, *The Harvest of Medieval Theology: Gabriel Biel and Late Medieval Nominalism* (Cambridge, Mass.: Harvard University Press, 1963), pp. 57–68, 120–21, and Wilhelm Ernst, *Gott und Mensch am Vorabend der Reformation* ("Erfurter Theologische Studien," 28 [Leipzig: St. Benno-Verlag, 1972]), esp. pp. 311–19.

(Peter Lombard, Anselm, and Thomas Aquinas) were permissible because the church had not defined its dogma on this point since the
Synod of Orange in 529.

Wilhelm Ernst[9] describes Biel's consistent application of Ockham's
razor to the concept of the powers of the soul. He agrees with
Thomas that it is not possible to separate the soul into separate substantial parts. However, he goes beyond Thomas and rejects both the
distinctions among reason, will, and appetites and between them and
the soul itself. Terms such as "reason" and "will" both refer to the
soul itself and are simply a convenient way of describing what the soul
is able to do: to know and to will. The appetites are simply a way of
describing what the soul wants and wills. However, we can never
speak of reason, will, or appetite without referring to the whole soul.
Biel then describes the soul as being created by God with limited
knowledge. The basic human problem thus is not the concupiscence
of the flesh but the lack of knowledge. This lack is remedied by the
gift of faith. Faith is understood as the knowledge of the truth.
Anyone who knows the truth about God will love him and choose the
good.

This style of thinking opened a whole new perspective. If theological statements could be made about the whole soul without regard
to its parts (if any), theological statements no longer needed to pre-
suppose a particular psychology—although each theologian would of
course continue to have his own view of psychological questions.
Equally important, since theological statements could now be made
using the soul as subject without regard for the differentiation of parts,
other applications of the principle of conceptual parsimony were
possible. Perhaps it was also possible not to speak of the soul at all,
but rather to refer to the individual person as an entity. Biel seems
to have done so. If so, new perspectives on original sin became possible. These new perspectives acquired a dynamic force when Luther
defined the basic relationship to God as trust rather than love. Trust,
however, is the primal human relationship, resulting from an act of
neither the will nor the intellect but solely dependent on the experience
of being loved. Original sin, then, is *not* trusting the God who is
love. The Lutheran Reformation for a time explored these possibilities
and seemed to be developing new approaches to the doctrine of sin.
Then, however, as the progression of this essay will indicate, the focus

9. Ernst, *Gott und Mensch,* pp. 256–85.

on the individual necessary for these new approaches was abandoned, and the new approaches remained largely unexplored.

As a result of this basic shift in perspective, Luther could describe both sin and salvation in terms of people's relationship to God without needing to describe the interior structure of human personality. Original sin affects the relation of body to soul, and the relation of the powers of the soul to one another; but the real problem of original sin is in our personal relationship to God. Luther did indeed have his own views of the soul and its structure, but this view was not constitutive for his theology.[10] Original sin is described in terms of not fearing, not loving, not trusting God. Such unbelief is accompanied by disorder within the person, and acting contrary to the law is one form of this disorder. This makes concupiscence sinful. However, whenever a person does not trust God, he sins whether he breaks the law or conforms to it. Given this assertion, sin also no longer needs to be a conscious, deliberate act. Concupiscence is sin whether or not the reason and the will are involved. Since no one in this life fears, loves, or trusts in God perfectly, all people, including Christians, remain sinners who, when judged by this norm, are completely sinners before God. Even the sacraments do not remove this sin; it is destroyed only through the death of the person and the perfect regeneration of the resurrection from the dead.

For Luther, the primary focus of original sin is not what man is or has, but his relationship to God.[11] Unbelief—not fearing, not loving, not trusting God—does not mean that relationship has been lost. The personal relationship to God remains but it has been converted into its opposite. Mistrust is not the absence of trust but an active relationship which not only results in the commission of sins but is the essence of sin itself. The medieval distinction between nature and supernature is no longer necessary.[12]

---

10. Werner Elert, *The Structure of Lutheranism,* trans. Walter A. Hansen (St. Louis: Concordia Publishing House, 1962), repeatedly emphasizes this personal relationship. Wilfried Joest, *Ontologie der Person bei Luther* (Göttingen: Vandenhoeck & Ruprecht, 1967), is very instructive on Luther's understanding of the structure of the person.

11. The question is of course not new. Thomas Aquinas was also seeking this in his categories of "aversion from God" and "conversion to the creature." Cf. G. K. Chesterton, *St. Thomas Aquinas* (Garden City, N.Y.: Image Books, 1956), p. 37.

12. For a fuller treatment of Luther's doctrine of original sin, see Paul Althaus, *The Theology of Martin Luther,* trans. Robert C. Schultz (Philadelphia: Fortress Press, 1966), pp. 141–60; Elert, *Structure,* pp. 28–35; Lauri Haikola, *Studien zu*

Luther's radical shift in perspective was in one sense the next step in the medieval development; but that next step was also a radical reorientation of the doctrine of original sin. The openings for new conceptual formulations provided by theologians like Biel helped Luther to form and shape his new approach. Those conceptual possibilities helped Luther assimilate his own traumatic experiences in personal relationships, particularly to his parents, into his theology.[13] Luther reconstructed the doctrine of original sin in terms of his own experience rather than Augustine's. Not everyone shared the intensity of Luther's experiences in their own lives; they found, however, that Luther's approach enabled them to comprehend more of their experience of evil under the doctrine of sin and hence of salvation than did the medieval schemes. As a result, they understood Luther's claim that his understanding of sin permitted a broader, deeper understanding of the gospel.

One of Luther's closest supporters was Philipp Melanchthon. Personal competence and historical necessity made him rather than Luther the teacher who formed and shaped the systematic statements of Lutheran theology. If Luther's interpersonal relationships were determined by unresolved questions of mistrust, shame, and guilt in relation to his parents, Melanchthon's were determined by the distant relationships and cool emotional climate that characterized his family and by the early death of his father. During Melanchthon's youth his father was frequently absent and then ill. The grandfather who took the father's place in Philipp's life died a few days before the father. In addition, neither Melanchthon's mother nor her mother who served as surrogate mother was noted for personal warmth and affection. All this resulted in a style of interpersonal relationships and personal development radically different from Luther's. Melanchthon himself commented on the effect of these childhood experiences on his personal psychological development.[14]

Luther und zum Luthertum ("Uppsala Universitets Årsskrift," 1958:2 [Uppsala: A.-B. Lundequistska Bokhandlen, 1958]), pp. 7–55, 69–103; Otto Hermann Pesch, *Theologie der Rechtfertigung bei Martin Luther und Thomas von Aquin* (Mainz: Matthias-Gruenewald, 1967), pp. 77–122.

13. Erik Erikson, *Young Man Luther* (New York: Norton, 1958), describes the psychological dimensions of those experiences. Cf. Roger Johnson, ed., *Psychohistory and Religion: The Case of Young Man Luther* (Philadelphia: Fortress Press, 1977).

14. Wilhelm Maurer, *Der junge Melanchthon zwischen Humanismus und Reformation* (Göttingen: Vandenhoeck & Ruprecht, 1967), vol. 1, pp. 14–15, gives a brief but insightful overview of this data.

Frightened by the loss of his father and particularly aware of his own ambivalent feelings toward those whom he loved and needed, Melanchthon was cautious and careful both in thought and in action. Melanchthon published his *Loci Communes* in 1521, the year in which he was so immobilized by fear of sin that he lost control of the Wittenberg Reformation to Carlstadt and the Zwickau prophets. Luther's admonition to "sin boldly," and thus to do something to establish his leadership, fell on deaf ears. It is not surprising, then, that the *Loci* of 1521 discuss the doctrine of original sin primarily in terms of concupiscence rather than the relationship to God. Indeed, the relationship to God is discussed not as a personal relationship but as a relationship through the law.

Subsequent editions of the *Loci* are characterized by a return to typical medieval approaches and by a blunting of Luther's more intuitive, but also more radical, doctrinal formulations. Thus by 1555, the relationship between God and man is discussed in terms of God's wrath and man's blindness and doubt. The awareness of active mistrust and rebellion is submerged in the discussion of concupiscence:

> To be in original sin is to be in God's disgrace and wrath, to be damned on account of the fall of Adam and Eve. On account of the wretched loss of the divine presence, light, and activity in us, on account of our blindness and doubt about God, and our perverted, evil tendencies which are opposed to God, we are sinful and damned.[15]

Not the human person, but our evil tendencies are opposed to God. For Luther, concupiscence had been a personal expression of unbelief. Melanchthon localizes the impersonal tendencies as the point at which opposition to God is expressed. It is Melanchthon's blunted, often impersonal reductions of Luther's dynamic interpersonal analogies that shaped Lutherans' systematic statements of the doctrine of sin.[16] That was the situation both before and after the Formula of Concord.

Catholic theologians could not help but perceive such new ways of thinking as blatant heresies. The simple identification of concupiscence with original sin removed the safeguards established by Peter Lombard and Thomas Aquinas and seemed to be a clear denial of the goodness

---

15. *Melanchthon on Christian Doctrine: Loci Communes, 1555,* ed. and trans. Clyde Manschreck (New York: Oxford University Press, 1965), p. 75; cf. *Corpus Reformatorum (CR)* 21:669.

16. Elert, *Structure,* p. 32, shows how Melanchthon could sometimes use Luther's language but that even then the sense of a direct personal relationship is missing.

of God's creation. The Son of God could not assume such human nature. Salvation by faith alone without providing the means for overcoming the weaknesses of human nature looked like a denial of the reality of salvation. This righteousness which could never be described as man's own righteousness did not seem worthy of the name! Since there was no clarity about the radical shift in perspective from the structure of the person to interpersonal relationships, even meaningful conversation was impossible. Such conversation would become possible only when each recognized that both were describing the same reality of sin from different perspectives.

The intensity of Luther's personal experience kept him from being intimidated by the Catholic criticisms, but others, whose experience was less intense, could not help but be sensitive. As a consequence, Lutheran theologians generally found Melanchthon's approach more comfortable. Successive modifications of the more modulated Melanchthonian position tended to move closer to the medieval approach rather than toward a dynamic restatement of Luther's position. As the doctrine of original sin was more and more formulated in terms of the structure of the soul, Luther's statements increasingly lost the context which made them meaningful. Luther's interpretation of Paul's "Whatever does not proceed from faith is sin" (Rom. 14:23), was replaced by the simple clarity of John's "Sin is wrongdoing," translated as "Sin is every transgression of the law" (1 John 5:17). Faith and unbelief were increasingly intellectualized. Trust and hope increasingly became fruits of faith rather than manifestations of faith itself.[17] In practice, faith was defined in terms of knowledge rather than trust.

In this context the controversy between Flacius Illyricus and Viktor Strigel developed. Strigel was concerned to defend the Melanchthonian doctrine of original sin against the Catholic accusation that it denied the goodness of God's creation and made God, who had created concupiscible appetites, the cause of sin. Strigel asserted that God creates appetites and that appetites must seek their fulfillment in a variety of ways, some good, some evil. The choice is an accident. Strigel therewith returned to a position that was acceptable within the medieval frame of reference.

Flacius objected to Strigel's approach. He sensed that the basic

17. Richard R. Caemmerer, "The Melanchthonian Blight," *Concordia Theological Monthly* 18 (1947): 321–38.

insights of Luther were being lost through the use of this terminology. Flacius, however, operated in basically the same conceptual frame of reference as Strigel. It was therefore not possible for Flacius to challenge the conceptual frame of reference. Rather, he found himself trapped into the position of disagreeing with Strigel by describing original sin as the substance of human nature. Flacius's opponents pointed out that this seemed to make God the creator and cause of sin. Flacius could present no more convincing defense against this charge than that Luther had made the same kind of statements.

Flacius rightly considered himself more faithful to the heritage of Luther than his opponents. His position on original sin as the substance of human nature is therefore a specially good example of the way in which Luther's position found no consistently faithful representative after his death.

Flacius seems to begin as Luther does by looking at the whole (*totus*) man in relation to God. Like Luther, he rejects the medieval view that original righteousness is an additional gift to human nature. That view made original righteousness an accident as well as original sin.

The assertion of Flacius's opponents, including Article I of the Formula of Concord, has the effect even though not the intention of affirming the scholastic position. This is the point at which Flacius could claim to represent Luther.

Flacius varies from Luther, however, in describing this original righteousness as internal psychic harmony which enabled man to be righteous by keeping the law. Here he agrees against Luther with those who make keeping the law the ultimate standard of righteousness and thus ulitmately the principle even of grace.

This is related to Flacius's cautious moving away from Luther's focus on the whole man in relation to God. Flacius at first follows the position exemplified by Biel and treats the soul as a unity. As the nominalists did, he views the will as the highest expression of this unity. Since the will has lost its conformity to the law of God, original sin is a corruption of man's highest substance. Flacius thereby begins to break the unity of the soul.

Flacius's opponents focus on his definition of original sin as the "substance" of human nature. How can the sinner still be human? These opponents resolutely overlook Flacius's qualification that original sin affects the highest substance of man—his conformity to God's law. Other elements of the substance of human nature are weakened but not lost. Original sin is the substance of man only in terms of his relationship to God.

Flacius's position was thus closer both to Luther's and the basic intention of Article I of the Formula of Concord than were his opponents'. His opponents were using the basic medieval categories and thus working against the position they claimed to affirm. However, Flacius became involved in the same process as soon as he distinguished levels of the substance of human nature within the structure of the human person. He thereby took Luther's position out of its context in interpersonal relations and tried to explain it in the categories of the structure of the human person. His actual position was thus not basically different from his opponents'. They, however, could sense that he was struggling to say something different without being able to express it well. But as long as the terms of the controversy were not clarified, the real issue could not be defined. As in many another controversy, Flacius's opponents avoided hearing what he wanted to say by twisting his words to make him say what he did not mean.

At no point in the controversy was the discussion focused on Luther's radically different perspective. The actual assertions about people being made by Flacius and Strigel were not sufficiently different to explain the intensity of the controversy. The heat over substance and accident was the heat of mutual misunderstanding; Strigel's position was stated in terms compatible with Melanchthon's approach. Flacius was trying to use Melanchthon's system to describe insights of Luther that Melanchthon had lost. In the process, Flacius stretched Melanchthonian terminology to the point of distortion. Various participants in the controversy used the same terms in different senses. But as in the colloquies with Roman Catholics, the terms were hardly ever defined. Haikola's careful analysis of all the elements of the controversy leads to the conclusion: "The point at issue in the great controversy about original sin was ultimately a question of terminology."[18]

Flacius, like his opponents, could describe man's relationship to God only as a function of his relationship to the law. Given that limitation, he could not demonstrate his agreement with Luther or fulfill his intention of re-presenting Luther's description of sin in terms of man's direct personal relationship to God. This inability left Flacius defenseless against the charge that he alone among the Lutherans justly de-

18. Haikola, *Gesetz und Evangelium bei Matthias Flacius Illyricus*, p. 164. For references to detailed analysis of the controversy, see note 1, above.

served the condemnation of the Catholics that his doctrine of original sin contradicted the doctrines of creation, redemption, and sanctification (FC, SD I, 30–48). By condemning one of their most capable theologians in this way, Lutherans could demonstrate their seriousness in guarding against the heresy of which they were accused. Personal antipathies between theologians (Jacob Andreae, one of the authors of the Formula of Concord, was one of Flacius's most bitter opponents) made it easier and even more satisfying to scapegoat one for the sake of affirming the innocence of many. The pontificating style of the universal assertions about substance and accident in FC, SD I, 55–59 indicates that communication on this point or among the Lutherans was almost impossible.

This process was a costly one for the future of Lutheran theology. There can be no doubt that the Formula of Concord arrived at a position closer to those of Flacius and of Luther than to that of Strigel.[19] In so doing, however, it failed to explore the basic issues of the controversy; although rejecting the position of Strigel, it accepted his terminology. It not only accepted his terminology but made that terminology normative for Lutheran theology. Thus the road which might have led back through Flacius or through a more adequate expression of Flacius's concern to Luther's position was closed. In choosing this way of prematurely resolving a controversy, the Formula of Concord followed the pattern adopted earlier by the Council of Trent. Both were concerned to protect the church from error and confusion by establishing one single perspective and its accompanying terminology as the only acceptable form of theology. Pluralism was rejected and with it the church's ability to carry on meaningful dialogue within itself. The church also lost its capacity to respond to man's constantly changing experience of himself and of his world. Tied to terminology that even then was becoming antiquated, the church found itself increasingly unable to address a meaningful and understandable gospel to its contemporary world. That was more significant than any immediate contribution to sound doctrine.

Article I set the tone for the rest of the Formula of Concord, and it affirmed earlier confessional statements on original sin, but the style of affirmation robbed them of their vitality. The only new question

19. Elert, *Structure*, pp. 28–30; Friedrich Brunstaed, *Theologie der lutherischen Bekenntnisschriften* (Gütersloh: Bertelsmann, 1951), pp. 58–63; Fr. H. R. Frank, *Die Theologie der Concordienformel historisch-dogmatisch entwickelt und beleuchtet* (Erlangen: Theodore Blaesing, 1858), 1:50–112.

it discussed is whether original sin is to be described as the substance or as an accident of human nature. The Formula of Concord thereby turned away from the only opportunity to return to Luther's focus on interpersonal relationships. It is ironic that it did so by standardizing the terminology that was also adopted by the Council of Trent. The significance of this loss can only be hinted at by tracing the vagaries of the development of the doctrine of sin in succeeding generations. The language of medieval theology leads to a preoccupation with its questions.[20]

The whole terminology of substance and accident became increasingly less meaningful, and an ontological approach to psychology became increasingly less relevant. It was unavoidable that a doctrine of sin formulated in those categories would become increasingly less useful to Lutheran pastors and theologians.

The theologians of seventeenth century Lutheran orthodoxy were able to reassert the position of the Formula of Concord only by an almost imperceptible but still slow and steady process of eroding its intention.[21] For example, John Gerhard closes his discussion of original sin in the ninth locus of his *Loci Theologici* by simply equating a definition of original sin in medieval categories with the definition of original sin in the Augsburg Confession. There is no sense of tension between the two approaches.[22] This emphasis on concupiscence and the lack of original righteousness generally leads to a corresponding focus on sin in terms of breaking the law and of guilt. Other manifestations of sin, such as subjection to the demonic powers of death and corruption in all their manifold forms, shame, and failure to achieve one's own goals fade into insignificance along with the Reformation's emphasis on the terrors of conscience. Even today some who are most self-consciously loyal to the Formula of Concord are afflicted with a guilt-centered theological tunnel vision that has no precedent in the *Book of Concord*.

20. Theologians of the Vatican's Secretariat for Christian Unity are presently discussing the possible affirmation of the Augsburg Confession as a meaningful theological document from the church's history. Lutherans will do well to consider the affirmation of the Council of Trent as another way in which Christians tried to find answers to questions for which no entirely satisfactory answers were available. This would enable participants on both sides of the dialogue to put such confessional documents into an appropriate historical context.

21. Elert, *Structure,* pp. 28–29.

22. This basic similarity is described by Robert P. Scharlemann, *Thomas Aquinas and John Gerhard* (New Haven: Yale University Press, 1964), pp. 44–113, see esp. pp. 84–96.

Such an emphasis on guilt provides a clear focus for ministry in some situations but provides none in many others. The first to feel the inadequacy of the orthodox Lutheran doctrine of sin were the pietists. They recognized concupiscence and guilt as one part of the experience of sin. However, they experienced sin more as a problem of the will with the accompanying feeling of shame. For them, the problem was not so much one of doing wrong as of being wrong.[23] Pietists thereby paralleled but did not exactly repeat the medieval distinction between mortal and venial sins. In contrast to the medieval understanding of venial sins, they saw sins of weakness as damnable. Deliberate sin, however, was the real test of regeneration, for it combined concupiscence with an act of the will. Pietists, who overcame deliberate sin, had validated the reality of salvation in their own lives. In their revision of Lutheran orthodoxy, they were responding to Catholic criticism of Luther's assertion that the Christian under the law is totally a sinner. Catholics criticized that assertion as a denial of the reality of redemption and sanctification.

Rationalists, on the other hand, modified Lutheran orthodoxy by emphasizing the involvement of reason in sin. Sin is not only an expression of concupiscence and of will but also of reason. For example, a typical eighteenth century Lutheran rationalist emphasized, "Every actual sin arises from a vague conception," and, "Every actual sin arises from failure to make use of freedom."[24] The phrase "arises from" indicates that "a vague conception" and "failure to make use of freedom" are counterparts to original sin. As Elert points out, the development of the doctrine of sin is a constant process of moving away from Luther's insight that original sin is a reversal of man's personal relationship to God. I would add only that that reversal moves in the direction set by the Formula of Concord.

One more dimension of the nature of sin remained to be explored. Sin is not merely a failure to achieve God's standard, it also is a failure to be what I want to be for myself. Medieval theology recognized this by speaking of voluntarily accepted evangelical counsels. Immanuel Kant's categorical imperative which requires each individual to do the good without regard for reward or punishment became a

---

23. Osmo Tiililä, "Über den pietistischen Sündenbegriff," in *Bekenntnis zur Kirche, Festgabe für Ernst Sommerlath* (Berlin: Evangelische Verlagsanstalt, 1960), pp. 209–12.

24. Cited by Elert, *Structure*, p. 33.

Protestant parallel. In attempting to fulfill this for himself, Kant experienced sin as "radical evil," as the inability to live up to the standard which he had set for himself. His critics correctly recognized that he had thereby returned—in terms of his personal experience— to an Augustinian/Lutheran emphasis on original sin.

The development of the doctrine of sin from Luther to Kant may be seen as a Lutheran reappropriation of the questions and concepts of the medieval doctrine of sin. The schematic parallel is strikingly similar, from the emphasis first on the loss of original righteousness, then on concupiscence, then on the weakening of the will, then on the darkening of reason, and then on a new breakthrough of personal experience. The potential fullness of the medieval doctrine was, however, closed to Lutheran theologians, combining as they did the assertion that concupiscence is sin with a conceptual framework in which that simple assertion cannot be made. The identification of concupiscence as sin was the one remnant of the Reformation doctrine of sin that prevented a simple return to the medieval doctrine.

One more non-Pelagian possibility remained to be tested, the non-Augustinian Eastern approach to the doctrine of original sin. This approach describes man as stumbling along the road to fuller maturity. This less tragic view of sin matched the experience of theologians and philosophers at the end of the eighteenth and beginning of the nineteenth centuries. Philosophers like Lessing, theologians like Schleiermacher and Bretschneider, agree sin is a developmental problem.[25]

Man is in the process of finding out who he is just as each individual person must, and some rebellion, whether in the child or the adolescent, is not only an inevitable but, since we are the kind of people we are, a necessary part of the process. Like a good and wise father, God will not destroy or reject his children because of these mistakes but will support and guide them as they move to a higher stage of development.

There were important and significant attempts to recover and restate the doctrine of sin in the nineteenth century. The most important and

25. Gotthold Ephraim Lessing, "The Education of the Human Race," in *Lessing's Theological Writings,* ed. Henry Chadwick (London: Adam and Charles Black, 1956), p. 95; Friedrich Schleiermacher, *The Christian Faith,* 2d edition, ed. H. R. Mackintosh and J. S. Stewart (New York: Harper Torchbooks, 1963), 1:269–324 (§ § 65–78); Karl Gottlieb Bretschneider, *Handbuch der Dogmatik . . .,* 4th ed. (Leipzig: J. A. Barth, 1838), 2:127. Cf. Bretschneider, *Die Grundlage des evangelischen Pietismus; der die Lehren von Adams Fall, der Erbsünde und dem Opfer Christi* (Leipzig: Vogel, 1833).

popular of these simply rework earlier discussions and bring little that is fresh and new.[26]

The significant breakthrough in the doctrine of sin in the nineteenth century was made by Søren Kierkegaard. Like Luther's, his perspective on sin is determined by the radical nature of his personal experience. In dealing with that experience, he focused on categories such as trembling, dread, and anxiety, which indicate Kierkegaard's concern with man's personal relationship to God. These categories, remarkably similar to those of the early Reformation, were defined in books that were hardly noticed until the end of the century and became popular only as the experiences of World War I and the Great Depression in the United States gave many people the firsthand experience of evil that required a more adequate understanding of sin. In the context of such experience there was a wave of rediscovery of the uniqueness of Luther's approach. The discovery of Kierkegaard and the rediscovery of Luther thus were mutually reinforcing in focusing the doctrine of sin on the *whole* person in relationship to God rather than in focusing on various elements of the human personality and their relationship to one another. Trust is always a function of the whole person.

This period of theological rediscovery coincided with the beginning of a period of radical breakthroughs and a proliferation of viewpoints in the field of psychology. A bewildering multiplicity of viewpoints have emerged and are utilized by people to describe and interpret their experience. The data are too extensive to be adequately comprehended by any one theoretical approach. The theories are often incommensurable and even contradictory. Yet it is inevitable that the categories of a doctrine of sin be related to a view of man. Given this situation, the church can (as a whole or as individuals) follow the lead of the Formula of Concord (and the Council of Trent) and set one approach as basic to the doctrine of sin. This will give unity, consistency, predictability, and clarity to the church's and/or any

---

26. For example, Friedrich August Tholuck, *Die Lehre von der Sünde und vom Versöhner oder: Die wahre Weihe des Zweiflers* (Hamburg: Perthes, 1823). This book was written in opposition to Wilhelm de Wette's rationalist novel *Theodor oder des Zweiflers Weihe* (Berlin, 1822), which was published in eight editions by 1862. Cf. Paul Handschin, *Wilhelm Martin Leberecht de Wette als Prediger und Schriftsteller* (Basel: Verlag Helbing & Lichtenhahn, 1958), pp. 95–114. Julius Mueller, *The Christian Doctrine of Sin,* trans. William Urwick, 2 vols. (Edinburgh: T. & T. Clark, 1877), was first published in Germany in 1839 and was reprinted in six editions by 1877. There is an earlier English translation by William Pulsford (Edinburgh: T. & T. Clark, 1852–53).

individual pastor's position. At the same time, it will restrict the church's capacity to respond to the constantly changing categories of human self-awareness. Insofar as those categories differ from the categories normatized by the church, the proclamation of the gospel will become irrelevant and meaningless.

This essay proposes that the church consciously and deliberately choose the path of pluralism in its theological formulations and invite polymorphous approaches to the doctrine of sin. Following this path in relation to the doctrine of original sin, the church would ask any and all of its members who have formulated their own understanding of the structure of human personality and/or of interpersonal relationships to develop a doctrine of original sin that would be meaningful in terms of those understandings and make that doctrine available to the church together with a summary statement of the basic conceptual framework. These various formulations would thus be available to pastors who regularly deal with people who can be addressed only in varying contexts. Pastors could be trained to work theologically with people, not only in terms of the one or two psychological approaches which they find personally congenial but in terms of the broad spectrum of available perspectives.

Our historical overview has indicated that this would have been theoretically possible in the past. All of the various doctrines are characterized not so much by substantive disagreement with each other as by the different categories and perspectives that were dominant and by their authors' levels of personal experience. All of these theologians were talking about the same phenomenon of original sin but could not find a common language which would permit them to identify the theological dimensions of their agreement or disagreement. Strigel and Flacius are excellent examples of this problem. The Formula of Concord's failure to hear Luther's question is an example of the attempt to achieve agreement when there is no clarity about what is to be agreed upon. The pluralistic or polymorphous approach proposed here means that disagreement with and correction of someone else's statements can be attempted only after mastering that particular conceptual frame of reference and the specific categories being used in terms of their relevance for one's own personal experience and then risking one's own suggested formulation of the church's teaching in those same categories. Under those conditions, I am convinced that the history of doctrinal development in the church would have been characterized by far more agreement and much less disagreement than presently seems to be the case.

This approach to pluralism is radically different from the simplistic assertion that "all roads lead to the same place." Roads lead to many places, with many unexpected intersections and turnings. It is only possible to know where any road will lead by following it in one specific direction from one specific point. Then it is found that many, but not all roads do indeed lead to the same general vicinity provided they are traveled in the appropriate direction.

A more appropriate analogy is provided by the concept of equi-finality in general systems theory. In a closed system, there is only one starting part, one appropriate process, and one ending point. Up until now theologians have tended to operate with closed systems. Each has had his starting point, his process of theological thinking, and his conclusions. The time has come—and the ongoing dialogues offer us the opportunity—to switch deliberately to an open-systems approach to theology. In an open system, it is possible to start at many points. Those who start at different points and desire to reach the same goal must of necessity follow different processes. Starting at different points and following the same process leads to differing conclusions. All the Melanchthonians, orthodox, pietists, and rationalists who started at different points but did not appropriately modify their process discovered that. Their attempts to represent the evangelical position in their day were considerably less than successful. That has also been the tragedy of those who attempted to be faithful to the Lutheran confession. They were in fact operating in the reality of an open system but trying to function as though it were a closed system. We can learn from their experience and consistently attempt to work with the pluralism of an open system.

There is no better point at which to start than the doctrine of sin. There is no more fruitful context than the present inter-confessional dialogues which permit us not merely to identify the differences, but to test the meaning of the differences and then to ask whether the differences really represent any significant theological difference. How does, for example, *this* particular doctrine of sin help *me* express the gospel as *I* experience it?

Luther had dealt with sin as a problem of trust and mistrust. Melanchthon and orthodoxy focused on the concupiscent rebellion against God. The pietists focused on the weakness of the will and its inherent shame. Rationalists were particularly aware of sin as a rational act and of the need for reward and punishment. Idealism described sin in terms of the rebellion associated with the adolescent's search for identity. I have already commented on the parallel to the medieval development. The parallel of both the medieval and the post–Formula of Concord patterns of development to the sequence of tasks in personal development as described by Erik Erikson is even more striking. Indeed, this systematic exploration of the various experiential analogies is a major contribution made by Lutheran theology to theology's resources in exploring polymorphous doctrines of sin.

It may be objected that since these various doctrines of sin were accompanied by reductions of the gospel, their reappropriation in the contemporary context would also limit the understanding of the gospel. That is possible, but two factors indicate that it is not necessary. First, a pluralistic approach means that the church will have a wide perspective in its doctrine of sin that will prevent any one viewpoint from becoming dominant. Although any theologian or pastor will at various times emphasize one dimension more than another, his personal experience will move him from one to another in much the same way that theology moved from orthodoxy to idealism.[27] Thus a doctrine of sin formulated in terms of sin as demonic force requires a gospel of redemption; sin experienced as shame and self-doubt because of a failure of autonomy, a gospel of acceptance; the experience of sin as a conscious and deliberate act resulting in real guilt, a gospel of forgiveness; the experience of sin as the meaninglessness of life because of our failure to achieve our own goals and realize our own potential, a gospel in terms of incarnation and Christian liberty, and so forth.

A second corrective is even more important; we are now in a position to reappropriate the understanding of sin as a problem not primarily of inner personal structure but of a person's relationship to God. Sin now can be understood in its deepest sense regardless of the level or style of personal experience. Given this perspective, the simple moralism of Pelagianism and semi-Pelagianism is not possible for long. The reappropriation of Luther's perspective will also fulfill the intention of Article I of the Formula of Concord. But more important, it will be a major contribution to the theological resources of the whole church.

27. When asked at the end of his life about his failure to complete the *Summa theologica,* Thomas Aquinas thus commented: "I can't do any more. Such things have been revealed to me that everything I have written seems to be so much straw." This is not unlike Luther's judgment on his own works.

3

Melanchthonian Motifs in the Formula's Eucharistic Christology

Ralph W. Quere

Luther vs. Melanchthon the proto-Calvinist[1] or crypto-Calvinist:[2] that is how the eucharistic controversy that eventuated in articles VII and VIII of the Formula of Concord has usually been explained. The consensus has been that theologically "Melanchthonianism was put down in the Formula of 1577."[3] Indeed the Formula, which is in-

1. Heinrich Heppe, *Reformed Orthodoxy,* trans. G. T. Thomson (London: George Allen & Unwin, 1950); Hans Engelland, *Melanchthon, Glauben und Handeln* (Munich: Chr. Kaiser Verlag, 1931); Helmut Gollwitzer, *Coena Domini* (Munich: Chr. Kaiser Verlag, 1937); Wilhelm H. Neuser, *Die Abendmahlslehre Melanchthonis in ihrer geschichtlichen Entwicklung (1519–1530)* (Neukirchen-Vluyn: Neukirchener Verlag des Erziehungsvereins GmbH, 1968).

2. C. F. W. Walther, *Der Concordienformel: Kern und Stern* (St. Louis, 1877); Friedrich Bente, ed., *Concordia Triglotta* (St. Louis: Concordia Publishing House, 1921); Charles Porterfield Krauth, *The Conservative Reformation and Its Theology* (Minneapolis: Augsburg Publishing House, 1871).

3. Jaroslav Pelikan, *From Luther to Kierkegaard* (St. Louis: Concordia Publishing House, 1950). Cf. note 2 above and Heinrich Heppe, *Geschichte der lutherischen Concordienformel und Concordie* (Marburg: Elwert'sche Universitäts Buchhandlung, 1857). Philip Schaff, *The Creeds of Christendom* (Grand Rapids: Baker Book House, 1877); Henry E. Jacobs, *Historical Introduction . . . to the Book of Concord* (Philadelphia: Lutheran Publication Society, 1883); James W. Richard, *The Confessional History of the Lutheran Church* (Philadelphia: Lutheran Publication Society, 1909); Theodore E. Schmauk and C. Theodore Benze, *The Confessional Principle and the Confessions of the Lutheran Church* (Philadelphia: General Council Publication Board, 1911); George J. Fritschel, *The Formula of Concord* (Philadelphia: Lutheran Publication Society, 1916); Reinhold Seeberg, *Lehrbuch der Dogmengeschichte* (Erlangen: A. Deichertsche Verlagsbuchhandlung Werner Scholl, 1920), 4:2; C. H. Little, *Lutheran Confessional Theology* (St. Louis: Concordia Publishing House, 1943); Edmund Schlink, *Theology of the Lutheran Confessions,* trans. Paul F. Koehneke and Herbert J. A. Bouman

tended as a correct exposition of the controverted articles of the Augsburg Confession, claims Luther as the best interpreter of the Augustana.[4] This stands in marked contrast to the position of John Calvin who subscribed to the Augsburg Confession as Melanchthon had interpreted it in his 1540 *Variata* edition.[5] Our concern is whether the Formula is to be understood exclusively or at least primarily in the light of Luther's theology or whether themes from Melanchthon also emerge there.[6] Or does the Formula represent a third position fundamentally different from Luther's and Melanchthon's?[7]

The Formula follows the principle of defending and defining controverted doctrines by quoting Luther rather than the later Melanchthon's writings.[8] (Melanchthon's confessional writings through 1536 were regarded as orthodox. And such "profitable writings" as agree with the Book of Concord were not to be rejected or condemned.)[9] This is the ambiguous official status granted Melanchthon. My contention is that numerous Melanchthonian motifs make their way into the Formula—also in the controverted eucharistic doctrines. Demonstrating how and through whom this happened is a massive task and beyond the scope of this essay. My method is simple comparison: identifying characteristic or unique emphases in Melanchthon's theology and indicating where parallels exist in the Formula. It suffices here to show that teachings of the later Melanchthon—also on controverted matters—are affirmed in the Formula. What finally emerges

---

(Philadelphia: Fortress Press, 1961); Willard Dow Allbeck, *Studies in the Lutheran Confessions* (Philadelphia: Fortress Press, 1952). Hans-Werner Gensichen, *We Condemn: How Luther and 16th Century Lutheranism Condemned False Doctrine,* trans. Herbert J. A. Bouman (St. Louis: Concordia Publishing House, 1967).

4. Formula of Concord, Solid Declaration (hereafter cited as SD), VII, 41 (article, paragraph) in *The Book of Concord,* ed. Theodore G. Tappert (Philadelphia: Fortress Press, 1959), p. 576; hereafter cited as BC. Cf. *Die Bekenntnisschriften der evangelisch-lutherischen Kirche,* 4th edition (Göttingen: Vandenhoeck & Ruprecht, 1959), 984.36–985.9; hereafter cited as BK followed by page number(s) and line(s).

5. Bente, *Triglotta,* p. 174.

6. Friedrich Brunstad, *Theologie der lutherischen Bekenntnisschriften* (Gütersloh: C. Bertelsmann Verlag, 1951), pp. 154–57, 165–81. Cf. Schlink, *Theology,* pp. 170–71.

7. Cf. Wilhelm Niesel, *The Gospel and the Churches,* trans. David Lewis (Philadelphia: Westminster Press, 1962), pp. 275–83.

8. Fritschel, *The Formula,* p. 106.

9. Preface to *The Book of Concord, BC,* pp. 9–10; BK 10.17–22.

in the Formula's eucharistic doctrine is a kind of synthesis of the theologies of Luther and Melanchthon (not excluding the emphases and interpretations of the formulators themselves). In this process Melanchthon's thought supplements, corrects, and is corrected by the theology of Luther, who receives more than a nod from the writers of the Formula. What follows attempts to show that the Preceptor also made his mark on the Formula of Concord which his theology helped to occasion.

Christ's Efficacious Presence

Melanchthon steered a course between the Roman concept of efficacious signs and the Zwinglian attempt to reduce Christ's presence to efficacy. He early rejected the Roman Catholic understanding of efficacious signs on the basis of his Lutheran understanding of justification by faith. In 1521 he wrote: "(2) Faith is righteousness. (3) Works are the fruit of righteousness. (4) Signs are neither righteousness nor the fruit of righteousness."[10] In the Apology, Melanchthon stresses the necessity of faith in terms of the need to *receive* that which is offered in the sacrament: for "a promise is useless [*inutilis*] unless faith accepts it."[11] Similarly, he quotes Augustine: "faith in the sacrament, and not the sacrament, justifies." In the 1559 *Loci* he writes that "faith is necessary both in asking and receiving the remission of sins."[12]

Melanchthon also rejects the Zwinglian attempt to reduce Christ's presence to the presence of his power. In his study of the Fathers in 1529, he suggests: ". . . [Christ] can be truly present where he effects something."[13] In his 1530 negotiations with Bucer he argues for "not only the presence of the power but of the body." He also refuses to *substitute* the Spirit's presence for the Son. It is "Christ present who

10. *Propositions on the Mass,* 1521, in E. E. Black and L. J. Satre, eds., *Melanchthon: Selected Writings,* trans. Charles L. Hill (Minneapolis: Augsburg Publishing House, 1962), p. 65. Cf. Robert Stupperich, ed., *Melanchthons Werke in Auswahl* (Gütersloh: C. Bertelsmann Verlag/Gütersloher Verlagshaus Gerd Mohn, 1951–75), 1:163; hereafter cited as *MW*.

11. *Apology of the Augsburg Confession,* XIII, 20 (*BC,* p. 213, par. 20; *BK* 295.15).

12. *MW* 2/2:525.16–17.

13. Carl G. Bretschneider and H. E. Bindseil, eds., *Philippi Melanthonis Opera,* vol. 23 of *Corpus Reformatorum* (Brunsvigae: C. A. Schwetschke et Filium, 1834–60), p. 751; hereafter cited as *CR* (23:751).

distributes his body and blood to us."[14] In the 1535 *Loci* Melanchthon writes: "Christ is truly present in his sacrament and efficacious in us," and he "testifies that his benefits belong to us."[15]

What are these *benefits* and how are they related to the Lord's Supper? Melanchthon prefers the terms "use" (*usus*—based on the Augustinian *utor-fruor scheme*),[16] "purpose," or "goal" (*finis*).[17] The answer he gives, early and late, is: to strengthen and confirm faith. This is very different from Luther designating forgiveness, life, and salvation as the benefits of the sacrament. Or is it?

For Melanchthon, forgiveness is given in the sacrament in a derivative sense, that is, as faith is strengthened to grasp it anew. "For this, therefore, eating is useful to the penitent, namely, for confirming faith by which we take—it truly follows—remission of sins and the Holy Spirit."[18] This is as close as Melanchthon seems able to come to saying that forgiveness is given in or by the sacrament. Melanchthon is still trying to steer a course between the Roman and Reformed positions. So he wants to say that Christ, not the sacrament, gives the benefit and he gives it to and through faith.

Another characteristic expression of his view of the benefits is seen in the 1555 *Loci*: "With this bread and wine he gives *his body and blood* [italics translator's] to us and thereby attests [*bezeugnet*] that he accepts us, makes us his members, grants us forgiveness of sins, and that he has purified us with his blood, and will abide in us."[19] This careful distinction between the *Zeugnis* (Christ's attestation) and the *Zeichen* (the eating and drinking) is like his distinction between the sign and the thing signified: it refuses to make the sacrament as such a channel of grace. Rather, the Christ who is himself efficaciously present gives grace.

A final example of the new formula for Christ's efficacious presence may be pointed to in a letter of Melanchthon to Veit Dietrich written in 1537. Here the formula appears in its full and final form: "Christ

14. *Iudicium de Zwinglii doctrina*, July 25, 1530 (CR 2:223–24); cf. CR 21:468).
15. CR 21:479 and 477.
16. 1521 *Loci Communes*, MW 2/1:143.24–26; *"Propositions,"* 41, MW 1:165; 1535 *Loci*, CR 21:477.
17. 1559 *Loci*, MW 2/2:529.29. Cf. 523.34; CR 23:190.
18. 1559 *Loci*, MW 2/2:525.29–32.
19. *Melanchthon on Christian Doctrine: Loci Communes, 1555*, trans. Clyde L. Manschreck (New York: Oxford University Press, 1965), p. 218; hereafter cited as M 55. Cf. CR 22:471.

is truly and substantially present and is efficacious."[20] He locates the efficacy in Christ rather than affirming that the signs are efficacious, which would imply some kind of *ex opere operato* working or else identify Christ totally with the elements. This also avoids the Bucerian criticism that the Lutherans ascribed to the bread what belongs to God alone.

This central Melanchthonian motif is reflected in the Formula of Concord but only in the Solid Declaration: "Believers receive it as a certain pledge and assurance that their sins are truly forgiven, that Christ dwells and is efficacious in them. . . ."[21] There is a Melanchthonian ring to this discussion of the benefits (not forgiveness, but the assurance of forgiveness) and efficacy (i.e., that the Christ is dwelling in us efficaciously). The Latin text even has the characteristic Melanchthonian volitional emphasis: Christ *wills* to be efficacious in us (*efficax esse velit*).[22]

Christ's Ecclesial Presence

Incorporation into the body of Christ through the Lord's Supper becomes an important motif in Melanchthon's teachings in the 1530s. Luther had presented this as a central benefit of the Lord's Supper in his early writings.[23] Perhaps because Zwingli emphasized the church as the body of Christ as the *only* sense in which Christ was *bodily* present in the sacrament, Luther deemphasized it.[24] Oecolampadius's patristic study, the *Dialogus,* showing the importance of incorporation for the Fathers,[25] apparently influenced Melanchthon to reemphasize it. Our incorporation into the body of Christ through the sacrament and Christ's efficacious presence in his church in the sacrament are tied together for Melanchthon. The term I am suggesting for this linkage is "ecclesial presence." Melanchthon writes: "For Christ testifies that

20. Letter to Veit Dietrich, October 6, 1537 (*CR* 3:416–17).

21. SD VII, 63 (*BC*, p. 581; *BK* 993.43–994.4).

22. *BK* 994.1–6.

23. *The Blessed Sacrament,* 1519 in *Luther's Works,* American edition, ed. Helmut T. Lehmann (Philadelphia: Fortress Press, 1951ff.), 35:51; hereafter cited as *LW*. Cf. *D. Martin Luthers Werke* (Weimar, 1883ff.), 2:743; hereafter cited as *WA*.

24. Cf. Jaroslav Pelikan, "Neglected Aspects of Luther's Doctrine of the Lord's Supper," *Minutes of the . . . English District, the Lutheran Church-Missouri Synod* (1957): 12–33.

25. Ralph W. Quere, "Melanchthon on Sign, Presence, and Benefit: The Genesis of Melanchthon's Doctrine of Christ's Efficacious Presence" (Ph.D. dissertation, Princeton Theological Seminary, 1970), pp. 338–39.

his benefits belong to us when he imparts to us his body and unites us to himself as members. . . . Thus he testifies that he will be efficacious in us, because he himself is life; he gives us his blood to testify that he absolves us."[26] It is *Christ* who gives us peace and makes us his body, who forgives us and cleanses us with his blood, thereby assuring us that he will dwell and work in us."[27] Christ's presence in us is realized as his benefits are appropriated by faith. Melanchthon's new formula for the efficacious presence is conjoined to an affirmation of Christ indwelling and making us his members: "And Christ is truly present in his sacrament and efficacious in us just as Hilary says, '[We] who do this drinking and eating (do it) so that Christ may be in us and we in him.' " Thus "he imparts himself to us" and "we are joined to him as members."[28]

In the Wittenberg Concord of 1536 stands the Oecolampadian motif of the ecclesiological benefit of incorporation into Christ. Thus the Concord affirms: ". . . those who truly repent . . . are incorporated into Christ. . . ."[29] Since the Wittenberg Concord is itself incorporated into the Formula of Concord, it may not seem significant that its affirmation of the ecclesial benefit of incorporation is included. But the formulators were not at all hesitant to add the parenthetical explanation of transubstantiation or subtract the words connoting a "simultaneous presence" from the Wittenberg Concord.[30] Thus the inclusion of incorporation must be considered an affirmation of a theme often neglected among the Lutherans.

Article VIII of the Formula also affirms: "Christ can be and is present wherever he wills, and in particular that he is present with his church and community on earth as mediator, head, king and high priest."[31] Such ecclesial presence is immediately tied to Christ's eucharistic presence: ". . . he instituted his Holy Supper that he might be present with us, dwell in us, work and be mighty in us [*kräftig sein will/efficacem esse velle*]. . . ."[32] The juxtaposition of ecclesial and efficacious presence heightens the Melanchthonian flavor.

---

26. 1535 *Loci* (*CR* 21:477).
27. Ibid.
28. 1535 *Loci* (*CR* 21:479).
29. Wittenberg Concord cited in SD VII, 16 (*BC*, p. 572; *BK* 978.8–13).
30. See below, p. 64 and note 37; also pp. 68–69.
31. SD VIII, 78 (*BC*, pp. 606–607; *BK* 1043.28–35).
32. SD VIII, 79 (*BC*, p. 607; *BK* 1043.40–1044.5).

Christ's Ritual Presence

Not only are efficacious and ecclesial presence bridges for Melanchthon between Christ's eucharistic presence and his benefits, so is the "sacramental union" concept in the Wittenberg Concord. The sacramental union does not simply spell out the relationship between the elements and Christ's body or attempt to explain the mode of presence. It relates presence and efficacy in point of time by means of the sacramental action: "they grant that through the sacramental union the bread is the body of Christ, . . ." *that is, they think that when the bread has been held out the body of Christ is at the same time present and truly offered* [*exhiberi*].[33] (Italicized clause is omitted by German text of the Formula.) The offer, because it is *his* offer, has the power to deliver what it promises. This offer is made "when the bread is held out" and there and then—"at the same time"—Christ is present as gift and giver. It is this presence in the total eucharistic action (*in sacramento, in ritu, in ministerio, in actu*) that I am designating Christ's "ritual presence." Efficacious, ecclesial, and ritual presence are all set forth in Melanchthon's 1551 commentary on 1 Corinthians: ". . . the Son of God lives and reigns and wills to be present *in the sacrament in this instituted use,* and then joins us to himself as members, and without any doubt is efficacious there in those who eat in faith and who sustain themselves with this consolation" (italics mine).[34] Central to my concern is the concept of Christ present *"in Sacramento in hoc usu instituto."* In this passage *sacramento* and *usu* are joined, reflecting Melanchthon's concern for Christ's "sacramental" presence only in connection with man's participation in and use of the sacrament. Melanchthon implies here what he states elsewhere: Christ is not present *extra usum,* for example, in the reserved bread or in a *Corpus Christi* procession.

Melanchthon's clearest explanation of what he means by this way of explaining the presence comes in two letters to Veit Dietrich in 1538. On March 22, he wrote: ". . . the sacrament consists in the use, the body is offered for eating, and in the use Christ is present. . . ."[35] To put it in the theological shorthand of this paper, this is Christ's efficacious presence in the rite, himself offering us his body to eat.

In a letter to Dietrich dated April 23, 1538, Melanchthon wrote:

33. Wittenberg Concord (*BK* 977.26–30).
34. *CR* 15:1112.
35. *CR* 3:504. Cf. *CR* 3:933; *MW* 6:399.32–40.

"So that I do not move too far away from the Fathers, I have placed the sacramental presence in the use and I have said that when [the elements] have been given, Christ is truly present and efficacious."[36]

Another statement of the relation of efficacy to action comes from a letter to Dietrich written on October 25, 1543. "Just as Christ acting freely is present in the instituted action, after the action he does not will to be included with the bread, he does not will that he be bound there."[37]

In his 1551 Saxon Confession, Melanchthon again uses this ritual presence formulation: ". . . in the instituted use in this communion Christ is truly and substantially present."[38] The 1555 *Loci* makes the same point in a different way: "a sacrament is a sacrament only in its instituted use."[39] Only in the use Christ commanded has Christ promised to be efficaciously present. In his 1559 answer to the Weimar Confutation by the Gnesio-Lutherans, Melanchthon affirms: "in the instituted use, the Lord Christ is truly living and really present."[40] Noting that Melanchthon focuses on the *rite* rather than the elements in the 1559 *Loci*, Fraenkel comments that the Preceptor's emphasis is on *event*, not *est*![41] Niesel explains this emphasis well: "According to Melanchthon, Christ is present in the whole action of the Supper, not just in the bread and wine." His presence happens "together with and concurrent with" the action of the Lord's Supper.[42]

Schlink's explanation of the Formula's teaching expresses well its understanding of the relationship between physical and spiritual eating in the Lord's Supper: ". . . in the act of eating the bread, I eat Christ's body."[43] The Melanchthon ring is also accurate! The emphasis on "act," and not just the elements of bread and wine, gives the Formula its basis for affirming an end point of Christ's eucharistic presence. It is also a way to deal with all the knotty questions connected with the Roman Catholic practice of reservation of the host. The Formula's

---

36. *CR* 3:514.

37. *CR* 23:308.

38. *Confessio Saxonica*, 1551, *MW* 6:130.9–12.

39. *M* 55, p. 222; *CR* 22:477.

40. *CR* 9:626.

41. Peter Fraenkel, "Ten Questions Concerning Melanchthon, the Fathers, and the Eucharist," *Luther and Melanchthon,* ed. Vilmos Vajta (Philadelphia: Fortress Press, 1961), p. 148.

42. Niesel, *The Gospel,* p. 280.

43. Schlink, *Theology,* p. 173.

Melanchthonian solution is that Christ is not present apart from (or after) the designated sacramental use in the liturgical action. In theological shorthand, Christ's ritual presence is *non extra usum!*[44] This is affirmed not only in the Wittenberg Concord (denying a permanent union with the bread "apart from the use"[45]) but also in the Formula's subsequent interpretation of that somewhat suspect Wittenberg Concord. "There has also arisen a misunderstanding and dissension among some teachers of the Augsburg Confession concerning the consecration and the common rule that there is no sacrament apart from the instituted use."[46] The consensus reached by the formulators is as follows: "No man's word or work . . . can effect the true presence of the body and blood of Christ in the Supper. This is ascribed only to the almighty power of God and the Word, institution, and ordinance of our Lord Jesus Christ. . . . For wherever we observe his institution and speak his words over the bread and cup and distribute the blessed bread and cup, Christ himself is still active through the spoken words. . . ."[47] In the first and in subsequent meals, Christ is present and active in the rite—also to consecrate. Chrysostom is cited to reinforce this point: "Christ himself prepares this table and blesses it. No human being, but only Christ himself who was crucified for us, can make of the bread and wine set before us the body and blood of Christ."[48] This patristic version of ritual presence underlies the teaching that, in the sacrament, Christ is the host, priest, and giver of the gift.

What is the "divinely instituted," "entire external and visible action," administration, or use of the Supper?[49] The Formula is quite precise about what that action includes: ". . . in a Christian assembly we take bread and wine, consecrate it, distribute it, receive it, eat and drink it, and therewith proclaim the Lord's death. . . ."[50] Christ is present in the rite as priest (to consecrate), as host (to distribute), and as gift (to be received in faith). Therefore "apart from this use it

44. Cf. Augustus Muecke, *De Philippi Melanchthonis doctrina de coena domini* (inaugural dissertation in Academia Georgia Augusta; Gotha: Formis Perthesianis, 1867).

45. SD VII, 14 (*BC,* p. 571; *BK* 977.34).

46. SD VII, 73 (*BC,* pp. 582–83; *BK* 997.34–998.4).

47. SD VII, 74–75 (*BC,* p. 583; *BK* 998.7–38).

48. SD VII, 76 (*BC,* p. 583; *BK* 998.41–44).

49. SD VII, 79–87 (*BC,* pp. 584–85; *BK* 999–1001).

50. SD VII, 84 (*BC,* p. 584; *BK* 1000.37–40).

is not to be deemed a sacrament," for example, when "offered up" (in the sacrifice of the mass), "locked up" (reserved in the tabernacle on the altar), "carried about" (in *Corpus Christi* processions), or "exposed for adoration" (in Benediction services, sometimes referred to to as "putting Jesus to bed").[51] In the instituted use Jesus is present. That "ritual presence" is circumscribed by his command and promise and ascribed to "the omnipotence óf our Lord and Savior, Jesus Christ."[52]

Elemental Presence

The prepositional approach to the real presence must be seen against the background of Luther's use of "in and under" in the catechisms and Melanchthon's use of the Lateran paraphrase *"unter des Gestalts"* in the Augsburg Confession. Given the continuing objection to and misunderstanding of the formula, *in pane,* on the part of the Reformed, it is not strange that the formula, *cum pane,* appeared in the Apology. When this formula is understood in light of the ritual presence, new possibilities of interpretation and agreement open up. The ecclesial presence as benefit, paralleling the body and blood which *"exhibeantur cum . . . pane et vino,"*[53] gives further evidence that a new relationship is being drawn: the presence is more concrete (*substantialiter!*) than ever,[54] for Christ's body is given with the element in the rite in the church.[55]

In a memorandum in 1536, Melanchthon, Brenz, and others affirm that "with the bread and wine the Son of God is truly and substantially present. . . ."[56] In the Wittenberg Concord itself both the *cum pane* and the *simul adesse* are affirmed.[57] In Melanchthon's theology this allows for a temporally conceived "simultaneous presence"; this is

---

51. SD VII, 87 (*BC,* p. 585; *BK* 1001.25–29).

52. SD VII, 90 (*BC,* p. 585; *BK* 1002.36–37).

53. *BK* 248.1, 21–39.

54. See Quere, "Sign, Presence, and Benefits," pp. 296–310.

55. In 1530 Melanchthon had ignored the affirmation of ecclesial presence by Bucer (Brück's Summary in vol. 17 of *D. Martin Luthers sämmtliche Schriften,* ed. Joh. Georg Walch [St. Louis: Concordia Publishing House, 1880–1910], p. 1985) in his *Iudicium* (*CR* 2:224).

56. Henricus E. Bindseil, ed., *Philippi Melanchthonis epistolae, iudicia, consilia, testimonia aliorumque ad eum epistolae quae in Corpore Reformatorum desiderantur* (Halle, 1874), p. 109.

57. *BK* 977.20, 29.

ruled out by the Formula's editing of the Wittenberg Concord.[58]   A final quotation from the 1555 *Loci* will suffice to show the continuance of this *cum* formula and the implications this mode of presence has for believers: "With this bread and wine he gives his body and blood to us, and thereby attests that he accepts us, makes us his members, grants us forgiveness of sins, and that he has purified us with his blood, and will abide in us."[59]   The new formula is joined here to the full, careful, and characteristic exposition of the benefits.   The relationship drawn between presence and benefits is familiar: the eucharistic body is the sign of what Christ himself effects, that is, our incorporation into his body, the church, where forgiveness is granted. The distinction remains carefully drawn: participating in the sacrament does not grant grace automatically.   It is his presence that is efficacious —not the sign with which that presence is given.   Yet there is a point of identification too—a point where presence becomes benefit, that is, where, through the body given with the bread, he makes us his body.

Pelikan suggests that the Formula's prepositional approach to Christ's eucharistic presence "in, with, and under" the bread and wine derives from Heshusius.[60]   The famous Lutheran shibboleth can be traced directly to Luther's "Great Confession" of 1528.[61]   But it is also clear in that treatise that "in" and "under" the bread are Luther's favorite prepositions for describing Christ's presence.[62]   This is confirmed by his choice of these terms in the catechisms.[63]   It should be equally clear from the above discussion that Melanchthon's favorite preposition was "with" (*cum*).   The Formula of Concord is best understood in its use of the "in, with, and under" shibboleth (*not* in Luther's precise form) as a synthesis of Luther's and Melanchthon's emphases.   For the prepositional phrases are used to explain not only Luther's concept that the bread *is* the true body of Christ, but also Melanchthon's concept of sacramental union.   Thus "the union of the body and blood of Christ with the bread and wine is . . . a sacramental union. . . ."[64]

Thus Luther's "in" and "under" are qualified by Melanchthon's

58. See above, pp. 63–64.
59. *M* 55, p. 218; *CR* 22:471.
60. Jaroslav Pelikan, "Neglected Aspects," p. 27.
61. *Confession Concerning Christ's Supper,* 1528 (*LW* 37:306; *WA* 26:447.26).
62. *LW* 37:166–67, 230, 276, 309.
63. SD VI, 2 (*BC,* p. 351; *BK* 519.42); LC V, 8 (*BC,* p. 447; *BK* 709.24).
64. SD VII, 38 (*BC,* pp. 575–76; *BK* 983.12–984.3).

"with." Oral eating is balanced by a spiritual-supernatural mode and a rejection of Capernaitic language. Melanchthon's preference for temporal over spatial categories to describe Christ's presence never fully emerges in the Formula, except insofar as *non extra usum* implies presence in the *rite*. To that extent Luther's motif of elemental presence (Christ's presence in/under bread and wine) is modified not only by Melanchthon's *cum*, but also by the whole concept of Christ's ritual presence.

Personal Presence

The question is: whether it is the *body* of Christ or the *person* of Christ that is present in the sacrament. This has been seen as a decisive difference between Luther and Melanchthon. I would like to suggest that both reformers say both the body and the person of Christ are present for opposite reasons. Luther starts from the *verba* and argues that because Christ's body is present his person is also present. Luther's use of ubiquity is primarily to show that Christ's body *can* be present. It *is* present for us because he promised it. Melanchthon's starting point is Christ's personal presence, promised, for example, in Matthew 28:18. From that he moves to the bodily presence, or Christ present *substantialiter*. Gollwitzer says that Melanchthon affirms Christ's *corporalis praesentia* but does not emphasize it.[65] Melanchthon himself employs this kind of distinction in his 1534 *Iudicium de coena sacra* for Philip of Hesse: "Because he is God, he gives us his body as a witness that he is really [*wesentlich*] with us always . . . therefore I conclude that truly, not figuratively, the body and blood of Christ, that is the real [*wesentlich*] Christ, is with [*mit*] the bread and wine."[66] This implies the *person*al (*sic!*) and real presence of the whole Christ. The point of the second sentence is that *the body and blood of Christ truly present* means that the real or substantial Christ is really present.

Seeberg has set forth considerable evidence for Melanchthon's denial of ubiquity (i.e., the omnipresence of the body of Christ).[67] Yet, in 1558, Melanchthon makes a distinction, like Luther's distinction between the repletive (omnipresent) and the definitive (eucharistic)

---

65. Gollwitzer, *Coena Domini*, p. 68.
66. *CR* 2:801.
67. Reinhold Seeberg, *Textbook of the History of Doctrine,* trans. Charles E. Hay (Grand Rapids: Baker Book House, 1964), 2:350–51.

modes[68] of Christ's presence: "For there is a great difference between the universal presence and this special presence of the Son of God in the administration. And in this action, he himself bestows himself upon us and his benefits; he is efficacious in us and makes us his members, and the word of Paul is a clear witness that apart from the eating there is no sacrament: the bread which we break is the fellowship of the body. Now there is no fellowship apart from the eating."[69] This full statement of what Christ effects in the administration or action of the sacrament shows beautifully the interrelation of the ritual, efficacious, and ecclesial presence and the benefits. And he teaches that Christ gives both himself and his benefits. Knowing and receiving him includes but cannot be equated with his presence. The presence is not reduced to our apprehension of it.

Although Melanchthon had argued with Oecolampadius about the latter's view which left Christ's body sitting "incarcerated" in heaven,[70] he had no particular trouble with a literal understanding of the ascension and session of Christ. For, as he wrote in 1551, "all antiquity wrote that Christ may be, with respect to the location of his body, in any other place wherever he wills."[71] Melanchthon's understanding of the ascension in terms of Christ's lordship helps him avoid misunderstanding the eucharist as if it were "the tragedy of Hercules or Theseus, where remembrance [recordatio] of the dead and absent is made, but the Son of God lives and reigns and wills to be present in the sacrament in this instituted use. . . ."[72]

This kind of language leads Sasse to speak of Melanchthon's concept of "multiple presence."[73] The volitional element led to the designations "multivoli" or "ubivoli presence." Melanchthon writes: ". . . we say therefore that it can be in different places concurrently, whether this happens in some spatial manner or in some other mysterious way, by which all places are present to the person of Christ at the same time as one point."[74] Seeberg calls this "spiritual presence," which at

68. *Confession Concerning Christ's Supper,* 1528 (*LW* 37:215–24; *WA* 26:437.5–330.11; 335.29–336.27).

69. *Responsum Melanchthonis,* 1558 (*CR* 9:627).

70. Black and Satre, eds., *Melanchthon: Selected Writings,* p. 126.

71. 1551 Colossians Commentary (*CR* 7:884).

72. 1551 1 Corinthians Commentary (*CR* 15:1112). Cf. *MW* 1:298.27–28.

73. Hermann Sasse, *This Is My Body* (Minneapolis: Augsburg Publishing House, 1959), pp. 315–16.

74. *Iudicium* (*CR* 2:222). Cf. *WA* 26:330.9–11; *LW* 37:217: ". . . all creatures are . . . permeable and present to him. . . ."

first glance would seem to reiterate the crypto-Calvinist charge against Melanchthon.[75]   But it is strikingly similar to Luther's eucharistic mode of presence which he too calls "spiritual"![76]

Thus the Melanchthonian themes in the following passage are evident.   ". . . Christ's omnipotence and wisdom can readily provide that through his divine omnipotence Christ can be present with his body, which he has placed at the right hand of the majesty and power of God, *wherever he desires* and especially where he has promised his presence in his Word, as in the Holy Communion [italics mine]."[77]

That Melanchthon was uneasy about this supernatural, heavenly, ubiquitous mode of bodily presence is well known.[78]   In his refutation of the Weimar Confutation in 1559 he had written: "I do not like to speak before the young and unlearned concerning this matter of whether the body of Christ is in all places. . . . I have advised others to keep silent too."[79]   Melanchthon seemed to feel that bodily ubiquity was an illegitimate attempt to answer the how-question.   Moreover, it lacked precedent and parallel in the Fathers.   Here the Formula followed more closely Andreae and the Brenzian teaching of absolute ubiquity.

Present Promise

"To know Christ is to know his benefits."[80]   Remembering Christ in the sacrament is remembering and receiving his benefits by faith.[81] This equation which explicitly includes faith brings the sacrament unequivocally into the arena of soteriology.   In the Apology to the

75. Seeberg, *Textbook,* 2:350–51, citing *CR* 15:1112.

76. See above, note 68.   Cf. Vilmos Vajta, *Luther on Worship* (Philadelphia: Fortress Press, 1958), p. 85.

77. SD VIII, 92 (*BC,* p. 609; *BK* 1048.13–14).   Cf. *BC,* pp. 606–7 (78–79). Cf. Schlink, *Theology,* pp. 183-93.   The *ubivoli* motif makes the suggestion of Fritschel (*The Formula,* p. 203) of assigning this passage to Andreae seem highly unlikely.

78. Theodore G. Tappert, "Christology and Lord's Supper in the Perspective of History" in *Marburg Revisited,* ed. Paul C. Empie and James I. McCord (Minneapolis: Augsburg Publishing House, 1966), p. 62.   Cf. Seeberg, *Textbook,* 2:350–51.

79. Fraenkel, "Ten Questions," pp. 151–52, citing *CR* 9:766.

80. 1521 Loci (*MW* 2/1:7.10–11.; cf. Wilhelm Pauck, ed., *Melanchthon and Bucer, Library of Christian Classics* [Philadelphia: Westminster Press, 1969] 19:21).

81. Apol. XXIV, 72 (*BC,* p. 262; *BK* 370.7–26).   Cf. Apol. XXIV, 90 (*BC,* p. 266; *BK* 374.26–32) and IV, 76–78 (*BC,* p. 117; *BK* 175.31–39).

Augsburg Confession, he spells out the soteriological implications of the sacrament quite clearly. It is *per beneficia* that we are made alive by the living Christ who is truly present in the Supper.[82] For the sacrament is a *rite* with God's command and his promise of grace. "When we eat the Lord's body" thus "our hearts should firmly believe that God really forgives us for Christ's sake. Through the Word and the rite God simultaneously moves hearts to believe. . . ."[83]

The sacrament is also a *sign* of the promise to be "used" in faith. So "the communicant should be certain that the free forgiveness of sins, promised in the New Testament, is being offered him. . . ."[84] Augustine's concepts of sign and "visible Word" are utilized to affirm that the offer of forgiveness is a present promise. The Word remains the dynamic tool of divine efficacy and faith grasps the promise of the New Testament—"remission of sins and reconciliation for the sake of Christ."[85] Thus the Lord's Supper is both a *reminder* and a *pledge*[86] of forgiveness.

Furthermore, "the sacrament is a ceremony added to the promise, in which God gives us something . . . forgiveness of sins and justification on account of Christ." God grants his gifts through the rite. "For Christ testifies to us that his benefits belong to us when he imparts his body to us and joins us to himself as members. . . ." Efficacy is again portrayed as Christ's personal effectiveness in the sacramental action: "Again he testifies that he will be efficacious in us because he himself is life; he gives us his blood so that he may cleanse us."[87]

Through participating in the Lord's Supper, faith remembers/knows that we are strengthened as Christ's body by the body given to us. So when the bread and wine are given in the Lord's Supper, "the body and blood of Christ are presented [*exhibentur*] . . . so that we may know that we are loved, cared for, and preserved by him."[88]

Although the Formula evidences an even greater concern for establishing Christ's eucharistic presence in terms of omnipotence and omni-

---

82. *BK* 370.18–19. Cf. Apol. X (*BC*, pp. 179–80).
83. Apol. XIII, 4–5 (*BC*, p. 211; *BK* 292.27–293.4).
84. *BC*, p. 213; *BK* 295.20–38.
85. 1535 *Loci* (*CR* 21:477).
86. *CR* 21:478.
87. *CR* 21:477.
88. *CR* 21:479.

presence than Luther or Melanchthon did, the reformers' concern for the promise is by no means lost. Regarding Christ's testament, the Preface to the *Book of Concord* asserts: "He is almighty and veracious, and hence he is able to accomplish what he has ordained and promised in his Word."[89] Melanchthon would comment: In the gospel embodied in the visible word of the sacrament, Christ promises and gives forgiveness. For in this ritual action, he is efficaciously present as giver and gift, giving and making us his body. Presence and benefit become one in his eucharistic presence as he makes the promise present for faith.

89. *BC*, p. 10; *BK* 10.40–43.

4

Politics, Liturgics, and
Integritas Sacramenti

Oliver K. Olson

What Is and What Is Not the Sacrament

It is possible to write a serious history of political science as a sub-division of liturgiology. The reciprocal influences between the form of the Holy Communion and the secular constitution—forms of the two earthly regiments—justify a synoptic treatment. American history, for example, hardly makes sense if one does not understand the issues of the English revolution, which was a conflict just as much about the form of the sacrament as about the distribution of power. If someone were to write such a history, the climactic chapter might be devoted to Article X of the Formula of Concord, which renders judgment on a controversy in which political and liturgical history enter on a collision course.

The political importance of Article X is that it makes a decisive judgment on the rival arguments of Wittenberg and Magdeburg on the question of resistance to tyranny. The Wittenbergers said that resistance was optional, a matter of Christian liberty.[1] The Magdeburgers insisted that resistance was obligatory. The decision was for Magdeburg.[2] Seldom in history has there been a comparable victory of turgid style over explosive content. Nevertheless, everyone who reads carefully can know that whatever its authority the Formula of Concord requires resistance to tyranny: "We reject and condemn as wrongful the opinion of those who hold that in a period of persecution

---

1. Clyde L. Manschreck. "The Role of Melanchthon in the Adiaphora Controversy," *Archive for Reformation History* 48 (1957): 175.
2. Manschreck, ibid., p. 176, calls it a "partial triumph" but does not explain why.

we may yield to enemies of the holy Gospel or conform to their practices, since this serves to imperil the truth."[3]

The liturgical significance of Article X is its check on the darker elements of ritual by making a clear distinction between Christ's institution of the sacrament and the ceremonies associated with it: "Therefore we reject and condemn as wrongful the view that the commandments of men are to be considered as of themselves worship of God or a part thereof."[4] Critics of Article X are correct when they say that the distinction between Christ's institution and things indifferent (*adiaphora*) has contributed to an attitude that secondary ritual matters were not important. The fault lies not in the distinction, however, but in the simplistic way it has been used. Of course, we must put first things first, but we must also learn better how to put second things second, and know their importance.

Behind both the political and liturgical decisions lies the clarification Luther undertook in *On the Babylonian Captivity of the Church,* distinguishing between what is and what is not the sacrament:

> . . . in order that we might safely and happily attain a true and free knowledge of the sacrament, we must be particularly careful to put aside whatever has been added to its original simple institution by the zeal and devotion of men; such things as vestments, ornaments, chants, prayers, organs, candles, and the whole pageantry of outward things. We must turn our eyes and hearts simply to the institution of Christ and this alone, and set nothing before us but the very word of Christ by which he instituted the sacrament, made it perfect, and committed it to us. For in that word, in that word alone, reside the power, the nature, and the whole substance of the mass. All the rest is the work of man, added to the word of Christ, and the mass can be held and remain a mass just as well without them.[5]

The Duty of Resistance

Since one of the many things ritual can do is to enhance political power, political leaders have appreciated the Christian liturgy. The ancient function of supporting the state by giving it ritual representation survived the conversion of Rome to Christianity, as the history of the papal title *pontifex maximus* shows. The unification of Europe in a later age had a great deal to do with the liturgical unification carried

---

3. Theodore G. Tappert, ed., *The Book of Concord* (Philadelphia: Fortress Press, 1959), p. 615.
4. Ibid.
5. *Luther's Works,* American edition (Philadelphia: Fortress Press, 1959), 36:36.

out by Pepin and Charlemagne, who thereby asserted their claim to Roman authority. There has been a great deal of free use of Scripture in Western coronation orders in order to link somehow the local king with messianic themes. Even the history of the Advent season reveals how the kings' pomp in an official entry into a city had the overtone of Christ's entrance into Jerusalem.[6]

Although examples of royal use of the liturgy are almost limitless—one thinks of the way in which the mass was thought of as a cosmic ritual in the absolutist court of Louis XIV—in the long run the Christian liturgy has had quite an opposite effect, by robbing the king of just that element of divinity asserted in the sun rays of his crown and associated symbolism. The very circumstance that a people with the program-name "Israel" ("God rules") should appear on the scene, foreshadows a subdivision of royal claims to divinity; Israel worshiped and learned its laws without reference to a royal patronage. When lust to "be like the nations" brought a *rex sacerdos* into Jerusalem, he was considered "adopted," and the scandal was reduced. Later, when the temple—royal chapel!—was destroyed and the church decided that the Galilean was the real king, the Christian instinct denied the tribute *kyrie eleison* to the emperor and reserved it for God.

Nowhere is the coincidence of political and liturgical questions so clear as in the investiture controversy of the eleventh and twelfth centuries, which was at once a struggle for European political supremacy and a quarrel about the order of service at a bishop's consecration. One important effect of the long controversy was to erode a good deal of the pagan *charisma* of the kings. There is great significance, for example, in the medieval liturgical decisions to remove the cosmic canopy in processions from its function of enhancing the emperor's person to the enhancement of the *corpus Christi* or the demotion of the emperor to the office of mere deacon.

But it remained for Luther to give the emperor the liturgical *coup de grâce*. Somehow the imperial house had survived even the depredations of Gregory VII and Innocent III; the authority Luther faced continued to surround himself with symbols proper to the Emperor of the Heavens.[7]

There is an *integritas sacramenti,* Luther insisted, in the biblical ac-

6. Cf. Ernest H. Kantorowicz, "The King's Advent and the Enigmatic Panels in the Doors of Santa Sabina" in *Selected Studies* (Locust Valley, N.Y.: J. J. Augustin, 1965), pp. 37–75.

7. Cf. Friedrich Heer, *The Holy Roman Empire* (New York: Praeger, 1968), p. 3.

counts, given once and for all. It was obvious, then, that nothing the government could decree would make any difference one way or the other in the performance of the sacrament. It followed that if the emperor was powerless in this central religious matter he was on the way to final desacralization, like poor Louis the Pious at the Field of Lies. Society, eventually, would have to make other arrangements.

It is not saying too much to claim that modern democratic structures began with Lutheran doctrines of selective obedience based on a perception that the emperor's competence did not extend to religious matters. While the political effect of the sense of inward authority among the "radical reformers" is well understood, it is not often that the political effect of Lutheran confidence in having been given "pure doctrine" is perceived. It was that certainty about what later would be called *reine Lehre* (pure doctrine) which unites such disparate episodes of resistance to the imperial authority as Luther's appearance at Worms, the 1532 Nuremberg Recess, the 1539 Frankfurt Truce, and the Magdeburg Revolt of 1550–51.

As historians and political scientists continue to uncover the effects the Magdeburg pastors' doctrine of obligatory resistance on French, Dutch, English, and Scottish history, the significance of the Formula of Concord's approval of the Magdeburg position grows.[8] The doctrine that "Lesser Magistrates" must necessarily resist tyranny exercised by higher levels of government is a very important, though little known, Lutheran contribution to international political thought.[9] Kurt Wolzendorff made the claim that such other arguments as popular sovereignty or the feudal contract had far less significance in actually effecting political change than the doctrine of the "Lesser Magisrates."[10] "The *Untere Obrigkeit* [Lesser Magistracy] of the Magdeburg tract," J. W. Allen noticed in a 1928 discussion of seventeenth century political tracts, "becomes the 'officiers du royaume' [officers of the kingdom]

---

8. Cf. Cynthia Grant Shoenberger, "The Confession of Magdeburg and the Lutheran Doctrine of Resistance" (Ph.D. dissertation, political science, Columbia University, 1972); Richard Roy Benert, "Inferior Magistrates in Sixteenth-Century Political and Legal Thought" (Ph.D. dissertation, history, University of Minnesota, 1964); Oliver K. Olson, "Theology of Revolution: Magdeburg, 1550–1551," *The Sixteenth Century Journal* 3:1 (April 1972): 56–79.

9. See my essay "The Revolution and the Reformation," in *The Left Hand of God*, ed. William Lazareth (Philadelphia: Fortress Press, 1976), pp. 1–30.

10. Kurt Wolzendorff, *Staatrecht und Naturrecht in der Lebre vom Widerstandsrecht des Volkes gegen rechtswidrige Ausübung der Staatsgewalt* (Breslau: M. & H. Marcu, 1916; reprinted, Aalen: Scientia Verlag, 1961), p. 12.

of the *Du Droit,* the 'regni proceres' of the *Vindiciae,* the 'ministri regni' [royal ministers] of Boucher."[11]   Robert M. Kingdon found that the doctrine of the "Lesser Magistrates" is the consistent thread running through the otherwise varied justifications for resistance movements in France and the Low Countries.[12]   Although attempts have been made to trace the doctrine to Calvin, it seems well enough established that resistance involving armed intervention derives not from Calvin, but from Theodore Beza's use of the Magdeburg pastors' *Confession, Instruction and Warning* of 1550.[13]   The foundation of the doctrine of the "Lesser Magistrates," the duty of resistance, is, of course, a restatement of the *clausula Petri:* "We must obey God rather than men" (Acts 5:29), which turns up again and again in the literature of resistance.   But it is of crucial significance that the Magdeburg pastors avoided the notion of the "radical reformation" that each human being had some inherent right to resist.   The distinction from the "radical reformers" or the *Schwärmer,* as they once were called, is that the Magdeburg pastors specified that the obligatory resistance was to be carried out through the structures of concrete Christian vocations (*Ämter*).   Rom. 13:1–3, a biblical passage which has been used more than once to camouflage tyrannical regimes, was understood to mean that each person was responsible to God not indirectly through the social hierarchy, but directly.   That responsibility was clearly understood to involve the use of the "power of the sword," if appropriate, against higher levels of authority.   It was that combination, the doctrine of obligatory resistance (approved by the Formula of Concord) and the related doctrine of vocation, which made up the historically successful doctrine of the "Lesser Magistrates."

Understood better by the Calvinists who took it over than by the Lutherans, this position makes room for a prophetic corrective while preserving the principle of legitimacy in government and avoids the profound problems in establishing a new legal system experienced by revolutionary regimes, who have only an ideology of a small group of society as basis.   If the Lesser Magistrates doctrine became better

---

11. J. W. Allen, *A History of Political Thought in the Sixteenth Century* (London: Methuen & Co., 1928; reprinted, New York: Barnes and Noble, 1960), p. 106.

12. Robert M. Kingdon, "The Political Resistance of the Calvinists in France and the Low Countries," *Church History* 26 (September 1958): 227.

13. Cf. Olson, "Theology of Revolution," pp. 56–79.

known, the existence of those unruly magistrates, conscious of direct divine obligation to resist, might justify a subtle adjustment in the connotation of the term "magisterial Reformation."

Putting Second Things Second

The Declaration of the Imperial Roman Majesty on How Religious Matters Should Be Regulated until the Convocation of a Common Council of May 1548, which began the controversy behind Article X of the Formula of Concord, was not understood as an act of tyranny by the imperial court, of course, but as an instrument for preserving the *concordia* of Christendom. No matter that the rituals it required evangelical churches to reintroduce were syncretistic mixtures of Christian and pagan elements. These rituals had been a powerful cement for society and must be backed by the great personage who was the mystical representation of that society.

Four hundred years later the emperors are dead and the world is vastly different. It is astonishing, then, to become aware of the persistent sameness of the rituals Emperor Charles V insisted be forced on the Protestants. The very same liturgical orders are being pressed on us in the name of ecumenism. The mass canon, emphatically rejected by Luther, now renamed the "eucharistic prayer" and reinterpreted by *Mysterientheologie,* is the prime cause of a new "liturgical consensus." And the argument is brought home in an emphatic fashion that if we do not accept that liturgical *concordia* we will be sectarian.

The disturbing thing about the consensus, however, is that it was developed with the tacit understanding that what Luther (devisively!) said about the *integritas sacramenti* would simply be ignored. Lutherans generally have not been interested enough in following the fashion in which the mass canon has been fought for in the Faith and Order conferences, for example. It may be symbolic that the German delegation was unable to attend the 1937 Faith and Order Conference in Edinburgh, which is considered a milestone in developing the "liturgical consensus."

But although the mass canon is justified by biblical terms—eucharist, anamnesis, sacrifice—the important issue for Luther was that it turned the sacrament one hundred and eighty degrees from what it should be. Luther insisted that the mass was a testament, in the direction from God to man; the "consensus" assumes that the direction is from man to God. However innovative the secondary literature of the liturgical movement may seem to be, most of it varies in no point from the rigid decree of Trent that the mass, somehow, is the same sacrifice as the one on Calvary.

In the long tradition of the Western church since St. Augustine, what is most important in the sacrament—the *res sacramenti*—has been understood as borne to the believer through the Word. The medieval understanding of the ministry, unfortunately, helped create the impression that the Words of Institution were the priest's words—consecratory "action." For laymen, the words *hoc est corpus meum,* this is my body, became "hocus pocus."

It was to avoid the impression of verbal magic that liturgiologists have urged that less emphasis be laid on the "hocus pocus" words. Rather than emphasizing one action, they write, one should emphasize the *whole* action of the church. Presupposed, of course, is that the sacrament is essentially the church's self-sacrifice. The abandonment of the Augustinian tradition in favor of "action," however, has created new problems. Since the notion of the "whole action" is open-ended, it can comprehend a great variety of ritual expressions. Indeed, the new emphasis has stimulated a great deal of interest in ritual as a phenomenon.

Against the background of this new ritualist interest, it comes as a surprise that Aidan Kavanaugh of Notre Dame University has noticed that

> . . . ritual behavior has its own grammar and syntax. If these go unlearned, the liturgical act itself not only suffers, but those who engage in it may well find themselves split rather than united by it. If these go unlearned, the power of ritual for evil as well as for good goes unfactored, and those who engage in it may find themselves unknowingly gripped by the viciousness they would not rather than the good they would.[14]

The implications of ritual behavior are vast, and the difficulty most Lutheran theologians have in taking the problem seriously is that their theological training has not prepared them for the overwhelming complexity of liturgical discussions. But perhaps I can illustrate by taking one of the ritualist themes which is being used currently—the notion of liturgy as "play." That theme was popularized primarily by the Munich theologian and priest Romano Guardini. Play, he says, "is not a medium which can be used to achieve a certain effect, but, up to a

---

14. James D. Shaugnessy, ed., *The Roots of Ritual* (Grand Rapids, Mich.: William B. Eerdmans Publishing Company, 1973), pp. 7–8.

certain point at least, it is an end.in itself."[15]   But if we are seriously attempting to get to the bottom of things, and not merely casting about for ways to make Sunday morning services more interesting, we must make further inquiries about the "certain point" Guardini airily dismisses.   The researches of Johan Huizinga on the same subject of play reveal the tendency within it to reproduce the very pagan ritual dynamic Christianity meant to replace.

> The holy action is a *dromenon,* that is, something done.   That which is represented is a *drama,* that is, an action, whether the action takes the form of a performance or a contest.   It represents a cosmic event, but not merely as representation, but as identification.   It repeats that which has happened.   The cult brings about the reality which is represented visually in the action.   Its function is not merely an imitation, but a sharing or participation.   It is "helping the action out."[16]

The dangerous presupposition, of course, is that Christian worship can be imposed on universal ritual patterns, thus transforming or fulfilling them.   How radically the possibility of such syncretism is being pursued is illustrated by a claim made in a recent *Concilium* volume. "We can orientate the Hindu ascetical and mystical ways of worship towards a sharper and deeper experience of the mystery of Christ," says Mariasusai Dhavamany.   "The mythical-ritual way of apprehending ultimate truth becomes a 'power unto salvation,' a dynamic force whose very embodiment brings forth the sacred reality in everyday existence."[17]

The ultimate folly of such liturgical syncretism has been seen quite clearly by another Roman Catholic scholar, Alfons Kirchgässner:

> A complete melting down of pagan elements into Christian practice is not possible.   There is always an indissoluble remainder.   The origin keeps working like tinder. . . . When one domesticates an animal, he

15. Romano Guardini, *Vom Geist der Liturgie* (Freiburg: Herder, 1953), p. 53.

16. Johan Huizinga, *Homo Ludens* (Hamburg: Rowohlt, 1956), pp. 21–22.   It is revealing to find the identical structure in the mystery theology of Odo Casel, whose activity has had a great deal to do with the Constitution of the Sacred Liturgy of Vatican II: "Christ's salvation must be made reality in us.   This does not come about through a 'justification' from 'faith,' or by an application of the grace of Christ, where we have only to clear things out of the way in a negative fashion, to receive it.   Rather, what is necessary is a living, active sharing in the redeeming deed of Christ," *The Mystery of Christian Worship and Other Writings* (Westminster, Md.: Newman Press, 1962), p. 14.

17. Mariasusai Dhavamany, "Oriental Religions and Worship" in *Liturgical Experience of Faith,* ed. Hermann Schmidt and David Powers (New York: Herder and Herder, 1973), pp. 107–13.

must always be prepared for surprises: suddenly it can return to an earlier way of life and become disagreeable. It is similar with ritual: it is taken over not as an empty shell, but as a living thing. There is not a symbol in which content and form can be distinguished clearly from each other. Whoever dares to adopt a symbol, takes it over as a whole, that is, with its provenance, its own life, and destiny under many a lordship of gods and demons. Everything natural has the tendency to absolutize itself and to come into competition with the Gospel. The numinous in creation easily causes God's transcendence and his personal revelation to be forgotten.[18]

Kirchgässner's is a healthy warning; perhaps it will help to encourage our church leaders and theologians to begin taking seriously liturgics as a discipline, rather than as an aesthetic appendage to the life of the church. The present state of liturgical thought, going after novelty and absorbed in phenomenological narcissism, has managed to eliminate the prophetic element. One longs for the fiery sword of some angel-protector of the church to mark a firm boundary between Christ's gracious supper and the lush undergrowth of human ritualism. Or at least a clear ecclesiastical decision, like the one in Article X: "Therefore we reject and condemn as wrongful the view that the commandments of men are to be considered as of themselves worship of God or a part thereof."[19]

Compared to that primary theological consideration, the concern of Wilhelm Stählin, who can speak for any number of liturgically concerned Lutherans, must be considered secondary.

> . . . the recognition that certain regulations are not necessary for salvation does not relieve us of the responsibility of determining what is right in each individual situation. The insight of the Reformers that there is no one form of worship or church order necessary for salvation, and thereby above discussion, has time and again been misleading, causing men to overlook questions of what is right, or not to take such questions seriously."[20]

There is no doubt that Lutherans have neglected the discipline of liturgics. And there is no doubt that the distinction between the *integritas sacramenti* and indifferent matters—*adiaphora*—has in a

18. Alfons Kirchgässner, *Die mächtigen Zeichen: Ursprünge, Formen und Gesetze des Kultes* (Basel, Freiburg, Vienna: Herder, 1959), pp. 46ff.

19. Tappert, ed., *Book of Concord,* p. 615.

20. Wilhelm Stählin, "Resurrection and Calendar Reform," *Response* 9:3 and 4 (Epiphany and Easter, 1970): 70, translated from "Christus und die Zeit," *Manipulierte Zeit?* (Stuttgart: Evangelisches Verlagswerk, 1968), pp. 21–22.

curious fashion contributed to the indifference Lutheran theological schools have had for the practical theological discipline of liturgics. Words very often have subtle suggestive powers in themselves which are not necessarily in the minds of those who first use them. But the fault lies not in the distinction. Rather, it is far deeper, in that idealistic tendency which considers theology basically intellectual and therefore consigns the disciplines of practical theology to inconsequence.

Kavanaugh is quite correct. We must learn the grammar and syntax of ritual. Stählin is right, too. We must make the effort to determine what is right in each individual situation and take liturgical questions seriously in their relationship to other disciplines. It is not enough, for example, to choose to make use of modern music. We must know the elements of that modern music in detail and only in terms of that detailed knowledge apply it to the church. It makes no sense, for instance, to use a highly individualized and improvisatory jazz idiom to express the common praise of a congregation. Improvisation is the expression of one individual, not of a community. We must, in other words, learn seriously to put second things second and not merely content ourselves with having settled primary theological issues.

But I suspect that the most fruitful liturgical interaction between Lutherans and Roman Catholics in the future could be arranged by beginning with the warning notes sounded about the ritual process itself by Roman Catholic Kavanaugh and Kirchgässner. Just where is the line that separates Christian from Hindu worship? A "liturgical consensus" arrived at by stealth, by ignoring the serious issues which concerned Luther when he described the *integritas sacramenti,* will, to use Kavanaugh's words, split rather than unite. An ecumenical consensus must take account of the concerns which led to the liturgical *caveat* in Article X of the Formula of Concord.

Concordia

Finally, we must look at Article X in its context in a formula of *concordia*. Whereas it is our modern nonsectarian instinct to formulate *concordia* by eliminating prophetic rebuke, the Formula of Concord does not shy away from including the very elements—the duty of resistance, the check on ritualism—otherwise considered productive of *discordia* in politics and liturgics. A look at Article X after four hundred years can well include a comparison with attempts at unity in church and state today.

Take the American *concordia* as an example from the political realm.

The "civil religion," being studied so avidly these days in university religion departments, turns out to have been constructed largely of positive elements from our religious heritage—grace, destiny, election. But there is very little of the prophetic critique which in the biblical sources went with that religious heritage. And the United States reflects a kind of national impenitence which all the world knows. A new discovery on the part of the church of the obligation to resist "the enemies of Christ" wherever they may show themselves, in terms of one's specific vocation, would supply an element from the 1577 *formula* lacking in the American *concordia*. Clearly, the prophetic critique must come from the church, since our national ideology admits only flattering elements.

Take the ecumenical "liturgical consensus" as an example of the attempt to achieve concordia in the religious realm. It, too, has elements of the Christian tradition—sacrifice, remembrance, action. But the direction of it all, from man to God, assumes a goodness which makes us suitable to be incorporated in the "mystical body" of Christ and participants in his sacrifice. It leaves out the prophetic note that we are still sinners as we approach God's altar.

Beyond that, the new "consensus," open to new aspects of human ritual activity as never before, is largely unaware of the dark side of human ceremonial. Having rejected Augustine's emphasis on the centrality of the Word in the sacrament and Luther's emphasis on the mass as a gift from God, in the direction of man with its own integrity, the ecumenical liturgical consensus lacks the check of a serious prophetic element.

The stimulating passage by Arend van Leeuwen on the story of the Tower of Babel as the paradigm of the human search for *concordia*[21] suggests that the prophetic element can be abandoned only at great peril. It may be that prophetic *veritas* and human *concordia* are incompatible, to be realized only at the eschaton. The turbulent history of Western society, which can be understood as a history of their rival claims, may suggest that. The theologians of 1577, patiently weaving together whatever unity could be salvaged in a Germany exhausted by a heroic and discordant age, knew that combining clear biblical thought and human consensus was a difficult task.

The delicate term "the enemies of Christ," rather than the frank

---

21. Arend van Leeuwen, *Christianity in World History* (New York: Charles Scribner's Sons, 1964), pp. 74–75.

naming of Caesar as the problem, and even the dull style indicate that the formulators realized that some of their themes were more likely to produce discord than concord. Still, they did not avoid the most provocative themes in politics and liturgics, and one may assume that they suspected that Christ has his own notion of *concordia*.

Jorg Baur wonders, "Was it not the Germans' misfortune that with Luther and his followers they let the Revolution take place only in heaven and in the conscience?"[22] The particular group of followers of Luther whose concerns are reflected in Article X—concrete questions of political action and liturgical order—cannot be included in Baur's critique. The Lutheran tradition has neglected these areas and must pay a good deal more attention to the specific forms of the earthly regiments. One good starting point is Article X of the Formula of Concord, whose surprising content is a good deal more lively than we have thought.

22. Jorg Baur, "Flacius—Radikale Theologie," *Matthias Flacius Illyricus 1575–1975* (*Schriften Reihe des Regensburger Osteuropainstituts;* Regensburg: Verlag Lassleben, 1975), 2:38.

5

The Influence of
the Formula of Concord
on the Later Lutheran Orthodoxy

Robert D. Preus

The Influence of the Formula of Concord on the Later Lutheran Orthodoxy is an interesting and instructive topic. The title might better be
stated: The Influence of the Theology of the Formula of Concord on
the Most Fruitful of the Following Generations of Orthodox Theologians. For then we could easily demonstrate the way in which
Quenstedt and others of his era, often without any originality, followed
at points Chemnitz or Chytraeus, or Selnecker in many of their theological discussions.[1] I believe the matter of the influence of the
Formula of Concord and its theology on later Lutheran theologians
of the seventeenth century will be convincingly settled to the reader's
satisfaction by a simple sampling of how later seventeenth century
orthodoxy was affected by the Formula of Concord and its authors. A
massive assembling of evidence (or nonevidence) which very assuredly
exists in abundance is hardly necessary.

We can see where the later orthodox theologians follow Chemnitz,
Selnecker, Chytraeus, and, to a lesser degree, the other authors of the
Formula of Concord, again where they went back to the earlier confessions and more commonly to Luther and in some cases to Melanchthon, and then in some instances where they launched out on their own

---

1. One need only compare the Christology of John Andrew Quenstedt in his
Theologie Didactico-Polemica sive Systema Theologiae with that of John Gerhard's
Loci Theologici and particularly Martin Chemnitz's *De Duabus Naturis* to note an
almost utter dependence upon not only the thought but even the terminology. In
many cases Quenstedt simply quotes verbatim at great length without even mentioning the fact or giving references, a practice not uncommon in those days.

and showed almost no dependence upon the Formula of Concord or sometimes any of the confessions.[2]

In this essay I propose to comment on the subject of the relationship between the theology of the Formula of Concord and the later orthodox theology with, I trust, sufficient evidence, to show just how deeply the Formula of Concord itself affected the orthodox theologians of the following century. The conclusions drawn are significant if for no other reason because the seventeenth century theologians, with their giant tomes in dogmatical and exegetical theology, have exerted a strong influence on nineteenth and twentieth century theologians, who in turn have left their mark on the theology and on entire church bodies of our day.

Strong Influence—Articles I, II, and III

In their discussions of original sin the theologians of the late sixteenth and seventeenth centuries follow very closely the treatment of the Formula of Concord which in turn defines original sin in terms

2. Not only authors of the Formula of Concord such as Chytraeus and Selnecker wrote books on the confessions, but later orthodox Lutherans of all succeeding generations did the same. Most were written on the Augsburg Confession; but several were devoted to the theology of the Formula of Concord, most notable of which were *Nikolaus Selnecker, Erklärung etlicher streitiger Artikel aus der Concordienformel* (Leipzig, 1582); Leonard Hutter, *Concordia Concors, de Origine et Progressu Formulae Concordiae Ecclesiarum Confessionis Augustanae* (Wittenberg, 1614); and Sebastian Schmidt, *Articulorum Formulae Concordiae Repetitio* (Strasbourg, 1696). It is interesting that the seventeenth century dogmaticians in their dogmatical or exegetical works seldom cite the confessions; even less do nineteenth and twentieth century confessional Lutherans, e.g., Gisle Johnson, *Den Systematiske Teologi* (Oslo: Dybwad, 1897) and K. Krogh-Tonning, *Den Christelige Dogmatik* (Christiania: P. T. Mallings Boghandel, 1885) among the Norwegians; Friedrich A. Philippi, *Kirchliche Glaubenslehre* (Stuttgart: Samuel Gottlieb Liesching, 1854) among the Germans; and Francis Pieper, *Christian Dogmatics,* trans. Theodore Engelder, John T. Mueller, and Walter W. F. Albrecht (St. Louis: Concordia Publishing House, 1951—) and Adolph Hoenecke, *Evangelish-Lutherische Dogmatik* (Milwaukee: Northwestern Publishing House, 1909) among the American. Why? Perhaps it is because they were writing to some extent for non-Lutheran readers, but more likely because of their convictions, conscious or unconscious, that exegesis just does not require a confessional basis of any kind. This is not to say that later Lutherans were not guilty of dogmatic exegesis (see John Gerhard, *Annotationes Posthumae in Evangelium D. Matthaei* [Jena, 1663] and many of the shorter exegetical treatises of the day). Friedrich Balduin's *Commentarius in Omnes Epistolas Beati Apostoli Pauli* (Frankfurt on the Main, 1710) is a good example of the better quality of the dogmatic exegesis of that day. But all this does not mean that the "dogmatic exegesis of that day" (which I suppose is common also to our day) was based on the confessions *per se.* It was not.

identical with the Augsburg Confession. The same is true of their discussions of the freedom of the human will; and here, too, the Formula of Concord consciously follows Luther.

The Formula of Concord, in treating the doctrine of original sin, is combating two opposite errors: that of Flacius, which made sin the very substance of man and thus opened up a Pandora's box of misunderstandings and aberrations; and that of Viktor Strigel who was a synergist. I regard Article I of the Formula of Concord as a commentary on the history, not so much the text, of Genesis 3, with rather little regard to Romans 5 and other evidence for the fact of original sin. Thus, the article takes for granted an historical Fall (SD I, 6, 9, 11, 23, 27, 28; cf. SA III, II, 1; AC II, 1) whereby Adam, the progenitor of the entire human race, brought sin, guilt, and eternal punishment upon the entire human race. The definition of original sin as inherited, propagated sin (*Erbsünde*), which consists of a lack of fear and trust in God and of concupiscence, is simply taken from the Augsburg Confession. The polemic is almost exclusively against the Flacian error and its impossible consequences. The context of the entire discussion is a certain Pauline understanding of the image of God. Man in his state of integrity possessed this image which consisted in righteousness and knowledge of God. The loss of the image was not the loss of man's humanity, nature, or essence (Epit. I, 17ff.), much less a mere "external impediment" of some kind but a corruption of man's nature and a "complete deprivation or loss" of all his spiritual powers (Epit. I, 15).

This doctrine, with all its details, is completely taken over by the later Lutheran dogmaticians.[3] But a great mass of biblical evidence is assembled to press certain points, particularly that original sin is a total corruption, that it is propagated, and that it is an active and dynamic concupiscence. Quenstedt says that original sin encompasses and controls all our powers, our members, indeed, the total man. Like a garment original sin encircles and clings to us and hinders us in our course toward true piety. It produces its own germs or fruits. It is the "root," as Luther puts it in SA III, II, 1–2, of all vices and is the common source of all sin. And what is of paramount importance, original sin is an active following after hostile attitudes and

---

3. See, for instance Abraham Calov, *Socinismus Profligatus, hoc est, Errorum Socinianorum Luculenta Confutatio* (Wittenberg, 1668), pp. 259ff., and John Andrew Quenstedt, *Theologia Didactico-Polemica sive Systema Theologiae* (Leipzig, 1702), part II, chap. II, sec. II (1:914–1076).

wicked traits (*positio pravae concupiscentiae & successio contrarii habitus & vitiosae qualitatis*), and active rebellion, a desire for all that is base, a hatred of God.[4] This active nature of original sin, so commonly emphasized by the early reformers and the Formula of Concord, is stressed with the same vigor by the dogmaticians. Speaking of man's habitual inclination toward evil (Matt. 15:19; Mk. 7:21), Quenstedt remarks that even such initial and involuntary movements of our concupiscence are truly sin (Romans 7). And when Jesus says that evil thoughts proceed from the heart and Paul says we will what is evil, they are not speaking metonymically, but of an actual warring against the law of the mind, a sinful willing of evil even in the regenerated man (Rom. 7:13).[5]

The soteriological backdrop out of which Article I of the Formula of Concord is written is also shared by the later Lutherans, sometimes as they follow closely the Formula's discussions of the consequences of the Flacian error,[6] but also at times out of an evangelical concern of their own. Erik Adhelius[7] insists that the correct understanding of the human situation is so important because it alone shows a sinner his need for a savior. The fact to be stressed is that all sin (and this includes at the outset man's sinful condition) is against God's law and therefore against God. And man's tragic situation can only be remedied by Christ. Thus, original sin must be taught out of such a soteriological concern.[8] Only if a proper understanding of sin is

4. Quenstedt, Theologia *Didactico-Polemica,* sec. I, thesis 34 (1:918). Cf. Melanchthon's statement in his *Loci Communes* of 1521 in *Melanchthons Werke in Auswahl,* 2:1, ed. Hans Engelland (Gütersloh: C. Bertelsmann Verlag, 1952), p. 21: "Original sin is a sort of living power (*vivax quaedam energia*) in no way and at no time bringing forth any other fruit than vice. For when does the soul of man not burn with evil desires, desires in which the most base and offensive things are not checked? Avarice, ambition, hatred, jealousy, rivalry, the flame of lust, wrath; and who does not feel these things? Pride, scorn, Pharisaic bigheadedness, contempt of God, distrust of God, blasphemy. . . ." Such language is typical of the Formula of Concord and the later Lutheran theologians.

5. Quenstedt, *Theologica Didactico-Polemica,* thesis 35 (1:119).

6. Ibid., sec. II, ques. 10 (1:1021). Cf. Martin Chemnitz, *Loci Theologici* (Frankfurt and Wittenberg, 1653), 1:244–45.

7. Erik Adhelius, *Disputationum Homologeticarum in Augustanam Confessionem prima—sexta* (Uppsala, 1653), p. 83: "*Sed nihilominus sincera hujus peccati agnitio valde necessaria nobis peccatoribus, ut eo avidius medicinam per Christum amplectamur. Necque enim potest intelligi magnitudo gratiae Christi, nisi morbis nostris cognitio. Tota hominis justitia mera est hypocrisis coram Deo, nisi agnoverimus cor naturaliter vacare amore, timore, fiducia Dei.*"

8. Ibid., pp. 92–95.

preached in the church will a proper understanding of Christ and his work result in the church. One repents of "propagated" sin and turns to Christ.[9]

Very little is made in the Formula of Concord about the imputation of Adam's sin or guilt to the entire human race, probably because the concern was primarily centered in the anthropological aspect of the doctrine, the nature of man's sin as propagated. The imputation of course is implied when the Formula describes original sin as involving guilt (*reatus, Schuld*) and brings God's wrath and damnation (SD I, 13–19; cf. AC II, 2). The dogmaticians are more explicit about the imputation of Adam's sin, or guilt, to all posterity. When Rom. 5:12ff says that all men sinned in Adam, it does not mean that all did precisely as Adam did, but that all "participated in his guilt," and thus in God's reckoning.[10] Because all participated in Adam's sin, the two notions, inherited sin and imputed guilt, go together.[11] The reason that this matter, barely touched upon by our confessions, was stressed by the later dogmaticians was due to the Socinian threat. Quenstedt devotes one entire question to the forensic imputation of Adam's sin and guilt to the entire human race, using almost exclusively Rom. 5:12–19 as his exegetical basis.[12] The exegetical works of the later orthodox Lutherans take up the matter in greater detail, again at least in part for polemical reasons, also against papists and Arminians.[13]

One would suppose that with such close dependence upon the the-

9. Ibid., pp. 1, 4, 5.

10. Calov, *Socinismus Profligatus,* p. 243.

11. Ibid.

12. Quenstedt, *Theologica Didactico-Polemica,* sec. II, ques. 7 (1:993–98).

13. E.g., see Calov, *Biblia Novi Testamenti Illustrata* (Dresden and Leipzig, 1719), vol. I, book II, p. 99: *"Uti enim hic peccatores constituti sunt imputatione in obedientiae Adami, sic justi nos constituimur imputatione vel justitiae Christi."* Again Calov says, *"Quomodo autem poena esset in posteris peccati primi, nisi posteris primum illud peccatum imputaretur?"* Calov, in such typical statements, is polemicizing against Bellarmine, Becan, and other papists, but his soteriological concern is clearly apparent. Cf. also Balduin, *Commentarius,* p. 183, *passim.* Aegidius Hunnius, in his *Thesaurus Apostolicus Complectens Commentarios in omnes Novi Testamenti Epistolas* (Wittenberg, 1705), pp. 51–52 is more careful to relate the inherited nature of original sin with God's imputation of guilt. *"Non solum reatus alieni peccati imputatur posteris, sed ipsum quoque vitium in illos propagatur. . . ."* Also: *"Peccatum originis non definitur imputatione nuda lapsus alieni primorum parentum, sine vitio & corruptione propria; sicut Scholastici Theologi censuerunt: sed ea ratione & peccatum, & cum peccato mors in nos propagata scribitur, quatenus ipsi quoque peccavimus. Hoc palam affirmat Apostolus."*

ology of the Formula of Concord in its doctrine of original sin, the later Lutherans would also lean heavily upon the same source as they treat the subject of Article II of the Formula of Concord, that is, freedom of the will. This is true, particularly among the earlier post-Reformation theologians (e.g., Leonard Hutter, John Gerhard) and all the Scandinavians (e.g., Jesper Brochmand, Kort Aslaksøn, and Olav Laurelius). Aslaksøn simply and unabashedly takes over the doctrine of the Formula of Concord,[14] as does Laurelius, although the latter subsumes the subject under the doctrine of original sin.[15] At times, however, later theologians tend to depart from the theology of the Formula of Concord on the matter of the freedom of the will. They accepted Luther's strong emphasis upon man's utter passivity in conversion and his "block," "stone," "log," "pillar of salt" imagery (SD II, 19, 20, 24), although God works in man as in a rational creature (SD II, 49, 50). But in the discussion of other subjects synergism definitely crops up. Hollaz,[16] for instance, poses the question why God does not grant all men saving faith, and finds the answer in the theory that all unregenerated men do not resist the work of the Holy Spirit with the same intensity.

Article III of the Formula of Concord is a masterful discussion on the nature of justification, just as Melanchthon's treatment of justification by faith in the Apology is one of the finest ever written on the subject. The two notable discussions complement each other and afford a total picture of the doctrine of justification. Earlier Lutheran orthodoxy, taking its cue from these two great sections of our Book of Concord, combine the work of Christ, his obedience of doing and suffering, his life and death (SD III, 15–16, 55–88), later called active and passive obedience, under one heading, namely justification (Chemnitz and Gerhard). This is in keeping with both the intent of Melanchthon and the Formula of Concord. For Melanchthon offers his most explicit treatment of the work of Christ in his discussions of justification. In a sense this procedure of Gerhard and Chemnitz retains

14. Kort Aslaksøn, *De Libero Hominis Arbitrio* (Copenhagen, 1612), p. Blv.

15. Olav Laurelius, *Syntagma Theologicum* (Uppsala, 1641), pp. 149ff. Cf. also Abraham Calov, *Historica Syncretistica* (Wittenberg, 1682), p. 663.

16. David Hollaz, *Examen Theologicum Acromaticum* (Rostock and Leipzig, 1718, part III, sec. I, chap. I, quest. 9 (p. 602): *"Dist. inter resistentiam naturalem, & malitiosam. Illam Spiritus S. per gratiam praevenientem frangit & refrenat: haec in aliis hominibus minor, in aliis maior & ferocior est, quae saepe impedit, quo minus vera fides in corde hominis irregeniri accendatur."*

justification as the center and chief theme (*praecipuus locus*) of Melanchthon in the Apology (IV, 2) and at the same time retains Luther's strong emphasis in the Smalcald Articles that "the first and chief article" of Christian doctrine is the article of Christ and his saving work. This procedure by the earlier dogmaticians retains the atoning work of Christ not simply as the basis of a sinner's justification, but also as an element and form of the very declaration of justification itself. Like the Formula of Concord and Luther and Melanchthon, the dogmaticians make much of the imputation of Christ's righteousness (his obedience) to the believer (Apol. IV, 305, 307; in fact, this is Melanchthon's definition of justification!).[17]

A statement by Balthasar Mentzer may serve to show the dependence of later Lutherans on the theology of the confessions and particularly the Formula of Concord as they work out their Christocentric doctrine of justification.

> The basis which merits our justification is Jesus Christ the God-man who in both of his natures is the one mediator and redeemer of the entire human race. Although he was Lord over the law for our sake he was made under the law to redeem those who were under the law, that we might receive the adoption of children (Gal. 4:4, 5). He not only observed the whole divine law, but fulfilled it completely and exactly (Matt. 5:17, 18). Thus he is called the end (*telos*) and the perfection of the law (Rom. 10:4). But he also sustained the punishment which we deserved by our sins, he suffered and died in our place, as the whole gospel history abundantly testifies. This entire obedience of his, both in what he did and what he suffered (which is commonly termed active and passive obedience) is called the righteousness of Christ, i.e., the righteousness which is revealed in the gospel, and the righteousness of faith, i.e., the righteousness which is apprehended by faith and counted for righteousness to us who believe.[18]

Lutheran orthodoxy almost slavishly, but albeit with great vigor and real warmth, adheres to the Reformation doctrine of justification, to its centrality in the theological enterprise, to the reality of the imputation

---

17. Cf. SD III, 4, 9. Perhaps more than any of the other of the dogmaticians Gerhard emphasizes this fact in his lengthy discussion of the meritorious cause of our justification (*Loci Theologici,* 7:30–72) and again in his treatment of the nature of justification (*causa formalis justificationis*) as the nonimputation of our sin for Christ's sake and the gracious imputation of Christ's righteousness to us through faith (ibid., 257–315). This definition of the nature of justification is clearly taken from the Formula of Concord and Chemnitz, although, as shown above, it can be traced back to Luther and the earlier confessions.

18. Balthasar Mentzer, *Opera Latina* (Frankfurt, 1669), 1:60.

of Christ's righteousness to the believer, to the *sola fide* and the *sola gratia,* to Luther's understanding of faith directed always toward Christ.[19]   But exactly here at the point of justification *propter Christum* it takes much from the masterful treatment of the Formula of Concord.

No Appreciable Influence—Articles IV–X

After Luther's emphases upon the necessity of good works in so many treatises and after Melanchthon's excellent discussion of the subject of "Love and the Keeping of the Law" in the Apology (IV, 122–400), by far the longest discussion in all the Lutheran confessions, one can only marvel that the theologians who wrote the Formula of Concord would be compelled to treat the matter again and marvel still more that Roman theology persistently misunderstood the Lutheran position, thus compelling the later Lutheran dogmaticians to address themselves to this issue at great length, not merely for the sake of the subject itself, but for the sake of clarifying their position.   Because Majorism did not persist with its various subtleties long after the Formula of Concord, the subjects of good works, love, and the fruits of faith (of the Spirit) were handled by the later Lutherans primarily on the basis of Scripture and earlier Lutheran theologians.   Jesper Brochmand wrote a commentary on the book of James simply to prove that the Lutherans took the theology of James and good works seriously.[20]   A perusal of the great dogmatical works of the era, with their sections on the law, repentance, confession, good works, prayer, and the cross (sections not found in many modern dogmatics) should indicate the seriousness of Lutheran orthodoxy to maintain a proper emphasis upon the Christian life.   But the theology of the Formula of Concord had little influence upon their work.   Luther in his several discussions of the Ten Commandments did influence the later Lutheran orthodox theologians, and so did Melanchthon in his treatment of the subject in Apology IV.

Articles V and VI of the Formula of Concord, which belong together, had little influence upon later Lutheran orthodoxy, although the dogmaticians treated the subjects of the proper distinction between law and gospel and the Third Use of the law.   Once again the imme-

19. I believe I have clearly demonstrated this fact in my article "The Doctrine of Justification in the Theology of Classical Lutheran Orthodoxy," in *The Springfielder* 29:1 (Spring 1965): 24–39.

20. Jesper Rasmus Brochmand, *In Canonicam et Catholicam Jacobi Epistolam Commentarius* (Copenhagen, 1706).

diate occasion for the articles was no longer an issue. The theologians of the seventeenth century simply went back to Luther, Melanchthon, and to the Bible itself as they addressed themselves to the issue of distinguishing the law from the gospel and the threefold function of the law. Hollaz,[21] for instance, never cites Luther or the confessions as he delineates the word of the law and the word of the gospel. Chemnitz first discusses the law at great length and then the gospel under his section on justification, but does not treat the distinction *per se*.[22] He treats the threefold use of the law on only two pages of his immense *Loci Theologici*.[23] This is significant because Chemnitz is one of the authors of the Formula of Concord. Apparently the theologians after the Formula of Concord, indeed even its authors, did not think that the subject matter of Articles V and VI merited extended discussions in their theological works, perhaps because they believed the matter had been settled once and for all by the Formula itself.

Once again the later theologians simply pass over Articles VII and VIII of the Formula to Luther and the Scriptures in the case of the Lord's Supper, and to the Church Fathers and the Scriptures in the case of the Person of Christ. This was only natural. The Formula of Concord, while settling the two issues for Lutherans, simply did not do so in respect to the Lutheran and Reformed controversy. To us today the two articles in the Formula might appear quite thorough and conclusive, but they were hardly adequate to use as a basis to carry on the controversy with the Reformed who immediately attacked both articles on biblical and patristic grounds.[24] Searching the Scriptures and Luther's interpretation of them on the points of difference and a thorough study of the patristic doctrine of the Person of Christ was the only way the Lutherans, beginning with Chemnitz, could go.

A couple of observations might be made, however, before leaving

---

21. Hollaz, *Examen,* part III, sec. II, chap. I, quest. 6—chap. II, quest. 10 (pp. 996–1039). Cf. also Gerhard's section on the subject (*Loci Theologici* 6:132–42) which makes no use of the confessions and little of Luther. He cites a few Bible passages, and is not particularly heartwarming.

22. Chemnitz, *Loci Theologici,* 2:202–15.

23. Ibid., 2:99–100. Cf. also Laurelius, *Syntagma Theologicum,* who presents a rather edifying discourse on the threefold use of the law.

24. It is not necessary and would be fruitless to trace all the Reformed and Lutheran polemics which followed the signing of the Formula of Concord. Rudolph Hospinian's *Concordia Discors* (Zurich, 1611) was only the beginning of the vast discussion that ensued, centering on the articles of the Sacrament of the Altar and the Person of Christ and never settled anything.

these two articles. First, the intensity of the debate between the Lutherans and the Reformed in many cases tended to freeze further biblical research on the subject of the Lord's Supper to the point where little more than the doctrine of the real presence and what appeared immediately adjunct to it was ever discussed. This unbalanced treatment of the subject is already discernible in the Formula of Concord itself which limits its discussion to the doctrine of the real presence (which under the peculiar circumstances obtaining at the time was justified) except for a short discussion on worthy participation and the comfort offered in the Supper to poor and weak sinners who need God's grace and encouragement (SD VII, 68–71). The memorial aspect of the Supper is indeed mentioned by the later theologians. And the emphasis upon the "whole action" (words of institution, distribution, and consumption) found in the Formula itself is marked. But the soteriological purpose of the sacrament (SD VII, 62, 68–71) does not receive the emphasis in the later theologians that one would wish for, except often in a rather perfunctory manner.[25] And the relationship between the real presence and the blessing it brings (as expressed in the *huper humon* of 1 Cor. 11:24) is scarcely mentioned. This is not the case with the earlier Lutherans.

Johann Brenz closely relates the real presence of Christ's body and blood in the sacrament with the blessings which Christ has secured for us by his body and blood. I would like to quote some of his presentation to illustrate its uniqueness when compared with that of the later theologians.[26] He asks,

> What has Christ therefore bequeathed to us here? That which he had as his very own and his most precious possession, namely his own body and his own blood. Do not think that this is just an ordinary bequest! He could not have left his church anything greater or more beneficial. For in his body and blood which he expended to God the Father to pay for our sins he has bequeathed to us the remission of sins. And what greater, more marvelous thing can happen to us than that? Where there is remission of sins, we have also a gracious God, righteousness, life, eternal salvation. What then can harm us? Poverty, shame, sickness, death, hell? But where there is no remission of sins, nothing does

25. Hollaz, *Examen,* part III, sec. II, chap. V, quest. 22 (pp. 1137–39). Quenstedt is hardly better, *Theologica Didactico-Polemica* part IV, chap. VI, sec. II, quest. 10 (2:1282–89).

26. Johann Brenz, *De Majestate Domini Nostri Jesu Christ ad Dextram Dei Patris et Vera Praesentia Corporis & Sanguinis ejus in Coena* (Frankfurt, 1562), pp. 177ff.

any good, not wealth nor power nor health nor anything else which this world esteems and admires. Wherefore, since Christ in his testament has left to the church his body and blood, and thereby also the remission of sins which was procured through the sacrifice of his body and blood, we must see that he has left it the highest, finest, most useful and by far the most necessary things for our salvation.

The theologians after the Formula seldom talked this way. To Brenz the presence of Christ's body and blood in the sacrament conveys to us what he accomplished for us by his body and blood. The sacrament is the way in which the objective work of Christ is made ours. Sacramentology is the arm or vehicle of Christology.

Brenz proceeds:

> Now all these things are said that we might make use of this testament, just as we are wont to make use of mundane wills and testaments. For if a person has been made an heir in a testament of this world, but is prevented from receiving his bequest because of the injustice of coheirs or other parties he will straightway appeal to the terms of the testament, bring them to the fore, inspect and weigh them, throw them in the face of his adversaries, and consider all the objects according to these terms, in order that he might finally be permitted to receive his portion. Now we make use of the New Testament of Christ in much the same way. Remission of sins and an inheritance of eternal life have been promised for the sake of Christ our Lord. Now the terms of this testament were executed at the institution of the Lord's Supper. Satan, our adversary, tries to keep us from receiving this inheritance. He throws up at us the multitude and enormity of our sins. Our sins which are to be remitted by God are so great and so many, he says. Then he seeks to deny that we will inherit the kingdom of heaven. Oh, he concedes that God is forebearing and merciful, but only if we love him (as the law prescribes) and observe his commandments. But then he says, you have not loved God with your whole heart, you have not observed even the least of his commandments perfectly. Why should you expect or hope for eternal life. These are the fiery darts of the adversary. What can we do about it? We can produce the terms of our testament, we can partake of the Lord's Supper, and then we are made certain of our inheritance, of the remission of sins and of eternal life. Of course, we do not deny that our sins are great and many; on the contrary, we frankly confess them before God. Nor do we deny that we have never perfectly followed God's law. But we have the terms of the Lord's testament, we have the Lord's Supper. And since he has there committed unto us his body and blood, he has *eo ipso* bequeathed to us also the remission of sins and life eternal. What about this? Will Christ revoke the truth of his testament because our sins are many and great? Will he become a liar because I have been disobedient? Never! Heaven and earth will pass away, he says, but my Word will not pass

away. Therefore let us see from the word "testament" what a broad application the Lord's Supper has. As Christ has called this Supper his testament, our great divines have called it, not inappropriately or without purpose, a viaticum. . . . What then is that viaticum through which we can extricate ourselves from destruction? We know of course that Christ is our *hilasmos,* that is, the price of our redemption. But because he has given himself to us to be eaten and drunk along with his body and blood in the Supper, we can correctly say that the Lord's Supper is the viaticum which pays our way on our pilgrimage and protects us from the attacks of thieves and the tyranny of Satan. You see, if Satan, in the hostel of poverty or of sicknesses or of death, exacts the claim he has over us because of our sins and threatens us with eternal destruction, then we have the Lord's Supper in which Christ's body and blood, the price of our redemption, are given us to feed upon with the bread and wine. . . . When we partake of the body and blood of Christ, who has conquered death and risen from the dead and enjoys eternal blessedness, then it can only follow that we too conquer death in him; and when death is defeated, we have reached eternal happiness.

I have found nothing on the real presence and purpose of the Lord's Supper like this quotation from Brenz in those theologians who wrote after the Formula of Concord.

The post-Reformation Lutheran theologians almost totally bypass the Formula of Concord as they present their doctrine of Christology. This is to be expected. Chemnitz, himself one of the authors of the Formula of Concord, had written a great and definitive work on the subject of the two natures of Christ.[27] And Chemnitz supplied the "Catalog of Testimonies" which supported the Formula of Concord on this subject. The later theologians of the seventeenth century, notably Gerhard, Calov, and Quenstedt, follow the theology of Chemnitz who leaned heavily upon the early Church Fathers (especially John of Damascus), except that they reverse the second and third genus (classification) of the communication of attributes. Their theology is that of the Formula of Concord at every point, but it is to Chemnitz, the Church Fathers, and ultimately to the Scriptures that they repair as they work out their Christology.

The occasions for Article X of the Formula of Concord were long gone even at the time of its writing. For this reason little attention is given this article by later Lutheran orthodoxy, except that their doctrine of church fellowship (*concordia*) is based upon agreement in

27. Martin Chemnitz, *De Duabus Naturis in Christo* (Frankfurt and Wittenberg, 1653). English translation by J. A. O. Preus, *Martin Chemnitz on the Two Natures of Christ* (St. Louis: Concordia Publishing House, 1971).

the gospel and all its articles (SD X, 31), like the Formula itself. In the seventeenth century, controversies, not unlike those that followed Luther's death, arose, and the same *modus operandi* was employed by Lutherans to overcome them and reach unanimity. That such efforts failed, even among Lutherans as in the case of Calov's *Consensus Repetitus*,[28] indicates not a departure from the position of the confessions concerning adiaphora, but an adherence to a position which demanded only agreement in the doctrine of the gospel for unity and concord in the church.

Departure from the Formula of Concord—Article XI

In only one article is there clearly a departure from the theology of the Formula of Concord on the part of seventeenth century Lutheranism: the doctrine of predestination and election. The Formula of Concord presents the doctrine of the election of grace as a great mystery. God in his grace has elected a certain number to faith and eternal life (SD XI, 24, 45, 82). This choosing must not be viewed *nude* to search out God's hidden will apart from God's giving Christ to be the savior of all men. And it must be distinguished from God's foreknowledge in the ecclesiastical sense of knowing all things in advance of their occurrence. But this choosing is a decree (SD XI, 5), which pertains to all who believe in Christ; it offers gospel comfort (SD XI, 26); it particularizes the universal grace of God, just as absolution particularizes the universal grace of God (SD XI, 27–28, 33). Especially is it to be taught and urged to support and affirm the *sola gratia* (SD XI, 43, 44). It is *propter Christum*. And with such an evangelical treatment our confessions stop: there can be no probing of the secret will of God, no asking why he does not convert all. Such questions must remain a mystery (SD XI, 53–59). With perfect justice God could damn all men (SD XI, 60).

I think the dogmaticians honestly try to follow the Formula of

---

28. Abraham Calov, *Consensus Repetitus Fide vere Lutheranae* (Wittenberg, 1666). Calov, Dannhauer, and other theologians of the day wrote dozens of books and pamphlets on the subject of syncretism, in every case following the principles of the Formula of Concord on what constituted adiaphora and what was necessary for harmony and fellowship in the church. Calov himself wrote some twenty books. But the Roman menace and the Augsburg and Leipzig Interims were in no sense the context of their discussions. Rather, it was the negotiations with more liberal Lutherans, such as Georg Calixtus, and the Reformed that prompted their discussions. See Robert Preus, *The Theology of Post-Reformation Lutheranism* (St. Louis: Concordia Publishing House, 1970–72), 1:117–54.

Concord as they develop a new approach and doctrine. In their discussions of election they cite the Formula more than in almost any other article they treat. But beginning with Aegidius Hunnius[29] the *intuitu Christi meriti fide apprehendendi* and the simple *intuitu fidei* formulae are brought into the picture; and in the end the election *eis uiothesian* (Eph. 1:5) is denied; speculation replaces simple biblical theology, and the purpose of the doctrine to comfort and lead one to the *sola gratia* is vitiated. We have already seen the synergistic error into which Hollaz fell as he sought to answer the question of why all are not chosen. Hunnius and his successors sincerely tried to combat with their formulae the supralapsarian or sublapsarian doctrines of the Calvinists and the bizarre doctrine of Samuel Huber that all human beings were elect. But they succeeded only in muddying the waters. Hunnius's position is almost impossible to understand. Does he or does he not include the eight points in the Formula of Concord (SD XI, 15–22) as a part of election or as an evangelical context in which the doctrine must always be treated? Gerhard, the systematician, and his followers make the matter quite clear. The eight points are a part of election itself; and thus in effect election becomes no more than God's decree (the dogmaticians do not hesitate to call election a decree, as did the Calvinists) to save those who he already knows will believe, a clear misunderstanding of Paul's use of *proorizo* and of the theology of the Formula on this point.[30] It is significant that Gerhard and those after him treated the decrees of election and reprobation as parallel, both contingent upon God's foreknowledge. Like Calvin, he treats the doctrine prior to the work of Christ or justification and in the context of divine providence, fate, and the cause of sin, thus depriving his treatment of the evangelical context he thought he was offering, and falling into a position radically different, but parallel to Calvinism. All the dogmaticians of the seventeenth century follow Gerhard's doctrine of election.

Striking Out on Their Own—Article XII

Article XII of the Formula of Concord is no doubt the least noticed and studied of all the articles offered there. This article touches topics not under debate among the Lutherans, and therefore one wonders

---

29. Aegidius Hunnius, *Articulus de Providentia Dei et Aeterna Praedestinatione Filiorum Dei ad Salutem* (Frankfurt, 1596).
30. Chemnitz, *Loci Theologici,* 3:145ff.

whether it is needed at all. Ironically the only other article not debated by Lutherans at the time was Article XI, and at just this point alone the later dogmaticians departed from the theology of the Formula of Concord. Article XII deals with "Other Factions and Sects Which Never Embraced the Augsburg Confession." Looking back, one observes that it was most propitious that the three items discussed in this final article were included. For the theologies of the Anabaptists, the Schwenkfelder (*Schwärmer*), and the "new anti-Trinitarians" are very contemporary indeed, and it is well that Lutheranism spoke on these issues in the final pages of the Book of Concord.

The theology of later Lutheranism followed closely the polemics and the entire approach of Luther and the early reformers when they addressed themselves to the threats of the Anabaptists and *Schwärmer*, and thus they offered little new on the subjects of baptism and the means of grace. But in reference to the doctrine of the Trinity they did something which had never been done before. Never had the doctrine of the Trinity been given the amount of attention in terms of its biblical basis as during the time of the post-Reformation era.[31] The early Church Fathers and creeds articulated the doctrine and defended it against all kinds of heresies. But somehow they were hampered from presenting a total and convincing biblical and exegetical basis for the doctrine. Luther and the early reformers were apparently too busy with other concerns. They wrote commentaries on the creeds; they included mention of the Trinity in their confessions (AC I; Apol. I; SA I); and Luther's presentation in the catechisms of God as Triune as seen by his external works (*opera ad extra*) is an original and masterful exposition. But they never found time to expend the arduous exegetical labors necessary to nail down the biblical basis for the doctrine, as for instance Luther did in his presentations of justification, or the Lord's Supper. It remained for Lutheran orthodoxy to do this; and this stands as one of the great accomplishments of the age. Perhaps they could not add much to what our confessions and the Formula of Concord have stated on the other articles of faith. But here was an area where the confessions had merely assumed what had been taught so many years by the church catholic and had reiterated the theology of the creeds and to some extent that of the medieval scholastic theologians (AC I). It remained for Lutheran orthodoxy to furnish the

31. See Werner Elert, *The Structure of Lutheranism,* trans. Walter A. Hansen (St. Louis: Concordia Publishing House, 1962), pp. 219–20. Cf. also Preus, *The Theology of Post-Reformation Lutheranism,* 2:113–63.

fullest exegetical basis for the doctrine yet provided. It was more the Socinian menace than the concern for catholicity or thoroughness that inspired such arduous labors. But the fact remains that John Gerhard, Abraham Calov, John Dorsch, John Quenstedt, Jacob Martini, Leonard Hutter, Martin Chemnitz, and a host of other Lutheran divines, including some exegetes, did a job that had never been achieved before. They followed faithfully the leads, the arguments, and the nomenclature of the great Church Fathers; but the biblical basis, especially for the deity and person of the Holy Spirit, they dug out of Scripture itself. If modern theology does not like their exegesis, contemporary theologians will need to do the job all over again; for no one has so thoroughly presented the doctrine of the Trinity from an exegetical basis since that time.

Conclusion

Our study has been brief and perhaps not apparently very productive. Possibly the reader has experienced something of the frustration of the writer as he pursued the subject. For we seem to have proved a negative thesis. The Formula of Concord as such did not exert a formative influence upon the theological works of classical Lutheran orthodoxy which immediately followed. The rest of the Book of Concord exerted more influence.

But we have not emerged from the study empty-handed. The *theology* of the Formula of Concord clearly corresponds to that of later orthodoxy on every point of doctrine except the doctrine of election. Perhaps we might have expected this agreement, for the Lutherans had the highest respect for their confessional heritage and their forebears.[32] But the facts assembled are, I believe, still significant evidence for the close continuity and agreement in doctrine which prevailed among Lutherans from 1577 until almost the turn of the eighteenth century. And this is a remarkable fact indeed.

32. The allegation of Edmund Schlink, *Theology of the Lutheran Confessions,* trans. Paul F. Koehneke and Herbert J. A. Bouman (Philadelphia: Fortress Press, 1961), pp. xxi-xxii, is utterly without foundation. Perhaps Schlink follows Friedrich A. Nitzch, *Lehrbuch der evangelischen Dogmatik,* 3d ed. (Tübingen: J. C. B. Mohr, 1912), p. 26 or Ernst Ludwig Th. Henke, *Georg Calixtus und eine Zeit* (Halle: Buchhandlung des Waisenhauses, 1853), vol. II, part 2, p. 182, or some other secondary sources. Modern historians such as Jörg Baur in *Die Vernunft zwischen Ontologie und Evangelium* (Gütersloh: Gerd Mohn, 1962) and Johannes Wallmann in *Der Theologiebegriff bis Johann Gerhard und Georg Calixt* (Tübingen: J. C. B. Mohr [Paul Siebeck], 1961) have come to the exact opposite conclusions.

6

Confessio and *Scientia:*
Life and Truth in Theology

Robert P. Scharlemann

A clear grasp of the problematics involved in the relation between *confessio* and *scientia* or *sapientia*[1] in Lutheran theology has been hampered by the fact that from its start this theology rested on a dual principle involving confession of the gospel and authority of the Scripture. The faith was formulated, by force of circumstance, as a confession; but it was elaborated and defended by appeal to the authority of Scripture. This circumstance, which had often been noted, was brought into relief again by the way in which Barthian theology reinvigorated the principle of Scripture as well as by the recovery of a confessional theology which took place when developments under German National Socialism led to calling the First Confessional Synod of Barmen in 1934. Lutheran confessional theology, reshaped in the wake of these events in the present century, brought with it a corresponding discussion of the relation between Scripture and confession. Peter Brunner's observation in that discussion is representative of the position taken as well as of the rationale for it. In 1957 he wrote, "Where

---

1. The dinstinction between *scientia* (as having to do with knowledge based on derivative principles) and *sapientia* (as having to do with first principles), which was important in the formation of theological science in the Middle Ages has had, since the time of Kant, little significance for understanding the relation between confession and science or between nontheological and theological science. For that reason the present essay will use *scientia,* or "science," as a general term, disregarding the distinction between *scientia* and *sapientia* in favor of the distinction between practical and theoretical, which not only shaped the early Protestant conception of theology but also gained importance through the influence of the Kantian critiques of reason. On the rise of theological science, see Ulrich Köpf, *Die Anfänge der theologischen Wissenschaftstheorie im 13. Jahrhundert* (Tübingen: J. C. B. Mohr [Paul Siebeck], 1974).

the authority of the scripture is lost, the *hairesis* of a school replaces the *confessio* of the church."[2]

Two factors in current theological discussion make it desirable to put the question of the relation of confession and science anew. Those factors are, first, a renewed interest in the theory of science and its effect on theology, and, second, the increasingly important role being assumed by universities and academic institutions in modern society, a development which obliges theologians to deal with the issue of how theology is aligned among the disciplines that constitute the world of *Wissenschaft*. Is theology a knowledge methodically achieved and testable by reference to the subject matter of its investigations and thought? Or does it present only a *Gegenbild* of science,[3] a picture of what science is not and should not be, so that its presence in an academic institution might be understood as that of a negative mirror whose purpose is to show the sciences what they should not be or become? Or does theology, when it undertakes to be a disciplined knowledge, perhaps reduce to a branch of historical science, capable of determining what the authors of writings and sayings assert about the one they call God, but incapable of deciding whether what they say is true?

In the post-Reformation period Protestant theology sought to understand the Scriptures as a *principium cognoscendi* in such a way as to give theology a place among the disciplines. This was done by construing the Scripture according to the Aristotelian definition of principle. Thus John Gerhard contended in his *Loci* that "Scripture itself is the sole and distinguishing principle of theology"[4] because it possessed the properties that Aristotle requires of a principle—whatever agrees with it is certain and firm and whatever contradicts it is obviously fallacious. That such an effort at a theological science independent of confession needed to be made at all can be explained by the fact that confession alone cannot verify what it professes. None-

---

2. Peter Brunner, *Pro Ecclesia: Gesammelte Aufsätze zur dogmatischen Theologie* (Berlin: Lutherisches Verlagshaus, 1962), 1:48.

3. Trutz Rendtorff's characterization of the situation in Germany in 1973 would apply elsewhere as well: "In the general scientific consciousness [theology] defines, or represents, that which is not science. And theology plays this role in a quite general way, without more precise connotation and without reference to a definite theology or theology as actually carried on." Trutz Rendtorff and Eduard Lohse, *Kirchenleitung und wissenschaftliche Theologie: Eine Ortsbestimmung* (Munich: Chr. Kaiser Verlag, 1974), p. 22.

4. John Gerhard, *Loci Theologici,* I (Leipzig: J. C. Hinrichs, 1885), prooem., §19.

theless, the orthodox conception of the principle collapsed as soon as it became apparent that what is evident to one person (a Protestant believer) may not be evident to another, so that the Scripture in point of fact did not meet the qualification demanded of the principle of a discipline. Karl Heim provided what is perhaps still the acutest account of the nature of this collapse in his history of the problem of certainty in systematic theology.[5]

Limitations of space prevent treating the whole problem of *confessio* and *scientia* here. But the central question of whether a confessional theology can ever be *true* or whether, on the contrary, truth can be attained only from the standpoint of *scientia* can be illuminated with reference to two points of conflict between confession and science—the matters of certainty and distinction in relation to truth.

Truth and Certainty

Assertions made as a matter of confession seem incapable of surviving a critical scrutiny of whether they are true. Confession, drawing its meaning in part from the testimony of martyrs, connects truth with the willingness of a witness to give his life on behalf of what he professes. In Kantian terminology this involves a "practical" test of certitude. If we are willing to risk, say, only a day's wages on something we assert to be true, we are less certain of it than if we are willing to risk our reputation. Our certainty is absolute when we are willing to risk our very being—the whole of what and who we are—on behalf of what we hold to be true. Martyrs are those who have proved the truth of their contention by giving their lives for it. Why is such a witness even necessary? The Apology to the Augsburg Confession explained its need by reference to the work of Satan, who is ever seeking to distort and suppress the truth of the gospel. Thus, the erroneous doctrine of work-righteousness was said to have been sowed by Satan "to suppress the right doctrine of the gospel so that no one, or few, might be taught what is law or gospel, what is repentance and faith, and what the benefit of Christ is" (XII, 141). The weapon employed against such satanic activity is the confession of the saints; Christ sets their confession against the kingdom of the devil in order to maintain the gospel among men (IV, 189).

But is martyrdom, or the willingness to sacrifice oneself on behalf of

---

5. Karl Heim, *Das Gewissheitsproblem in der systematischen Theologie bis zu Schleiermacher* (Leipzig: J. C. Hinrichs, 1911).

a profession, a test of the truth of what is professed? Is it conceivable that someone might be willing to die, indeed to give up his right to be anyone or anything at all, on behalf of something that is not true? Is it possible to be absolutely convinced of the truth of something and yet to be in error? This is one point where *scientia* and *confessio* clash. A martyr cannot believe he is giving himself to falsehood, but a scientist cannot see that such a practical certitude is ever more than subjective. A martyr can say, in view of that for which he takes his risk, "I *am* certain of it," but he cannot assert, "*It is* certain." In theology, accordingly, one of the motives behind the rise of theological science is the desire to find a basis and a criterion for turning the "I believe" of a confession into an "It is true" of theology. Between *credo* and *verum est* there is a gap that confession apparently cannot span but must leave to science. Or must it? A confessionalism which opposes such a subordination to science in the matter of truth is obliged to show how confession can be not only certain but true. That is a formidable difficulty. But an indication of how it might be done can be gained by considering the conception of dogmatics as *Religionswissenschaft* as that conception was represented in the speculative idealism of the nineteenth century Heidelberg systematician Karl Daub.

Idealism in general replaced the orthodox *principium scripturae* as well as natural theology by a philosophy of religion. One direction taken was that of Schleiermacher, who located religious consciousness in feeling, namely, in the feeling of absolute dependence, and made dogmatics a systematic reflection of that feeling. A second direction was that of Daub, who located religion in an idea, specifically the idea of God. "Idea" here has the technical sense given it by idealism; it means not just any abstract concept, such as "cause" or "end," but a concrete concept in which the thought and the reality it means are co-present. Daub called attention to the impossibility of basing theology on a scriptural principle. To regard the Scripture as incontestably sacred—a standpoint taken by the reformers in their opposition to clericalism, violation of conscience, and suppression of spirit—was adequate in the battle against superstition but it is inadequate, Daub contended, for a battle against unbelief. For no one who denies the divine origin of the Scripture can be convinced of its divinity by proof. Every proof—whether based on miracles or on prophecies fulfilled or on whatever else—would have to be drawn from that source itself. Hence, the proof always commits the fallacy of *petitio principii*, begging the question. But, Daub concluded, theology is necessary not only against superstition but also against unbelief, "particularly so in the present age," and if it is to be effective, then theologians must take their standpoint not in "the consciousness of the sacred books which are the vehicle of religion but in the consciousness of God, or in religion itself." From that consciousness the truth of particular teachings and even of the dogma of the divine origin of the Scripture can be drawn through diligent investigation. A theology so produced would be the best defense of religion; no special apologetic theology would be required in addition to this sort of dogmatics.[6]

Contrary to a widespread assumption, what was at issue in this nineteenth century idealism was not whether theology was based on revelation; rather, the question had to do with where the revelation is located and how its truth is to be shown. Daub's contention was that the place where revelation occurs is not, in the first instance, a consciousness of the sacredness of a book but the consciousness of God. The point of reference for theological science—dogmatics as *Religionswissenschaft*—accordingly was the "suprasensible consciousness of the suprasensible" rather than the "view of the Holy Scriptures as divine." This suprasensible consciousness was seen as the "eternal revelation of God in the reason and the spirit of man, *ho logos theou.*"[7] It provides the seed which flowers into a theological science through the work of reflection, distinction, and construction. Conscious of God and thus a participant in truth itself, man reflects on this consciousness in order to understand its basis (*Grund*). But the reflection itself must be theological, that is, conditioned by the religious consciousness on which it reflects. "Only with and in God's revelation, only with and in religion, can man reflect on religion in such a manner that by means of his reflecting a cognition (*Erkenntnis*) of it is actually produced."[8] What this requires specifically is that the reflecting thinker abstract both from himself as an individual subject and also from nature and

6. Carl Daub, *Einleitung in das Studium der christlichen Dogmatik aus dem Standpunkte der Religion* (Heidelberg: Mohr und Zimmer, 1810). Quotations in this paragraph are from p. 173.

7. Ibid., p. 201. "Reason" here is used in the idealist sense which contrasts *Vernunft* with *Verstand*. Such concepts as cause and substance are concepts of understanding (*Verstand*) because they are exhibited by empirical experience in time and space; such concepts as those of God and the universe are concepts of reason (*Vernunft*) because they formulate conditions of the possibility of any empirical experience at all—they are transcendental instead of objective in their reference.

8. Ibid., p. 256.

the world in their objectivity in order to think of religion from the standpoint of religion itself, seeking the basis of the consciousness of God in the God-consciousness itself rather than in something else. As a method this abstraction was called "absolute doubt."[9] It amounts to breaking the certainty not only of the objective world as that world presents itself, a fracture which Kant's critical idealism had already accomplished, but also of the standpoint of the reflecting self, which remained intact in Kantian critical idealism, so that what remains is no certainty at all but only an "interest" in the idea itself on the part of the absolutely doubting, self-emptied (the play on kenoticism is deliberate) subject. With that the thinker reaches the standpoint of religion, from which the reflection on the religious consciousness can be carried out.

If looking for the basis of the suprasensible consciousness in that consciousness itself is the way of finding the *principium* of theological science, the next two steps must with equal rigor be carried out from the standpoint of absolute abstraction. The distinctions worked out in this step are those found in the God-consciousness itself—such as the difference between religion as the consciousness of a particular person and religion as God's consciousness of himself. We are aware that our awareness of God is not God's awareness of himself. We do not need to look to the human subject or to the objective world in order to find such differences, for they are present in the God-consciousness itself, which is a consciousness of one who is not comprehended by that consciousness. Finally, the last step of working out the principle is one at which we bring together, or conclude, what the second step has distinguished. This connection of the elements with each other and with their basis, made possible by the idea itself, is the constructive work which completes the explication of the truth that is implicit in the consciousness of God. In knowing that there is an inner order to that idea, one knows it systematically; in knowing that the idea is true, one knows it scientifically.[10] The power of systematic thought resides, according to this idealist conception, in the fact that it can show the necessity of what is initially only a profession of faith. Faith participates in the truth but cannot know it as truth; theological sci-

9. Carl Daub, *Die dogmatische Theologie jetziger Zeit, oder die Selbstsucht in der Wissenschaft des Glaubens und seiner Artikel* (Heidelberg: J. C. B. Mohr [Paul Siebeck], 1833), pp. 413–37: "Der absolute Zweifel, als das Mittel der Entwickelung des dogmatischen Lehrbegriffs."
10. Daub, *Einleitung*, p. 213.

ence shows that what faith participates in is the truth. The showing is done by explicating faith's implicit principle so that at the end the system makes clear that what faith believes is true because we cannot think otherwise. But since this necessity of truth becomes manifest through the free activity of reflection, division, and construction on the part of the theological thinker, the system itself is a unity of freedom and necessity. The necessity of our thought, which the system manifests, corresponds to the freedom of what is the principle and object of that thought. Furthermore, the implanting of the idea in human reason, the act of revelation which is the principle of knowledge for theology, is, in respect to human consciousness, something unconscious and necessary; but the articulation of that principle, the actualization of the idea, is the work of human freedom and consciousness.[11]

On this reading, then, the principle of theology is the idea of God that is implanted in the human spirit; it is not the feeling of the sacredness or the authority of the Scripture. The *idea* of God is, in other words, the identity between the thought of God and the reality of God that is in the religious consciousness, the place where the revelation of God is to be found. In his later work Daub shifted the emphasis somewhat from the idea to the word, and in his "Über den Logos," an article treating the dogma of the Trinity, he endeavored to show how thinking can move from the word "God" to the reality of God which is identical with it.[12] In retrospect, at least until it has been given the close scrutiny it deserves but has not received, that *Logos*-essay of Daub might appear to be nothing more than an idealist curiosity—except for the fact that Karl Barth's book on Anselm, which he himself regarded as opening the path to his theological system, has a strikingly similar theme.[13] Disregarding the peculiarities of Daub's and Barth's language, one can see that Barth's *Fides quaerens intellectum* works with the same principle of identity between word and reality as does Daub's "Über den Logos," even though Barth was treating Anselm's formulation of the name of God as "that than which no greater can be thought" (*id quo majus cogitari nequit*) rather than the Trinitarian dogma. Specifically, Barth contended that the name, "that than which no greater can be thought," which is a phrase in

---

11. Ibid., pp. 273–74.
12. Carl Daub, "Über den Logos. Ein Beitrag zur Logik der göttlichen Namen," *Theologische Studien und Kritiken* 6 (1833): 355–410.
13. Karl Barth, *Fides quaerens intellectum: Anselms Beweis der Existenz Gottes* (Zollikon: Evangelischer Verlag, 1958), pp. 81–89, 135–37, 154–61.

normal language, was the presence of God, or the revelation of God, in the midst of our language. In the whole of language there is one word which thus is the word of God because in it God is identical with the name, he himself is at hand, presenting himself inescapably to anyone who thinks the meaning of the word. Just by following the rule of thought that this name of God contains, we can arrive at the knowledge that God really is someone outside of our own thought as well, one who places a limit upon our thinking. This word of ordinary language prevents us, the creatures, from denying the reality of God, the creator. It exercises its power over our thought in such a way that we find denial of the existence of God to be quite literally impossible. We may, of course, utter the words "God does not exist," but the "God" whom we thus deny is no longer the same as the one whose presence is manifest in the name "that than which no greater can be thought." The name gives us, therefore, only two choices. We can deny that there is any truth in it; but in that case the cost of doing so is that we must simultaneously deny the patent meaning of the phrase. Or we can think the thought contained in the plain sense of the words, and then we know that the one of whom they speak is real and not merely verbal or noetic.

Neither Barth's nor Daub's account offers a restoration of natural theology. No claim is made that we can come to a knowledge of the existence of God on the basis of a rational inference, whether it be an inference from the existence of the world to a first cause or some other kind of inference. But both Barth and Daub do offer an alternative to the post-Reformation conception of the principle of theology. The principle is not the Scriptures regarded as having a sacred character that enables them to be an Aristotelian *principium disciplinae* but a word or set of words which, set within the whole of ordinary human language, is the revelation of God. God is already manifest there; it is a mistake to think that theology must first look for a revelation with which to begin. It can begin with its proper beginning, with God who is present in the word that is his name. Furthermore, nothing in addition to the normal exercise of thinking—Daub would say the exercise of speculative thinking—is required in order to see that the word "God" or the phrase "that than which no greater can be thought" is God really manifest in the language in which we think.

The vulnerability of this bold conception of the theological principle is indicated by the way in which the negator must be treated. If God is thus manifest, how does one account for the existence of the denier?

Barth resorted to the notion of a miracle. The existence of the denier is wondrous; it is the existence of one who cannot actually be what he is. The denier does what, strictly speaking, cannot be done—he denies the existence of God, whose existence it is literally impossible to deny. What is impossible becomes a possibility. For that reason the negator is a wonder, a marvel. Daub on the other hand was thoroughly idealist in his explanation. He could regard the denier only as an egoist who refused to leave the level of critical reflection, with its standpoint in the certainty of the subjective self, in order to take the standpoint of absolute doubt from where the truth of religion might emerge. Egoism is an ethical fault, a matter of free willing. So the denier was not, as he was for Barth, a witness of the freedom of God which can bring about, as a wonder, the existence of a creature who does the impossible thing of denying his creator's existence; he was, rather, a person who had not yet willed to give up his egoism.

Daub in his idealist conception of the necessity of a system and Barth in his treatment of the Anselmian name of God—the rest of Barth's theology is not under discussion here—both root the *truth* of theology not in confession and faith but in theological science. Faith may be certain of its being in the truth. But whether that certainty is in truth the truth cannot be shown by reference to the profession of faith; it must be shown by explicating the knowledge faith contains on the basis of the principle resident in it. Quite apart from whatever vulnerability might be present in this kind of thought, one might raise the question whether the result achieved can be avoided, since it is a result that seems to say that the life of faith in confession and the truth of faith in science are separate. *Confessio* is a living act, without truth; *scientia* has truth, without life. Must the living act give itself over to reflection in order for its truth to come out as truth?

If we were to apply the confessional test of truth to the idea or word in which God himself is said to be manifest, then we should have to say that the certainty of the word involved is measured by its willingness to give itself up on behalf of that to which it testifies. But this is a notion difficult to grasp. We find it hard to think of a word or an idea as *doing* anything, as though a word were a personal agent. We have no difficulty imagining a person as willing to risk his life rather than to deny a confessional assertion, of being willing, let us say, to be devoured by lions rather than to deny that Jesus is his lord. But what sense is there to the assertion that a word or an idea must be willing to sacrifice itself on behalf of what it attests? What would it mean to say that the word "God" is a martyr, one that witnesses to the truth of what it asserts by being willing to sacrifice itself? How can we tell what a word or an idea is "willing" to do or not to do?

The hurdles indicated by such questions are formidable, but they are not, I think, insurmountable. Indeed, it is by pursuing such questions that we can see how confession might enter its test of truth in a manner that escapes from mere subjectivity. To maintain that a word or an idea is a witness is to say that when we form the idea of God and speak or hear the word "God," we are also led to think and understand that the idea or word can present the reality it intends only by ceasing to be an idea or a word. An idea of God is true, by this criterion, if it can cease to be an idea and in so doing make visible what it is an idea of; the word "God" is a true name if it can cease to be a word and yet make God audible. How does an idea or word cease to be? It is easy enough to tell when a person ceases to live physically (except for the ambiguity attendant on whether one uses breathing or brain waves as the index); it is not so easy to say what it means for a word or idea to "die" on behalf of what it points to. But we might expound the conception along the following lines, granting that the reformers' question of whether God was gracious is not the modern question of whether God is anything at all besides a word and an idea.

The contention here is that the *word* "God" is a witness to the *assertion* "God is someone; God is not nothing." This assertion, which we may here abbreviate to "God is," is true to the extent that the word "God" can give itself up rather than deny that God is. Such a contention applies a confessional, not a scientific, test to the truth of the assertion. The scientific principle says we cannot think of God as not existing, hence God exists; necessity of thought is here the obligating power. Confession says that, whatever may be the case with the necessity of thought, "God is" is attested by the fact that there is nothing in the word "God" which compels us to hold onto the word in order to live in the truth that God is, or in order to answer to the reality of God's being. The truth of the assertion "God is" lies, in this case, not in the necessity with which we must think of the existence of God but in the living experience that the word "God" (i.e., any particular name for God), in going out of existence (i.e., in losing its meaning), gives testimony to the assertion "God is not nothing." The word "God" can lose its meaning rather than cease to point to the being of God. That is to say, there is something in the word itself which enables us, who understand its meaning, to be willing to give up saying

111

and hearing it; and there is something in the idea of God that enables us, when we think the idea, to be willing to give up our thinking of it. When that quality of the word and idea becomes manifest, the certainty attaching to them is no longer merely a subjective practical certainty. It is no longer the case that *we* are as certain that God is not nothing as we are certain that we are human beings; rather, the *fact* that God is is more sure than is the fact that the word "God" is a word. The word "God," in ceasing to be what it is, attests the fact that God is the negation of nothing. Only in that way does the certainty of confession achieve the truth of a science, the truth that God is.

All of this is to say that the life of faith, which is usually found in confession rather than in science, and the truth of faith, which is usually found in science and not in confession, can come together where the word of faith is itself a confession. Practical certainty remains subjective, and for that reason the truth of confession as we make it remains problematic; we may be absolutely certain of something, but our being certain does not guarantee that we have not erred. But if the certainty is not merely practical, if instead it resides in the idea or word itself in such a way that the word or idea *enables* us to be willing to dispense with the word or the idea, then the certainty is no longer merely subjective; it lies outside of us in the word or idea itself. In that way "God," as a word or an idea, is a witness to God as the one who is. The life of faith and the truth of faith, *confessio* and *scientia,* can come together to the degree that the language of faith has in it something which enables us to do without that language itself.

Truth and Distinction

Truth may be defined as identity in difference so that, by way of example, the truth of such empirical assertions as "the leaf is green" has to do with the fact that although our understanding of the sense of the statement and our physical perception of the thing to which it refers remain different from each other, nonetheless what we understand as the sense and what we perceive as the object are the same. Sense as such and reference as such are and remain different from each other; but the content of the sense which we understand and that of the referent which we perceive are the same. Therein is the truth of the assertion. Truth cannot appear if either the difference or the identity is removed. "The leaf is green" is not true, if we cannot both distinguish between its elements (sense and referent) and also see an identity in the difference. That is the sense in which we can accept the definition of truth as the correspondence between *intellectus* and *res*.

Empirical judgments only illustrate what is the case with other judgments as well. If we cannot distinguish our understanding of what is said from our ascertaining of what is so, we cannot determine whether an assertion is true; and, contrariwise, if we cannot see that what is said and what is so are the same, we cannot regard the assertion as true. For that reason the act of confession presents us with a dilemma. A confession aims above all to witness to the truth; it intends to utter what is true. Yet, as the history of the Formula of Concord and, more recently, of Barmen shows, making a confession may solidify one group but it splits it from other groups who declare the same faith. Confession accordingly produces a difference between two sides, but it loses the identity that might enable it to be true, just because the issuance of the confession divides one faith into two distinct beliefs. And if the effect of making a confession is to divide a group holding a faith into two parties, then, from the standpoint of *scientia*, neither of the two parties can be speaking the truth. Each party contends that it professes the truth, in opposition to falsehood; but this truth cannot emerge as truth unless the difference between the parties is bridged. Distinction, or difference, is essential to truth; but truth does not lie in the distinction alone, it lies in the identity within the distinction.

The act of confession can therefore be a movement on the way to truth, but it cannot be an expression of the truth. The act of confession makes the necessary distinction in a previously undifferentiated identity, but it cannot "close" the distinction it thus opens. The truth of faith depends upon the distinction between belief and superstition —or, from a more neutral vantage point, between belief and other-belief. That distinction is accomplished by confessional declarations. But the truth of faith also depends upon there being an identity in that difference between belief and other-belief; and confession, as we know it historically and systematically, does not provide that element. The truth of faith does not eradicate the difference between belief and other-belief, but it appears as the identical content in both of them, just as the truth of an empirical assertion resides in a structure in which the same content appears in the perception of the fact and in the understanding of the sense. When it is possible to see that what a belief and what an other-belief profess, both of them confessionally, exhibit the same faith even though they remain different beliefs, then the truth, hidden in and unattainable through confession, emerges. From this point of view the twentieth century might be regarded as the epoch in which the truth of faith has begun to appear in the identity of the difference between Protestant belief (or other-belief) and Catholic other-belief (or belief).

But can the identity of faith ever be made a matter of confession since by its very character confession divides even what it intends to unite? The Lutheran confessions of the sixteenth century did indeed intend to express what was the teaching of the church catholic, not a school opinion; but that intention was in fact defeated. And such seems always to be the case with the production of confessions. They may unite some factions—as the Formula of Concord united the North German and Swabian views of the sacramental presence, and as Barmen united Reformed and Lutheran Protestants—but even while doing so, they split one group professing the Christian faith from another group professing the same faith, and they do so in such a way as to hide whatever identity might be there. A confession may start out by intending to be a confession of truth; in fact it ends by being a confession of untruth, or at least of a truth that is not yet truth, because it divides the elements which compose truth. In the name of one church a confession creates two or more churches; in the name of faith in the one God, it brings about belief in two Gods. It is not surprising then if the conclusion is drawn that the truth of faith can be seen only by theological science, even if it is a truth without life, whereas the life of faith, which moves in confession, is a life without truth.

There is one circumstance, however, in which a confession might nonetheless overcome this dilemma so as to attain a truth and come together with *scientia*. When it is possible to incorporate into a confession the assertion that the confessional assertion of truth is, by virtue of its confessional character, untrue, then the confession of belief transcends the limits of its own confessional character. If one can confess the untruth of one's own confession of truth, the confession might be true; otherwise it is false. Lutheran confessionalism in the twentieth century has recognized that a confession must always be a confession of the sin of the confessors themselves, but it has not made much headway in the rather more dizzying undertaking of recognizing how a confession is always a confession of the untruth of what is confessed as truth. Perhaps the quadricentennial of the Formula of Concord will be a spur toward working at that task.

Short of producing a confession of that nature, theology must remain divided between the life and the truth of the subject matter with which it deals.   If theology is more interested in the truth, it pursues its object through *scientia*; if it is more interested in the life, it pursues its object through confession.   But neither alternative can be satisfactory over the long run because a living confession does not continue to live when severed from truth, and truth does not continue to be important when severed from life.   Life without truth is deadly, as truth without life is blinding.

II

HISTORICAL ESSAYS

The Response to the Formula of Concord

7

The Reception in Silesia

Manfred P. Fleischer

The Formula of Concord was implemented in a country where the most representative Lutheran prince, Duke George II of Brieg (1523–1586), adhered to it in "spirit rather than to the letter," as the *Allgemeine Deutsche Biographie* puts it. Nevertheless, Duke George interdicted in 1573 disputes concerning the Person of Christ, the communication of attributes, the Lord's Supper, etc. The Formula of Concord appeared in the Lutheran "church orders" of the principalities of Liegnitz, Brieg, and Wohlau only in 1677 when these regions had reverted, after the expiration of the native dynasty, to the Hapsburg emperor, and the forcible "reduction" of the Lutheran churches to Catholicism had started. But the last of the Silesian Piasts, Duke George William (d. 1675), a Calvinist, who would not allow the Formula of Concord on the books, had implored Emperor Leopold I on his deathbed to preserve the Lutheranism of his territories. In the Silesian "hereditary principalities," where the Hapsburg overlords had been also the local dukes since 1526, the Formula of Concord did not surface in the church orders until 1654 when, after the reduction of all the other Lutheran churches to Catholicism, the predominantly Lutheran population was allowed to construct three "peace churches," and a spiritualist, the mystical poet Daniel Czepko, acted as defender of the Augsburg Confession.[1]

---

1. On the "church orders," see Ernst Siegmund-Schultze, "Kryptocalvinismus in den schlesischen Kirchenordnungen," *Jahrbuch der Schlesischen Friedrich-Wilhelms-Universität zu Breslau,* 5 (1960): 52–68. On Czepko, see Werner Milch, "Quellen zur schlesischen Geschichte des 17. Jahrhunderts aus Daniel Czepkos Werk," *Zeitschrift des Vereins für Geschichte Schlesiens,* 67 (1933): 46–84. For lack of space, footnotes have to be largely omitted. For pertinent sources, see the author's article, "The Institutionalization of Humanism in Protestant Silesia," *Archiv für Reformationsgeschichte,* 66 (1975): 256–74; his

In order to provide an historical denouement for these confessional incongruities, this essay will have first a general reference to Silesia's special significance for the cultural history of confessionalism; second, the introduction of a Silesian forerunner and namesake of the Formula of Concord; third, a discussion of the constitutional and cultural complexities which cautioned the Silesian Lutherans against the subscription to a new confessional statement; and finally a review of the ways and means by which the Formula of Concord was incorporated into the cultural ecology of the Lutheran countryside. Such a procedure seems to have been perfectly acceptable to the guardians of Lutheran orthodoxy in Wittenberg, if the cordial correspondence of Silesian pastors with Hunnius, Meissner, Calovius, and Hülsemann at the seat of Luther is a sign of approval. If the reason for the missing Silesian signatures to the Formula of Concord was the fact that their homelands did not qualify as an "immediate estate of the empire," then the Silesian Lutheran republic of the learned spent the following one and a half century at efforts to remedy this situation. It took a legal expert 326 pages to outline the historical precedents and constitutional arguments which the Silesian Lutheran humanists used to have their religious rights recognized.[2] Thus this essay will constantly hint at the resources other than confessional subscription to which Lutheranism resorted when its survival was at stake. This should reveal something of the "morphology" of Lutheranism in Werner Elert's sense, of which doctrines were only an outward, and not necessarily essential, expression.

According to Herbert Schöffler, Silesia is of special significance to the cultural history of confessionalism because its Lutheran section led Germany in literature and philosophy between the Reformation and the Enlightenment.[3] If Luther created the modern high German language, the Silesian Martin Opitz (1597–1639) laid down the laws

forthcoming article in the same yearbook entitled, *"Silesiographia:* The Rise of a Regional Historiography"; and his essay, "Die schlesische Irenik: Unter besonderer Berücksichtigung der Hapsburger Zeit," *Jahrbuch für Schlesische Kirchengeschichte,* 55 (1976): 87–107.

2. See Georg Jaeckel, "Die staatsrechtlichen Grundlagen des Kampfes der ev. Schlesier um ihre Religionsfreiheit," *Jahrbuch für Schlesische Kirchengeschichte,* 37 (1958): 102–36; 38 (1959): 74–109; 39 (1960): 51–90; 40 (1961): 7–30; 41 (1962): 46–74; 42 (1963): 25–49; 43 (1964): 67–88; 45 (1966): 71–110; 47 (1968): 7–40; 49 (1970): 64–116.

3. See Herbert Schöffler, *Deutsches Geistesleben zwischen Reformation und Aufklärung: Von Martin Opitz zu Christian Wolff,* 3d ed. (Frankfurt: Vittorio Klostermann, 1974).

for modern high German literature while his compatriot Christian Wolff (1679–1754) taught philosophy to speak in German. Lutheran Silesia was also the only landscape within the Hapsburg Empire which preserved the faith of the majority of its people throughout the period of the Counter-Reformation. Another Silesian peculiarity not evident anywhere else in world-Protestantism was the failure of hundreds of thousands of Lutherans who lived in close proximity to found a territorial university. When in 1525 an attempt to establish a Lutheran university in Liegnitz foundered on incipient Schwenkfelderism and insufficient funds, this default furthered the development of Silesian Lutheranism along the individualistic lines of late humanism, and goes far to explain the lack of Silesian signatures to the Formula of Concord. Confessional subscription was then to a territorial training center what the oath of allegiance is now to a state university.

In regard to the humanist element, Melanchthon reiterated in 1558 that no other tribe of Germany could boast of more learned men in all of the humanities than the Silesians, and in no other part of Germany were there more commoners who studied and understood the doctrinal differences, many of whom were also gifted for poetry and eloquence, so that they could express their preferences. Concerning the confessional ferment, the historical novelist Hermann Stehr attested that in no other region of Germany did the Reformation send through the veins of the lower classes in such rapid succession a wilder and more colorful delirium of denominationalism or fever of confessionalism than in Silesia.

The dynamics of humanism and denominationalism created currents which stirred at home and spilled abroad. Margrave George the Pius of Jägerndorf (1484–1543) and his brother-in-law, Frederick II of Liegnitz (1499–1547), used their dynastic relationships to help in spreading a network of Lutheran territorial churches from (East) Prussia to Franconia. In 1557, the city of Breslau exported its *Kirchenordnung,* an original import *via* Margrave George from Brandenburg-Nuremberg, to the cities of Danzig, Thorn (Torún), and Elbing. According to the lists compiled by Frederick Lucae in *Schlesiens curieuse Denckwürdigkeiten* (1689), Silesia sent into "foreign service," mostly during the time from 1500–1675, 27 bishops and abbots, 85 military leaders, 81 statesmen, 30 Reformed theologians, 75 Lutheran divines, 60 jurists, professors, and famous practitioners of medicine, and 52 philosophers, historians, and mathematicians. Lucae, himself an exiled Calvinist court preacher and historian from Brieg, did not take into account, besides the 105 Reformed and Lutheran churchmen, the emissaries of Silesian spiritualism and mysticism, such as Caspar von Schwenkfeld, Jacob Boehme, or Quirinus Kuhlmann.

Because of the successive waves of confessionalism, which rocked the ships of church and state at home, there was no Lutheran region more in need of self-definition and doctrinal distinction from other denominations than Silesia. The Formula of Concord looks as if it had been custom-tailored as a Lutheran resolution of Silesia's confessional conflicts. Since the beginning of the Protestant Reformation, Silesian Lutheranism had to establish, define, and defend itself in contradistinction to all of those "false teachings" condemned by the Formula of Concord. The Anabaptists, Anti-Trinitarians, the Zwinglians, or Sacramentarians, but above all the Schwenkfelder, Silesia's native sect, whose errors were rejected in the first part of the Formula of Concord, had beset the body of Lutheranism in Silesia, both from within and without, since the days of its birth, and affected the course of its development as well as the nature of its growth.

Moreover, in 1574, some Silesian Lutheran nobles and clergymen had given a friendly reception and open hearing to Matthias Flacius Illyricus (1520–1575) in his search for support to his view on the substantial nature of original sin. Thus the suspicion arose that Flacianism or Manichaeism was the latest swirl in Silesia's pool of confessional crosscurrents. Therefore, a convention of twenty-six Lutheran ministers from the districts of Strehlen and Nimptsch in the principality of Brieg signed the same year, at which not only the specter of Flacianism, but the prospect of the Counter-Reformation appeared on the horizon, the so-called Heidersdorf Formula of Concord (*formula concordiae Heidersdorfensis*). The subscribers disassociated themselves from the ancient heretics, the pope, Schwenkfeld, Zwingli, Calvin, Beza (a correspondent of the Silesian crypto-Calvinists), and Flacius Illyricus.[4] The Heidersdorf Formula of Concord (1574) paralleled those steps toward confessional consolidation in other parts of Lutheran Germany, such as the Swabian and Saxon Concordia (1574) or the Maulbronn Formula (1575/76), and attempted on a Silesian provincial scale what the Bergen Formula of Concord (1577) tried to accomplish among "the Electors, Princes, and Orders of the Empire."

4. For the text and the signatories, see Siegismund Justus Ehrhardt, *Presbyterologie des Evangelischen Schlesiens,* part II, main section 1 (Liegnitz: J. G. Pappaesche, 1782), pp. 22–23.

Then there was a long fuse which linked Silesia to the issue of the Formula of Concord at the former monastery of Bergen near Magdeburg in 1577. The crypto-Calvinist controversy in Saxony, which removed the last doubts from the minds of the leading German Lutheran princes about the necessity of such a confessional statement, had been ignited by the posthumous and anonymous publication of the Silesian Philippist Joachim Cureus, *Exegesis perspicua et ferme integra controversiae de sacra coena* (Leipzig, 1574). Cureus (1532–1573) had been the perfecter of Lutheran Silesiography, and died as court physician of Duke George II in Brieg.

In the light of these interactions, whether at cross-purposes or along parallel lines, it seems inconceivable that neither the names of the princes of Liegnitz, Brieg, and Wohlau, nor the signatures of the *consul et senatus* of the city republic of Breslau appeared after the Preface of the Book of Concord. Subscription to the Formula would have put the seal of approval on a set of common experiences and convictions which had been the outcome of fifty years of continuous cooperation between Lutheran Silesia and Wittenberg. During the sixteenth century, more Silesian Lutheran clergymen had been ordained in Wittenberg for service both at home and abroad than in any other place.

For confessional reasons, more than twenty Lutheran "imperial estates" had also abstained from requiring their professors and pastors to subscribe to the Formula of Concord, to say nothing of the kingdoms of Denmark and Sweden. But the absence of the Silesians involved more deeply than in other cases constitutional and cultural considerations. In contrast to Calvinism, which tried to reconstruct Christianity by repudiating much of the medieval past, or Anabaptism and spiritualism, which wanted to have heaven on earth here and now, the "Conservative Reformation," as Charles P. Krauth entitled his book on Lutheran theology (1871), aspired to "redeem" traditional values and existing conditions by working within their dispensations. In this endeavor, Silesian Lutheranism even drew public support, as initially stated, from pillars of society who privately preferred the Reformed faith or a spiritualist view of life. These outside buttresses may have seen in Lutheranism the only viable form of Protestantism which offered religious change in critical periods without cultural discontinuity and political disruption.

If culturally and confessionally Silesia was a centrally located country of crossroads and bridges, constitutionally it had evolved on the eve of the Reformation as a hinterland of the crowns of St. Stephen (Hungary) and St. Wenceslaus (Bohemia) as well as the Holy Roman Empire. The Silesian princes had become vassals of the king of Bohemia in the early fourteenth century. In the wake of the Hussite wars they transferred their allegiance in 1474 to King Matthias Corvinus of Hungary (d. 1490) who laid the foundation for the overall constitution of the country which was a conglomerate of twenty-odd principalities and "free estates." The constitution, consolidated under Corvinus's successors, Wladislaus II of Bohemia (d. 1516), and Louis II of Hungary (d. 1526), would remain in force at least through the Bohemian rebellion which started the Thirty Years' War (1618).

The three overlapping sources of sovereignty, upon whose successful handling the maintenance of religious freedom by the Silesian Lutherans depended, were first the authority of the suzerain, which after 1526 was held by the Austrian Hapsburgs in personal union with the scepters of Bohemia, Hungary, and the Holy Roman Empire. As suzerains over Silesia, the Hapsburg kings and emperors would not only be the *princeps supremus* of the province, but also the local dukes in the "hereditary principalities" of Breslau, Schweidnitz, Jauer, Troppau, Glogau, Münsterberg, Oppeln, Ratibor, and Sagan. Only the principalities of Liegnitz, Brieg, and Wohlau as well as Teschen were still headed by branches of the old Silesian dynasty, the Piasts. The principality of Oels was held by descendants of the "Hussite" King George of Podiebrad (d. 1471). Jägerndorf and Beuthen were in the hands of the margrave of Ansbach and Bayreuth, George the Pious (1484–1543), a Franconian Hohenzollern, who had been the guardian of Louis II, the late king of Hungary. The principality of Neisse and Grottkau belonged to the bishop of Breslau. Wartenberg, Militsch, Trachenberg, and Pless were "free estates," the last soon to be bought by the bishop of Breslau.

The titular heads of all of these territories formed the second source of sovereignty, the Silesian diet of princes (*Schlesischer Fürstentag*). Its president (*Oberhauptmann*) was appointed by the suzerain, who as head of the "hereditary principalities" commanded the largest block of votes in this provincial parliament. However, due to the financial embarrassment of the late Jagellionian and the new Hapsburg dynasties because of the Turkish campaigns, the principality of Glogau had been pawned to Duke Frederick II of Liegnitz, who introduced Lutheranism there. Likewise, the duchies of Ratimor and Oppeln were leased as collaterals to George the Pious, who became the "reformer of Upper Silesia." The city of Breslau, whose council had acquired the lordship

124

over the principality, also embraced Lutheranism, and the remaining dukes and magnates followed suit. The *princeps supremus* and the bishop of Breslau, who after 1536 was regularly appointed president of the diet of princes, were the only Catholics left.

With so many Lutheran delegates, the diet of princes could provide protective custody for their faith. The diet also served as a forum for the cultivation of cordial relations between the bishops of Breslau and the Lutheran princes over whose pastors the bishops would continue to exercise a certain degree of jurisdiction. Such a staunch Lutheran as Duke George II of Brieg had the portrait of the Breslau bishop, Martin Gerstmann (ca. 1575–85), always at his bedside, and inherited the bishop's most precious ring and his most expensive fur coat. One of Gerstmann's episcopal successors, the Polish Vasa-Hapsburg prince Charles Ferdinand, was represented at the diet of princes by the Lutheran Silesiographer and imperial counselor, Jacob Schickfus, as late as 1636. Such delicate dealings elucidate why, after the imperial recognition of the Augsburg Confession (1555), a new doctrinal definition had to be treated with circumspection.

However, the Silesian diet of princes was not only composed of the delegates of princes and magnates. Prelates, "knighthoods," and "townships," especially from the hereditary principalities, were represented too. It was within these groups that the third source of sovereignty, church patronage, primarily resided. As far as the spread of Protestantism and its subsequent rollback by the Counter-Reformation went, church patronage served as the leverage point. The history of Silesian church patronage is as involved as the development of the country's overall constitution. We must start *in media res* shortly after the outbreak of the Reformation when church patronage had reverted more or less to a state of a proprietary ecclesiastical system (*Eigenkirchentum*). "Each landowner (*Grundherr*) considered himself as lord over his church, and many enriched themselves with its property."[5]

Practically, the authority of the estates over the "government of doctrine," as Thomas Hobbes would call this new phenomenon, was exercised through their long-established or newly acquired rights as local church patrons. The difference between firmly rooted or recently usurped prerogatives (from deserted monasteries, for instance) would

---

5. Edmund Michael, *Das schlesische Patronat* (Weigwitz, Kr. Ohlau: Selbstverlag, 1923), p. 43.

decide, when the *princeps supremus* had become almost absolute by virtue of the Peace of Westphalia (1648) or after the expiration of the native Protestant dynasty (1675), which churches could remain Lutheran until the death of their pastors, whereupon they were to revert immediately to Catholicism, albeit without the parishioners. After their church buildings had been taken, or shortly before they were to be taken, the faithful adopted the Formula of Concord, as initially stated. But a century before, the Silesian Lutherans hesitated to jeopardize their ecclesiastical property rights by signing a later addition to the Augsburg Confession. Such a signature might have been interpreted by their Catholic opponents as an act by which they forsook the legally established and constitutionally recognized *terra firma* of the unalterable Augsburg Confession of 1530. An official warning to this effect would actually be issued by Emperor Rudolph II to a diet of princes in 1604.

To repeat, during the first decades of the Reformation, it had been the local church patrons, the city councils, nobles (including the princes and magnates), and prelates who geared the supply of pastors to the demands of the parishioners, and thus determined the confessional composition of the country. In the course of the sixteenth century, 1,500 congregations had been staffed with Lutheran clergymen while about 400, mainly monastic and episcopal dependencies, were left in Catholic hands. By 1618, when the legal battle over the rights of church patronage would be joined by a political power struggle over the law of reforming (*ius reformandi*), 1,285 Lutheran churches and chapels could still be counted in twenty Silesian principalities and "free estates."[6] For brevity's sake, only two partners involved in the triangular trade of church patronage can be presented: the kind of Lutheran "knighthood" which exercised its powers of appointment in the countryside, and the type of Lutheran "priesthood" which defended its faith, as the occasions arose, against the overt or covert agents of other confessions, whether they were princes, patrons, or fellow-pastors.

When Luther charged the "Christian nobility of the German nation" (1520) with the task of reforming the church, he conferred upon this estate a new mission which many of its members took seriously. If by the beginning of the sixteenth century the "von Zedlitz" family had sired Silesia's most notorious robber baron, "Black Christopher,"

6. Michael, *Das schlesische Patronat*, p. 52.

who was caught and executed in 1512 by Frederick II of Liegnitz in league with the surrounding cities, in 1575, a Sebastian von Zedlitz would found a hospital for the poor at the gates of his castle as a memorial to his teacher, Matthias Flacius Illyricus, whose student he had been in Wittenberg. Sebastian and his mother-in-law hosted the disputations of Flacius at *Burg* Lehnhaus and *Schloss* Langenau making them splendid social occasions for the neighboring clergy and nobility. As teenagers, Sebastian and his brothers had been educated at the Lutheran humanist *Gymnasium illustre* in Goldberg whose headmaster, Valentin Trozendorf, they honored by dedicating to him a costly church bell at Neukirch, where the family possessed church patronage.

In the second half of the sixteenth century, the academic pilgrimage of a Silesian Lutheran noble would lead from a school of humanism, such as pioneered by Trozendorf, or founded in 1568 by Duke George in Brieg, to further studies at a university like Wittenberg or Jena. Degrees in law and medicine, which were more frequently the goal of "burghers" who aimed at the status of nobility, would then be pursued in Italy, especially at the University of Padua where provisions had been made for Protestants to circumvent the profession of Tridentine faith. By earning a doctor's degree, distinguishing oneself in public service, and acquiring a landed estate whose place name would be linked with the word "von" to one's family name, one could easily obtain a patent of nobility from the emperor. Most intellectual leaders of Lutheran society in Silesia had received such titles of nobility, and many of them were sons of pastors.

The Lutheran "country squire" and rural church patron, whether of the old (*Uradel*) or new nobility (*Briefadel*), would then settle down to a life of learned leisure. He would manage his secular estate along the lines set forth in the *Oeconomia ruralis et domestica* (Wittenberg, 1591ff.) by Johann Colerus (ca. 1570–1639), and order his ecclesiastical affairs according to the guidance given in the *Oeconomia ecclesiastica* (Parchim, 1616) by the same writer. The author of these two paradigms of the Lutheran domestic and ecclesiastical "economy"[7] in the countryside had been born in Goldberg. Colerus's handbooks were an extension of the work of his father Jacob, whom we will meet later as the epitome of a Lutheran country pastor in Silesia. During his tenure as theology professor in Frankfurt on the Oder, Jacob

---

7. *Oikonomia Theou* (1 Eph. 18:2) was the patristic term for *Heilsgeschichte*.

Colerus had tried to combine the lessons of the ancient Roman agriculturists Cato, Columella, Varro, and Palladius with Lutheran vocational ethics. Although Johann Colerus, as Lutheran "archdeacon and senior minister" in Parchim, spent most of his life in the March of Brandenburg, and dedicated his *Oeconomia ecclesiastica* to three duchesses of Schleswig-Holstein, Mecklenburg, and Pomerania, the two "economies" of this *Aureo-Montanus Silesius,* as he called himself on their title pages, reflected the situation in Silesia. The *Oeconomia ruralis et domestica, worin das Ampt aller braven Hausväter und Hausmütter begriffen* underwent fourteen editions until the end of the eighteenth century, and has been recently reprinted.

Even if its companion piece, the *Oeconomia ecclesiastica,* did not become so popular, it is equally indicative of the confessional morphology and cultural ecology of Lutheranism under the auspices of late humanism. According to Luther's explanation of the Fourth Commandment in his Large Catechism (1529), God had entrusted the parental care for his creation to (1) fathers and mothers of families, (2) fathers of a nation, those who held governing positions, again, according to the Latin text of the Large Catechism, *heras* and *matres familias,* such as the duchesses to whom Colerus dedicated his work, and (3) spiritual fathers, who were to raise and rule their charges with the word of God, and faithfully feed and lead the flock. In the light of these *loci,* Colerus provided the Lutheran "patriarchs" and "matriarchs" who were to manage God's domestic and ecclesiastical economy in the countryside with an up-to-date technical know-how necessary to carry out the charge laid down by the Large Catechism.

The *Oeconomia ecclesiastica* was also an expanded version of the *Tabula oeconomica* attached to Luther's Small Catechism (1529), which were supposed to be posted in every household of the faith. In the *Oeconomia ecclesiastica,* the Book of Concord had been digested for the "simple layman," an understatement probably designed to counterpoise pride of authorship. In four parallel columns, sharp distinctions were drawn between the "faith which alone justifies" nowadays called the Lutheran, and the papal, Calvinist, and Turkish teachings. As an indirect introducer of the Formula of Concord explained in 1593 to the Lutheran faithful in St. Mary's church in Liegnitz, the anti-Christ at that time had three heads: papal pretense, Ottoman militancy, and Calvinism which posed as Lutheranism. Calvinism denied that God created sin, but attributed to him wholesale damnation. It limited God's presence on earth, especially in the Sacrament of the Altar. It turned God into an unjust judge, and made him appear a hypocrite who seemed to be friendly to all men, but had secretly decided to send most people to hell.[8]

Although the constitutional powers and the cultural inclinations to spread a network of Lutheranism over the Silesian landscape issued from the church patrons, the pastors as well as the cantors and schoolmasters were not merely appendages of "Latinized peasants" to the domestic and ecclesiastical economy of the landlords. The Lutheran pastorates all over the country constituted outposts of the late humanist republic of the learned in their own right. It was here that hymns and plays were composed, histories written, and art works commissioned, all of which expressed the confessional morphology and cultural ecology of Lutheranism. An instance of this will be given at the end of this essay.

In passing, a glance must be directed at the personnel in the rural parsonages. Not only in Silesia, but in all Lutheran lands, most theology professors and court preachers during the late sixteenth and early seventeenth century had been country pastors at one time or other. Partly because of the fickleness of church patronage, there was a constant circulation of theological degree-holders who were also well versed in all of those academic subjects considered to be handmaids of the "queen of the sciences," between city and countryside. In German Protestantism during the so-called *Epigonenzeit* when the second and third generations tried to follow meticulously in the footsteps of the various reformers, there were no "vicars of Bray" who would keep their positions by turning their confessional coats with the winds of political change. In cases of conflicts with rivals, superiors or inferiors, the caryatids of the different denominations in post-Reformation Germany would either win and stay, or lose and leave.

The author has previously used Jacob Colerus (1537–1612), the father of Johann, as an example of how a Lutheran-humanist pastor in Silesia had to prove himself during the decade before the Formula of Concord in order to stay in the Lord's business.[9] Colerus had been

---

8. See the sermon by Wolfgang Mamphrasius in *Ausführlicher Bericht von der Visitation im hochlöblichen Herzogthumb Lignitz in der Schlesien* . . . (Wittenberg: Matthes Welacks's Widow, 1595), pp. 100–101.

9. See the author's "The Institutionalization of Humanism in Protestant Silesia," pp. 258–59. The author has been able to fill in further details of Colerus's career. The name was obviously Colerus, not Colarus, as certain records suggested.

called in 1567 by Duke George II of Brieg from the village of Adelsdorf near Liegnitz to be pastor and senior of the local ministers for the city of Wohlau, where many nobles and the mayor were Schwenkfelder sympathizers, and where the court preacher at the castle church of the absentee prince was a crypto-Calvinist. The mayor served public notice that he would shoot the staunchly Lutheran Colerus, and gave up his assassination attempts only after Colerus had outsmarted the mayor's ambushes too often. Schwenkfeld's brother, who lived in Wohlau, tried to run down Colerus with his horse when he met him walking in the fields. Colerus saved his life by jumping over a ditch, a feat which Schwenkfeld's horse could not accomplish.[10] The crypto-Calvinist court preacher, Johann Ferinarius, complained to Duke George that Colerus was not true to the teachings of Luther. George had Colerus imprisoned in Brieg. Colerus vindicated himself by a disputation before the clergy of the whole country and returned in triumph to Wohlau. From Wohlau, he unmasked in 1572 the crypto-Calvinism of the court preacher in Liegnitz, Leonard Krentzheim, whom we will meet twenty years later. In 1573, patron Sebastian von Zedlitz called Colerus to the village church of Neukirch, from which he went in 1574 to the debate with Matthias Flacius Illyricus at *Burg* Lehnhaus and *Schloss* Langenau. The minutes of those meetings, kept by someone else, but later edited by Colerus, reveal his sense of humor, the courtesy and consideration of Flacius, and the social graces of the assembly.[11] In 1575, Colerus started, during his brief tenure as professor of Greek and Hebrew in Frankfurt (Oder), the agricultural and theological work to be continued by his son, and rapidly moved on to a leading ecclesiastical position as *Propst* in Berlin. He died as superintendent of the clergy in Güstrow, Mecklenburg. We do not know when and where after his departure from Silesia Colerus signed the Book of Concord (he would accuse Krentzheim of being against it). But while he was in the country, Colerus certainly qualifies as an outstanding example for Lutheran faithfulness without confessional subscription.

Once it has been established where and how Silesian Lutheranism

---

10. This is no reflection on the irenic Caspar von Schwenkfeld, who exhorted youthful Sebastian von Zedlitz, Colerus's later patron, to hunt hares rather than Schwenkfelder.

11. See Hermann Buschbeck, "Des Matthias Flacius Illyricus Religionsgespräche auf Burg Lehnhaus und Schloss Langenau im Jahre 1574," *Jahrbuch des Vereins für schlesische Kirchengeschichte,* 24 (1934): 3–23.

was culturally and constitutionally entrenched, the deflections and defusions of external and internal dangers to its confessional coherence can be more easily traced. From the moment of its inception, Silesian Lutheranism was "mixed up" with the spiritualist aspirations of its gatekeeper, Caspar von Schwenkfeld (1489–1561). Schwenkfeld became a partisan of Luther in 1518, was court counselor of Duke Frederick II of Liegnitz from 1518–23, whom he won for the Reformation in 1521, left Silesia for good in 1529, and spent his exile in southwestern Germany. The Formula of Concord grouped the Schwenkfelder, together with the Anabaptists, among those sects who never adhered to the Augsburg Confession of 1530.

The type of Lutheranism later to be endorsed by the Augsburg Confession was advocated in Silesia against the spiritualist reformers in Liegnitz by such humanists as Johann Hess, Ambrosius Moiban, Johannes Metzler, Laurentius Corvinus, and Valentin Trozendorf, then stationed in Breslau. These would keep the office of the priesthood, the preaching of the Word, preferably by classical scholars, the administration of the main sacraments, and many, if not most, traditional church decorations and ceremonies. Preserving the last two treasures would turn out to be of crucial importance for popular support. Because of the determined resistance of lower- and middle-class Lutherans against iconoclasm, Calvinism later would be confined to the courts and small circles of retired courtiers in the city of Breslau.

At the time of transition from Hungarian to Hapsburg suzerainty (1526), Frederick II of Liegnitz, Brieg, and Wohlau was not only won over from a Schwenkfelder type of Lutheranism by the better arguments of the Breslau humanists, but also by the sharper mandates of the new Spanish-born king. Ferdinand I insisted on the suppression or expulsion of Anabaptists and spiritualists, but suffered the toleration of the humanist kind of Lutheranism, because it posed fewer security risks. These policies must be seen in the light of the Turkish thunderbolt. Historians have recalled how from 1521 to 1555 Hapsburg concessions to Lutheranism coincided with the grants of aid by the Lutheran imperial estates against Turkish advances.

In Silesia, a Hapsburg domain in immediate danger of Ottoman invasion, this interchange of Hapsburg-Catholic religious concessions for Lutheran secular support took on a twofold form. The tax exemptions which the Silesian princes enjoyed from 1498 to 1526 have been blamed by the Lutheran Silesiographer Jacob Schickfus (1574–1636) for the downfall of Hungary in 1526 as the frontier guard of south-eastern Europe against the Turks. Now that, beginning with the reign of Ferdinand I (d. 1564; king of Bohemia and Hungary, 1526; Holy Roman emperor, 1556), the Ottoman Empire knocked at the Moravian Gate, Silesian Lutherans saw the necessity of contributing to the common defense of the Hapsburg "crown-lands" in terms of manpower, money, and prayers. The fulfillment of these reasonable demands strengthened the hand of the Catholic *princeps supremus* at the expense of the Lutheran provincial estates. When the regular collection of internal revenue led in 1558 to the opening of a Royal Chamber in Breslau, headed by the Schwenkfelder sympathizer Frederick von Redern, the Lutheran city clerk Francis Faber (1497–1565) was outraged, and wished in his passionate poem, *Sabothus sive Silesia,* that his homeland be conquered by the Turks rather than be subjected to such "Bohemian insolence."

On the other hand, Lutheran cooperation with the common defense facilitated the integration of the faith into the political system. The first indirect recognition by Ferdinand I, who in 1555 would conclude the Religious Peace of Augsburg, that the Lutherans were fellow Christians came in 1535 when he expressly asked that also the "disobedient" priests of the diocese of Breslau should pray for protection from the Turks.[12] Thus Lutheran religious "disobedience" toward Rome was overlooked because of continued civil obedience to the *corpus Christianum.*

Because the spread of Anabaptism and spiritualism, which peaked 1580–90 with the "peasant preachers" Michael Niedermayer, Antonius and Christopher Oelsner, and Martin John, was not "covered" by the Augsburg Confession, although Lutheran landlords and pastors patronized these eschatological movements here and there, the control of such sects concerned more the Hapsburg suzerain[13] than the Lutheran ecclesiastical establishment. It was an entirely different story with crypto-Calvinism which arose from the closed ranks of Lutheranism.

---

12. See [Paul] Konrad, "Die Protokolle des Breslauer Domkapitels aus der Reformationszeit," *Correspondenzblatt des Vereins für Geschichte der evangelischen Kirche Schlesiens,* 15:2 (1917): 215.

13. The repression of religious dissenters who would not participate in the fortification of towns and the founding of target practice societies (*Schützengilden*) along the close Moslem-Christian border, regrettable though it was, resembled the removal of "security risks" from the Pacific coast after Pearl Harbor rather than an exercise of bigoted brutality. The enthusiasm (*Schwärmerei*) of the 1580s had been partly provoked by Leonard Krentzheim's calendar for the Second Coming of Christ.

At the heart of crypto-Calvinism in Silesia were "Crato von Crafftheim and his friends," as the monograph by G. F. A. Gillet (1860) called this circle of humanists centered in Breslau. Johann Krafft (1519–1585), born and retired in Breslau, was a self-made noble who built on his landed estate in 1581 the first Reformed church on Silesian cultural territory. Krafft or Crato had been a protégé and table companion of Luther in Wittenberg. Luther counseled him to switch from theology to medicine, at which he was so successful that he became the personal physician of the three Hapsburg emperors during his lifetime. Crato carried on a nationwide correspondence to prevent the German princes and cities from signing the Formula of Concord. He also had his friends at all Silesian courts.

After Crato's death, one of his younger followers did not want to hide his crypto-Calvinism any longer. Adam Cureus, Jr. (b. 1556), a nephew of the posthumous prompter of the crypto-Calvinist contro-versy in Saxony (1574), by 1590 tried to use his teaching position at St. Mary Magdalene school in Breslau to introduce Calvinism to his pupils by opening a dictation which was to be translated from German into Latin with the sentence, "No honest Christian ever believed that [Christ's real presence in] the Lord's Supper resembled a shameful, despicable crucifix." After a friendly and understanding interrogation by the Breslau church and school inspector Johannes Fleischer (1540–1593), Cureus was "vacationed off" (*enturlaubt*), just as Zacharias Ursinus had been for similar reasons in 1560 by Cureus's father, Adam, Sr., who was then the church and school inspector. (Like many other Silesian Calvinists, Ursinus found a prominent position in the Palatinate where he co-authored the Heidelberg Catechism.)

To show the widespread ramifications and repercussions of the crypto-Calvinist "conspiracy," Cureus's subversive teaching activity became a *cause célèbre* in 1593 during the "vacationing off" of Leonard Krentzheim (d. 1598). As court preacher and supervisor of the Lutheran churches in the principality of Liegnitz for thirty-eight years, Krentzheim had been repeatedly charged with crypto-Calvinism by country pastors (such as Jacob Colerus) whom Krentzheim in turn heatedly dismissed as Flacians. In his public pronouncements, Krentz-heim pretended to be a Lutheran. In his private correspondence, he was in sympathy with Calvinism, a fact which could be partly deduced from a letter he had written in support of Adam Cureus, Jr., to Urban Pierius, a crypto-Calvinist at Wittenberg. This discovery contributed to the Liegnitz church visitation of 1593, at the request of Duke

Frederick IV, by Aegidius Hunnius (1550–1603), a replacement of Pierius in Wittenberg and prime mover behind the Formula of Concord, and Wolfgang Mamphrasius (1557–1616), a superintendent in Saxony, whose sermons in Liegnitz assuaged the public grief over Krentzheim's departure (with a well-filled traveling purse), and fortified the local Lutherans in the Formula of Concord.

In 1537, Liegnitz Lutheranism had been reclaimed from Schwenkfelderism by a book on Christ's commission of the office of preaching and his institution of the sacraments by Ambrosius Moiban, prefaced by Luther. In 1593, Liegnitz Lutheranism would be rescued from crypto-Calvinism by a Wittenberg church visitation. The next "foreign aids" Silesian Lutheranism would receive to give it new leases on religious liberty came from the elector of Saxony during the Dresden Accord (1621), from Sweden and the Lutheran "imperial estates" at the Peace of Westphalia (1648), from King Charles XII of Sweden as a guarantor of the Peace of Westphalia at the Altranstädt Convention (1707), and finally 1741, for the next two centuries, from Frederick the Great of Prussia. Its own life and inner strength, however, Silesian Lutheranism did not derive from foreign interventions, but from the confessional morphology and cultural ecology it had built up in the countryside.

In 1613, the Silesian Piasts had turned Reformed; their cousin and brother-in-law in Berlin converted to Calvinism; Bohemia would soon crown a Calvinist king whose entrance into Prague (1619), besides signaling the start of the Thirty Years' War, would be accompanied by acts of iconoclasm, as the conversion in Berlin had been; and conquest by the "image-breaking" Turks was another possibility or, as it would be with the Dutch dramatist Joost van Vondel, "tragic expectation." Under such circumstances, the Lutheran rural pastor Nikolaus Antherus (1590–1638), a former Hebrew professor at the *Gymnasium* in Brieg whose rector would turn Reformed in 1620, built a towering stone altar in his wooden town church at Loewen outside the city walls of Brieg. The three-tiered panels of the altar depicted the Lord's Supper, the crucifixion, the resurrection, and the ascension. Underneath, Antherus had engraved a verse of his own:

> *Tibi parvum hoc Altare dicatur.*
> *Sis illi praesens, sisque Patronus ei.*
> *Fac heic integrent et in omnia secla superstent*
> *Sacramenta, preces, cultus honorque Tui.*

Iconolatra, suo procul Iconoclasta furore
Exulet, optato splendicet augurio.

Great Jehovah, to you we dedicate this small altar.
Be present on it, and be its patron.
Resume and forever uphold on it
Your sacraments, prayers, praise, and honor.
Arouse with its imagery in the worshiper
A desire for the Word made flesh,
And your wrath drive iconoclasts far away.[14]

Apart from the context of cultural ecology, Antherus's prayer and expression of faith would not make sense. Pastor Antherus invoked the Lord as patron of his altar rather than the barons and later counts of Bees von Coelln und Ketzendorf who possessed the local church patronage, and who may or may not have resided then in Loewen as their descendants would for centuries after the Thirty Years' War. Antherus's wish to God that his wrath drive iconoclasts far away obviously referred to the Calvinist beachhead which had been established by then in nearby Brieg. The whole poem exposes a "theology of things to be done" (*Theologie der Tatsachen*) in regard to the Sacrament of the Altar rather than a "theology of rhetoric." With his unmistakable words, Antherus erected to the "structure" of Lutheranism which he supported without confessional subscription a monument more enduring than one of stone.

14. On Antherus, see Ehrhardt, *Presbyterologie*, part II, main section 1, 129–32. On his high altar, see Hermann Hoffmann, "Zwei Werke der Spätrenaissance als Zeugen der schlesischen Religionskämpfe," *Schlesische Heimatpflege*, Publication I, *"Kunst und Denkmalpflege"* (Breslau, 1935), 25–31. The original Latin text of the poem, which has been recorded by both Ehrhardt and Hoffman, runs as follows:

Magne Jehova, Tibi parvum hoc Altare dicatur.
Sis illi praesens, sisque Patronus ei.
Fac heic integrent et in omnia secla superstent
Sacramenta, preces, cultus honorque Tui.
Iconolatra, suo procul Iconoclasta furore
Exulet, optato splendicet augurio.

8

The Reaction in Scandinavia

Trygyve R. Skarsten

Probably no reaction to the Formula of Concord was so heated as that which it received in Denmark at the hands of King Frederick II (1559–88) where it literally went up in smoke! Yet over in Sweden, it occasioned so little attention as hardly to cause anyone to take notice. Two dominant principles underlie the confessional heritage of Scandinavian Lutheranism and help to explain the dissimilar reactions which the Formula of Concord received in Scandinavia, namely, the regal principle of *cuius regio eius religio* as found in Denmark-Norway-Iceland and that of popular sovereignty which prevailed in Sweden-Finland. In the latter case it was the will of the people which triumphed over that of the Swedish rulers while in the former instance, confessional subscription was all too often a matter of royal decree. In 1536, Christian III (1536–59), an ardent Lutheran who had been won over to the evangelical cause as a young prince at the famous Diet of Worms, decreed that Denmark-Norway-Iceland were henceforth to be Lutheran realms. The latter two countries would just as well have remained loyal to the papacy but they were politically impotent to assert themselves. Confessional subscription in the three countries was therefore determined by the Danish king.

Six years before Christian III ascended to the throne, some Danish evangelical reformers under the leadership of Hans Tausen and Peder Lauritzen had drawn up forty-three articles, popularly known as the Copenhagen Confession and presented them to the Catholic authorities. The confession represented the official expression of the Danish reformers' understanding of Christianity prior to the dominance of the Wittenberg-Melanchthonian theology as expressed in the Augsburg Confession. The Copenhagen Confession never gained official recognition in Denmark since it was overshadowed by the Augsburg Confession brought up from Wittenberg by John Bugenhagen in 1537. A comparison of the two reveals that the Danish confession is a much sharper, polemical Lutheran stance over against Roman Catholicism than is the Augsburg Confession.[1]

After three years of civil war (1533–36), Christian III moved swiftly in 1536 to consolidate his position.[2] He dismantled the ecclesiastical structure of the medieval church in Denmark and summoned Bugenhagen to set up an evangelical state church. For three years Bugenhagen labored in Denmark, crowning the new king and queen, ordaining seven new evangelical "superintendents" (bishops), thereby deliberately breaking the line of apostolic succession, revamping the University of Copenhagen into a Lutheran institution of higher learning and finally drawing up a Church Ordinance in 1539. While the Church Ordinance prescribed no formal symbolical obligation, its contents were clearly Lutheran. Every Danish clergyman was to have in his possession a copy of the Bible, Luther's *Postils,* the Apology to the Augsburg Confession and Melanchthon's *Loci communes,* Luther's Small Catechism, the Saxon Visitation Articles, and the Danish Church Ordinance.[3]

During these years when Lutheranism was being firmly planted in Denmark, many Danish students flocked to Wittenberg to study theology there. One Danish youth who matriculated in 1537 was Niels Hemmingsen (1513–1600). It is essential to look at his career in order to understand the actions of the Danish king in 1580 regarding the Formula of Concord.

Hemmingsen's prior schooling had been at Roskilde and Lund under Erasmian biblical humanists. When he arrived at Wittenberg, he became an ardent admirer of Philipp Melanchthon. Shortly after his return to Denmark in 1542, he was appointed professor of Greek at the University of Copenhagen. In 1545 he became professor of dialectics and exegesis and in 1553 professor of theology.

Thus a remarkable career got underway, and soon Hemmingsen became known throughout the learned circles of Europe; he attracted a considerable following and brought fame and renown to the University

1. Niels Knud Andersen, *Confessio Hafniensis* (Copenhagen: G. E. C. Gads Forlag, 1954), pp. 10–16.

2. Holger Rørdam, ed., *Historiske Kildeskrifter og Bearbejdelser af Dansk Historie* (Copenhagen: G. E. C. Gad, 1873), 1:133–99.

3. Max W. Olsen, ed., *Den danske Kirkeordinants af 1539* (Copenhagen: Nyt Nordisk Forlag, Arnold Busck, 1936), pp. 117–18.

of Copenhagen.[4]   His works were to be found in the leading libraries, often translated from the Latin or Danish into German, Dutch, or English and in multiple editions.   Toward the latter part of his life, scholars came to pay homage at his door; dignitaries and kings such as James VI of Scotland counted it an honor to have visited with the famous Danish theologian.

Three works quickly established Hemmingsen as a gifted theologian and pastor.   In 1557 his handbook on dogmatics and ethics (*Enchiridion theologicum*) was published.   This work was used abroad as well as in Denmark for many years as a systematics textbook.   Hemmingsen expressed himself humbly about the work as an introduction to Melanchthon's *Loci*.   This book quickly won acclaim, and within Lutheran circles became the first attempt at a systematic presentation of theological ethics.   Four years later came his *Evangeliepostil* which was published many times and translated into Danish, German, and English.   This work, which became the textbook in homiletics for a couple generations, was not a series of sermons but rather outlines and models for preaching that sought to force the pastor to undertake serious exegesis in order to uncover the wisdom and counsel of the text.   The third work which established Hemmingsen's career was his *Pastor* which appeared in 1562.   This became for many decades the textbook in pastoral theology and sought to present "all that belongs to the work of an evangelical pastor and curate of the soul's life and doctrine."   Hemmingsen's manuals on exegetical method and marriage counseling, his numerous commentaries on the New Testament and the Psalms, and a work on natural law in 1562 seen by many as a precursor to Hugo Grotius should also be mentioned here.[5]   By 1572 Hemmingsen was at the height of his career.   He set an illustrious example for his colleagues, and nothing seemed to transpire without his approval.[6]   But then troubles started to pile up rapidly, and his position became increasingly uncertain.

As we have seen, Niels Hemmingsen was a Melanchthonian with a warm, irenic spirit that tended to gloss over the differences that were

4. Hemmingsen served for a number of years as pastor of the Church of the Holy Spirit in Copenhagen in addition to his regular university duties.

5. For a complete listing of Niels Hemmingsen's works see: Kjell Barnekow, *Niels Hemmingsens Teologiska Åskådning* (Lund: C. W. K. Gleerup, 1940), pp. viii–xii.

6. Bjørn Kornerup, "Herlufsholms Skoleordinans af 30. Marts 1567," *Danske Magazin,* 7th series, 6 (1954–57): 67–81.

tearing apart the Lutherans in Germany. During the confessionally fluid years of the 1540s and '50s, Hemmingsen championed Melanchthon's *Variata,* which had seen the light of day when he was a student at Wittenberg. Toward the end of Christian III's reign, the king called upon Hemmingsen to draw up a "Statement on the Lord's Supper" (*Tavle om Herrens Nadvere,* 1557) which was subscribed by all the university professors and may be considered as a confessional statement of the Danish Church. In it Hemmingsen declared his unanimity with the Augsburg Confession (though he didn't say which version) and the Lutheran position on the Lord's Supper.[7]

Scholars have sought to determine when Hemmingsen's theology began to change from a Melanchthonian Lutheranism to an outright espousal of a Calvinist doctrine of Christology and the Lord's Supper. A consensus of scholarly opinion would seem to focus on some time after 1557.[8] Though called a Calvinist by his enemies, Hemmingsen never became a real Calvinist as his tract on the universal grace of God through Jesus Christ for all mankind would indicate.[9] It is clear, however, that in 1571 Hemmingsen attacked the Gnesio-Lutherans and the doctrine of ubiquity in his *Demonstratio indubitatae veritatis de Domino Jesu.* The following year an extended visit from some Saxon crypto-Calvinist teachers laid the groundwork for the impending crisis. In 1574, in a large dogmatic work entitled *Syntagma institutionum Christianarum,* Hemmingsen openly hailed the Calvinist doctrine of the Lord's Supper.

So strong was his support and following in Denmark that nothing would have come of all this had it not been for complaints from abroad. About this time the ardent Lutheran Elector Augustus of Saxony (brother-in-law of King Frederick of Denmark) was seeking to rid his territory of crypto-Calvinism only to have the Wittenberg

---

7. Holger Fr. Rørdam, *Kjøbenhavns Universitets Historie fra 1537 til 1621,* 4 vols. (Copenhagen: Bianco Lunos Bogtrykkeri, 1868–69), 2:430.

8. Barnekow, *Hemmingsens Teologiska Åskådning,* pp. 14–21, 115–39, 277–91; Erik M. Madsen, *Niels Hemmingsens Etik* (Copenhagen: G. E. C. Gads Forlag, 1943), pp. 206–28; idem, "Er Calvin Niels Hemmingsens eksegetiske Forbillede?" *Dansk Teologisk Tidsskrift* 9 (1946): 1–10; idem, "Om Forholdet mellem Niels Hemmingsens Enchiridion theologicum og Melanchthons Loci communes," *Dansk Teologisk Tidsskrift* 5 (1942): 137–51, 215–32; Bjørn Kornerup, "En svensk Disputats om Niels Hemmingsen," *Dansk Teologisk Tidsskrift* 4 (1941): 57–66; J. Oscar Andersen, "Om Niels Hemmingsens Teologi," *Kyrkohistorisk Årsskrift* 41 (1941): 108–31.

9. Nicolai Hemmingii, *Tractatvs de gratia vniversali salvtari omnibvs hominibvs* . . . (Copenhagen: I. Alburgensem, 1591).

Philippist theologians invoke the writings of Hemmingsen. A plot to import Calvinism into Saxony was also uncovered by the elector. When the defendants were questioned, they cited the views of Hemmingsen, whom they had recently visited in Copenhagen. A complaint was immediately lodged with Frederick II who called upon Hemmingsen to renounce his position on the Lord's Supper. Although it was very difficult for Hemmingsen, he finally conceded in 1576 so that the Danish Church could be free of any suspicion of false teaching. It was clear that he still held to the *Variata Augustana*, the altered Augsburg Confession as modified by Melanchthon in 1540 and 1542. Continued accusations came from Germany regarding Hemmingsen's ongoing teaching career. Finally on July 29, 1579, the king dismissed him from his position as professor, and recommended that he leave Copenhagen and take up residence in Roskilde. Far from fading away, Hemmingsen's works continued to come off the printing presses, and his fame only increased, especially in Calvinist sections of Europe where he was looked upon as a kind of martyr. The king continued to seek him out for counsel and guidance on difficult questions.[10] Hal Koch, in his multivolumed history of the Danish Church, calls the years 1569–1617 "Philippism's Finest Hour."[11] The honor and lofty esteem in which Hemmingsen was held can readily be seen in the diary of Sivert Grubbe, a young Danish theological student at Wittenberg in 1581. Grubbe had nothing but contempt for the Formula of Concord and the manner in which it was forced upon the Wittenberg professors by the Saxon elector.[12]

It is evident that Frederick II only reluctantly dismissed his famous university professor who had brought so much glory to Denmark. Hemmingsen became a sort of sacrificial victim in order to silence the complaints of the king's brother-in-law and any suspicions German Lutherans might have had regarding the doctrinal soundness of the Danish Church. Thus, when his sister, Anna, with the best of intentions, sent him two beautifully gold bound copies of the *Book of Concord*, Frederick II flew into a rage upon learning that the Formula of Concord was included and threw both copies into a nearby fireplace.

10. C. F. Bricka, ed., *Dansk Biografisk Lexikon* (Copenhagen: Gyldendalske Boghandels Forlag, 1893), 7:329–32.

11. Hal Koch, *Den Danske Kirkes Historie,* 8 vols. (Copenhagen: Gyldendalske Boghandel Nordisk Forlag, 1959), 4:135–220.

12. Holger Fr. Rørdam, ed., "Sivert Grubbes Dagbog," *Danske Magazin,* 4th series, 2 (1873): 369–70.

On July 24, 1580, the king issued a decree throughout Denmark, Norway, and Iceland stating that the Formula of Concord was an innovation which threatened the tranquility of the realm. Henceforth it was to be a capital offense for anyone to import, sell, or own a copy of the *Book of Concord!*[13]

Thus it was that the principle of *cuius regio eius religio* determined the reaction to the Formula of Concord in Denmark, Norway, and Iceland. Not until 1861 was the Formula translated into Dano-Norwegian, and to this day it has not become a part of the confessional heritage of these three Scandinavian churches.

When we turn to Sweden and its politically dependent duchy, Finland, we find an entirely different situation from that which prevailed in Denmark. In Sweden the problem was not Calvinism but rather Roman Catholicism. Therefore the Formula of Concord caused hardly a ripple since it basically addressed the crypto-Calvinist controversy in Germany. Had it not been for the determined opposition of the Swedish people and their leaders, Sweden and Finland might easily have gone over to the side of the Counter-Reformation during the latter part of the sixteenth century. In contrast to the principle of *cuius regio eius religio* which prevailed in Denmark-Norway-Iceland, the principle of popular sovereignty triumphed in Sweden-Finland.

Whether one wants to call what happened in Sweden-Finland during the sixteenth century a revolution, a reformation, or a transformation,[14] one is astounded to learn that it was not until 1593 that these two countries officially declared themselves to be Lutheran. This was accomplished not by royal decree but directly in the face of royal opposition by the representatives of a people who had, over the course of a century, peacefully swung away from the medieval church to become loyal children of the Reformation.

It was Olaus Petri (1493–1552) who introduced the Reformation into Sweden in 1518. He had arrived in Wittenberg just as Luther was about to begin his lectures on Galatians in 1516. He quickly became a supporter of Luther's stand against indulgences and was present in Wittenberg during the epoch-making days when the Ninety-

---

13. V. A. Secher, ed., *Corpus Constitutionum Daniae. Forordninger, Recesser og andre kongelige Breve, Danmarks Lovgivning vedkommende 1558–1660,* 3 vols. (Copenhagen: G. E. C. Gad, 1889–90), 2:166–67.

14. Paul B. Watson, *The Swedish Revolution under Gustavus Vasa* (Boston: Little, Brown and Co., 1889); Eric Yelverton, *An Archbishop of the Reformation* (London: The Epworth Press, 1958); Conrad Bergendoff, *Olavus Petri and the Ecclesiastical Transformation in Sweden* (Philadelphia: Fortress Press, 1965).

five Theses were published. Late in 1518, the young Swedish disciple of Luther returned to his homeland where he immediately began teaching and preaching his evangelical faith. There was no thought of a break with Rome. Luther had not yet met with John Eck for their famous debate in Leipzig. The Reformation treatises of 1520, to say nothing of the Augsburg Confession, were still well in the future. The reforming principles which motivated Olaus Petri were therefore very conservative and were to remain so all his life. Together with his younger brother, Laurentius Petri (1499–1573), who also studied at Wittenberg and who in 1531 became the first evangelical archbishop of Sweden, a gradual ecclesiastical transformation (as Conrad Bergendoff calls it) got underway.

The reform movement which the Petri brothers initiated saw no necessity for new confessional statements. These young disciples of Luther were convinced that the pure Word of God was all sufficient in the struggle against the aberrations of Rome. The *sola scriptura* theme of Luther's lectures came through loud and clear for the young Swedish reformers. The task of the pastor was to preach the Word of God as it was revealed in Holy Scripture. Herein was found all that was needed for salvation. One did not need the glosses and interpretations of men because the Scriptures were in themselves clear and understandable. All one needed was the Word of God. Thoughts similar to these were reiterated in the Preface of the Swedish New Testament which Olaus Petri published in 1526.[15] As the Reformation movement in Sweden progressed, there was never any attempt to draw up an evangelical confessional statement. One gets the feeling that such an endeavor would have been deemed contrary to the principle of *sola scriptura*. The ecumenical creeds of the early church were described as aids to sermon preparation and summaries of Scripture for those who did not have an opportunity to view the Bible as a whole, but never were the creeds regarded as confessional statements.[16]

During the turbulent decade of the 1520s, when Sweden was struggling for its political independence, King Gustav Vasa (1523–60) was hard pressed to control and unite his political supporters who were divided over the religious issue. In 1527, in the face of internal dissension and external pressure from Denmark and Lübeck of the

15. Bengt Hesselman, ed., *Olavus Petri Samlede Skrifter*, 4 vols. (Uppsala: Almqvist & Wiksells Boktryckeri, 1914), 1:233, 538–39.
16. Ibid., 1:134. See also Sven Ingebrand, *Olavus Petris Reformatoriska Åskådning* (Lund: C. W. K. Gleerup, 1964), pp. 32–33.

Hanseatic League, the Swedish Diet of Veseterås created in effect a national church independent from Rome. No confessional subscription was stipulated other than the call to teach and preach according to the Word of God.[17] It is difficult to find in the writings of the Petri brothers any explicit mention or discussion of the Lutheran confessional documents. Yet they consistently maintained a Lutheran posture commencing with the hymnal, the pastor's manual, and the Swedish Mass which Olaus Petri published in 1526, 1529, and 1531 respectively.[18]

It is clear that Gustav Vasa looked with alarm at the gradual development of a strong, independent church within his kingdom over which he would have little control. His goal was to duplicate the Danish model of ecclesiastical governance which made the church subservient to the state. To accomplish this end, he condemned Olaus Petri and a few others to death in 1539. The king needed subjects subservient to his will, and Olaus Petri was not one of them. Saner minds led by Olaus's brother the archbishop prevailed, and the condemned reformers were released.

It was in the 1560s under Gustav Vasa's son, Erik XIV (1560–68), that confessional subscription became an issue. As a result of the Peace of Augsburg in 1555, Lutheranism was given legal status. During the subsequent years many Calvinists fled to Sweden and sought to represent themselves as Lutherans.[19] In 1564 these Calvinists drew up the first confessional statement in Sweden and claimed it to be Lutheran. It was soon obvious that this was just a translation and revision of the Calvinistic Gallic Confession of 1559. The Augsburg Confession was quickly called upon to define the true Lutheran position thereby enhancing that document's prestige and authority, especially among the younger pastors and theologians.

Erik XIV early in his reign revealed that he himself had strong Calvinist sympathies when he opposed the Church Ordinance drawn up by Laurentius Petri in 1561.[20] Laurentius was quickly called upon to

17. B. J. Kidd, ed., *Documents Illustrative of the Continental Reformation* (Oxford: Clarendon Press, 1911), pp. 234–36.

18. Eric E. Yelverton, *The Manual of Olavus Petri* (London: SPCK, 1953); and Hesselman, *Olavus Petri Samlede Skrifter,* 2:389–426. No copy of the 1526 hymnbook is extant.

19. Sven Kjöllerström, *Striden kring Kalvinismen i Sverige under Erik XIV* (Lund: C. W. K. Gleerup, 1935), p. iii.

20. Emil Färnström, *Laurentius Petris Handskrivna Kyrkoordning av År 1561* (Stockholm: Svenska Kyrkans Diakonistyrelses Bokförlag, 1956), pp. 11–14.

defend his view of the Lord's Supper and drew upon the resources of the Lutheran confessions.[21] Through the stubborn opposition of the archbishop, who seemed to enjoy endless good health, Erik XIV was not able to introduce Calvinism by royal decree into Sweden.

Finally, in 1571, in the third year of the reign of the next king, John III (1568–92), Laurentius Petri succeeded in having his Church Ordinance adopted as the law of the land. No provision was made in the Church Ordinance or at the ordination of pastors for any confessional subscription.[22] Rather, the position that the Scriptures were the touchstone by which all other writings were to be judged was reiterated. Candidates for ordination were to promise "to remain steadfast in the pure Word of God and to flee all false and heretical doctrine."[23] It was a pastor's duty "to preach Christ's gospel in a pure and correct manner, neither taking away from nor adding to it, as had been the case under the pope." To preach the gospel, according to the archbishop, meant simply to preach repentance and the forgiveness of sins through Jesus Christ.[24] A promise to the Church Assembly in 1572 to draw up a confession similar to the Augsburg Confession failed to materialize when the archbishop died the following year.

In the years which ensued, Sweden found itself plunged into the intrigues of the Counter-Reformation. Through his revision of the Church Ordinance in 1573 (the so-called Red Book), John III revealed not only his strong liturgical interests but also a decided predilection which to many smacked of Romanism. Whether he actually converted to Roman Catholicism is still an open question[25] but there can be no doubt that John III was strongly influenced by the Jesuit chaplains of his Polish consort, Catherine Jagellonica, and especially his own father confessor, the Norwegian Jesuit, Laurentius Norvegus.[26]

So eager was the Roman curia to pursue John III's rumored conversion that the secretary of the Jesuit Order in Rome, Antonio

21. Bo Ahlberg, *Laurentius Petris Nattvards Uppfattning* (Lund: C. W. K. Gleerup, 1964), pp. 180–81, 213–16.

22. Yelverton, *Archbishop of the Reformation,* pp. 131–35.

23. Ibid., p. 133.

24. Vilmos Vajta and Hans Weissgerber, eds., *The Church and the Confessions* (Philadelphia: Fortress Press, 1963), p. 24.

25. Oskar Garstein, *Rome and the Counter-Reformation in Scandinavia* (Oslo: Universitetsforlaget, 1963), pp. 132–44.

26. Vello Helk, *Laurentius Nicolai Norvegus S.J.* (Copenhagen: G. E. C. Gad, 1966), pp. 110–20.

Possevino, was dispatched in 1577 to ascertain the facts. Possevino, was well received by John III, and by March 1578, the two had worked out details for the gradual reintroduction of Roman Catholicism into Sweden.

The main thrust of the Jesuits was to take over the recently established theological school in Stockholm which was known as the Collegium Regium Stockholmense. Ostensibly the school had been set up in 1576 by the king in order to educate a new generation of clergymen who would be sympathetic to the high church liturgical traditions espoused in his "Red Book," and at the same time undercut the influence of the University of Uppsala. With the arrival of Norvegus in April 1576, the Collegium soon became a highly secret instrument of the Jesuits for the indoctrination in post-Tridentine theology of young Swedish men who would serve as the vanguard for the Counter-Reformation takeover in Sweden.

It is important to observe that these events were transpiring during the years 1576–80 in order to understand why the reaction to the Formula of Concord was nil in Sweden. It was no longer a question of crypto-Calvinism or Lutheranism gaining the upper hand in Sweden. The very existence of Protestantism hung in the balance! The internal feuding within Lutheranism to the south seemed remote and irrelevant.

Few knew what really was going on, although some sensed something to be amiss. One such person was the new archbishop of Sweden, Laurentius Petri Gothus, who accidentally discovered the real identity of Norvegus. To his consternation, Gothus realized that the king's liturgical revisions (which Gothus had supported) went far beyond his wildest dreams. Gothus promptly renounced the king's designs and sought to arouse both clergy and laity. The archbishop's successor (in 1593), Abraham Andreae Angermannus, also joined the fray against Norvegus. Fleeing from the Åland Islands in the Gulf of Bothnia where he had been exiled by John III, Angermannus dramatically entered the pulpit of the Cathedral of Uppsala on September 21, 1578, and railed against the papists and "that ravenous wolf Closter Lasse."[27] The renowned German theologian, David Chytraeus, a personal acquaintance of John III, who had written in 1574 asking

---

27. "Lasse" is a nickname usually given to a boy named Lars or Laurits. The real name of Laurentius Norvegus (Latinized for Laurits the Norwegian) was Laurits Nilssøn. See Andreas Brandrud, *Klosterlasse* (Kristiania: Tr. Steens Forlagsexpedition, 1895), pp. 57–58; and Garstein, *Counter-Reformation in Scandinavia*, pp. 144–52.

him to send more students to the conservative Lutheran university in Rostock, renewed his correspondence with the Swedish king and strongly urged him to abandon his diplomatic maneuvers with the Hapsburgs and remain faithful to the Lutheran cause and the policy of his father, Gustav Vasa. But John III was playing for high stakes and had visions of turning the Baltic into a Swedish lake and of gaining control of Denmark in a Hapsburg-Vasa pincer move, so he was not about to be persuaded from these maneuvers.[28]

Meanwhile, the "operation Sweden" of the Jesuits began to gain momentum. By the end of the first academic year (1576–77), some thirty students in the Collegium Regium Stockholmense had renounced their Lutheran faith and embraced Roman Catholicism. Six of them were sent to Rome by Norvegus, their travel expenses paid by the king and hospitality shown them along the way by such famous Jesuits as Peter Canisius. Two years later Possevino brought with him 1,500 copies of the German edition of Canisius's famous Catechism along with a Swedish translation of the same. Plans were also made by the king to convert the house of St. Birgitta in Rome into a Swedish seminary for priests.[29]

It seemed that Sweden was on the verge of reverting to Roman Catholicism in 1580 when everything began to go sour for the Jesuits and their undertaking. John III, in spite of repeated admonitions to do so, hesitated to announce his new allegiance to Rome without certain conditions first being met. Among his stipulations was his insistence that the people be allowed to retain the vernacular in worship, receive communion under both kinds, and that the clergy be allowed to marry if they should so choose. In the post-Tridentine era, Pope Gregory XIII was in no mood to meet these demands. The troubles which Philip II was experiencing in the Netherlands and the rumored alliance of North German princes with Denmark against Sweden caused John III to be extremely cautious inasmuch as he had gained the throne in a somewhat dubious manner and feared a popular uprising.[30]

In March 1580, David Chytraeus of Rostock, who had previously

28. Sven Göransson, "Den svenska Konfessionspolitiken Grundlägges," *Kyrkohistorisk Årsskrift* 74 (1974): 17.

29. L. A. Anjou, *The History of the Reformation in Sweden,* trans. Henry M. Mason (New York: Pudney & Russell, 1859), pp. 508–16.

30. Michael Roberts, *The Early Vasas: A History of Sweden 1523–1611* (Cambridge: At the University Press, 1968), pp. 233–41.

dedicated his *Historia der Augspürgischen Confession* (1576) to John III in order to encourage the latter in his Lutheran convictions, wrote another, strongly worded, letter to the king admonishing him to make a public proclamation of his Lutheran faith as embodied in the *Book of Concord*. Suspicions of a North German–Danish alliance were increased by Chytraeus's letter. Possevino immediately composed a comprehensive refutation of the Formula of Concord in what was probably the only explicit reaction to the Formula in Sweden in order to fend off an attack against the Jesuits' "operation Sweden" should the Formula be used by the anti-liturgists (as the Lutherans were known). But such was not to be necessary, and Possevino's manuscript (*De Concordia Luteranorum*) took up its abode in the Vatican archives where it still resides.[31]

Just a few weeks prior to the arrival of Chytraeus's letter, the Jesuit fathers, out of sheer desperation, sought to force the hand of John III by publicly revealing their true identity and announcing the king's conversion to Roman Catholicism. This was a gross miscalculation on their part. Instead of publicly embracing Catholicism, John III publicly renounced it and ordered Norvegus and most of the Jesuits out of the country by August 1580. This left "operation Sweden" in shambles and the people thoroughly aroused. By 1583, when Queen Catherine passed away, the Jesuit efforts to rewin Sweden had come to an end.

But that did not mean Sweden was finished with the Counter-Reformation. Upon the death of John III in 1592, Sweden was again plunged into turmoil because the heir to the throne was none other than Sigismund, the Roman Catholic son of John III, who shortly before had been elected king of Poland. It was obvious that the Catholic Vasas were intent on setting up a dual monarchy which would force Sweden into the Roman camp.

In anticipation of the Catholic pressure, over three hundred clergymen, with the blessing of Duke Charles of Finland, met in March 1593 at Uppsala to draw up a confession of faith that would bind future monarchs to Lutheranism. John III's liturgy was rejected as "superstitious" and the unaltered Augsburg Confession was for the first time officially acknowledged and subscribed to by the Church of Sweden. The Church Assembly declared all divergent doctrines as "lamentable delusions." "We will remain by the clear and sanctifying Word of

31. Garstein, *Counter-Reformation in Scandinavia*, pp. 205 and 349 n. 10.

God," they declared. "The Holy Scriptures are the basis and support for a true Christian faith and the correct rule by which to judge, distinguish, and settle all religious disputes. . . . Furthermore, we affirm and acknowledge that we shall hold fast the Apostles' Creed, the Nicene Creed, and the Athanasian Creed, as well as to the correct and unaltered Augsburg Confession. . . ."[32] Papists and Calvinists were permitted to remain in the kingdom provided that they held no public services—and this on the eve of the arrival of the Catholic king and his Polish entourage. No mention was made of the Formula of Concord in the decrees which emanated from the Church Assembly at Uppsala in 1593. Ironically, only Antonio Possevino had seen fit to give it the honor of his attention.

During the period of Lutheran orthodoxy which followed in the seventeenth century, attempts were made to have the Formula of Concord recognized as part of the confessional subscription of the Church of Sweden. About 1650 one of the bishops asserted that the Formula of Concord did not really present anything new that was not already incorporated in the Augsburg Confession. Since it was a *repitio et declaratio confessionis Augustanae*, the Church of Sweden, it was maintained, had actually adopted the Formula of Concord as the correct exposition and interpretation when it had adopted the Augsburg Confession at its Uppsala Church Assembly in 1593. Powerful voices including that of Erik Benzelius demanded that the entire *Book of Concord* be subscribed to as a matter of church law. This was accomplished by the Church Assembly of 1686 when it stated that all should

> confess only and alone the Christian doctrine and faith which is grounded in the Holy Word of God, the Old and New Testament's prophetic and apostolic writings, further written in the three chief symbols, *Apostolico, Nicaeno,* and *Athanasiano,* together with the whole unaltered Augsburg Confession of 1530, established at the Uppsala *consilio* in 1593, together with the whole of the so-called *Libro concordiae* explanation. All teachers should be bound by oath to this doctrine when they are ordained, or when they receive their academic degrees.[33]

Benzelius was not completely satisfied with this statement, and subsequent years allowed a variety of interpretations which contended that

32. Vajta and Weissgerber, *The Church and the Confessions,* pp. 25–26.
33. Ibid., p. 28.

it was not the intent of the law to raise the entire *Book of Concord* to the status of a symbol of the Lutheran Church of Sweden. Eventually the archbishop declared that the Formula of Concord was only a *norma secundaria* even if it had been deemed a symbol.

What followed was years of controversy as to the exact status of the Formula of Concord in Sweden-Finland. In the nineteenth century the Swedish constitution of 1809 was pitted against the Church Assembly law of 1686. Not until after a century-long debate did the Church Assembly of Sweden (in 1893) vote to exercise veto power over the constitution. The old church law of 1686, entailing subscription to the entire *Book of Concord*, had taken precedent over the law of the land which affirmed only the Augsburg Confession as the confessional foundation for the Church of Sweden. Subsequent attempts in the twentieth century to reduce confessional subscription have repeatedly been rejected by the Church Assembly.[34]

The Church of Finland, which had always had the same confessional position as the Church of Sweden, continued with the old church law of 1686 into the nineteenth century because it was not bound by the new Swedish constitution of 1809.[35] However, the controversy in Sweden tended to spill over into Finland so that in 1869 the Church of Finland decided once and for all to end all doubts as to its confessional position by formally declaring the entire *Book of Concord* to be the symbol of the Church of Finland with no segment of it relegated to the rank of explanation.[36]

During the Reformation era and the centuries that followed, the churches of Sweden and Finland maintained their right to legislate confessional loyalty and subscription as it met in Church Assembly. In the face of threats from Calvinism and Roman Catholicism, the people of Sweden-Finland and their leaders sought to chart their own course against determined royal and later parliamentary opposition. In the end, rather than the king determining the religious affiliation and confessional subscription of the people as in Denmark-Norway-Iceland, the people of Sweden-Finland, exercising the right of popular sovereignty, determined the confessional subscription of the king.

---

34. Ibid., pp. 28–38.
35. Due to the Napoleonic wars, Sweden had been forced to cede Finland to Russia in 1809.
36. Vajta and Weissgerber, *The Church and the Confessions,* p. 8.

9

The Anglican Reaction

W. Brown Patterson

Although few early English Protestants seem to have been rigorous and consistent Lutherans, Lutheran influences were pervasive in England in the first several decades of the Reformation. Luther's ideas had penetrated into England as early as 1518, and in the next few years his books, though forbidden, found a ready market there. At Cambridge the scholars who met for conversation at the White Horse Inn, known as "Little Germany," were evidently deeply impressed by the new theology on the continent. The Ten Articles of Faith which Henry VIII laid before his bishops in 1536 were heavily indebted to the Augsburg Confession. The Order of Communion of 1548, the immediate predecessor of the first Book of Common Prayer, was strongly influenced by Lutheran church orders, particularly that of Cologne.[1] Such key figures as William Tyndale, the translator of the New Testament, Thomas Cranmer, the compiler of the Prayer Book, and Thomas Cromwell, the chief minister of Henry VIII during the crucial sessions of the Reformation Parliament, were influenced decisively by Lutheran

---

1. For Lutheran influences in England during Henry VIII's reign, see E. Gordon Rupp, *Studies in the Making of the English Protestant Tradition (Mainly in the Reign of Henry VIII)* (Cambridge: Cambridge University Press, 1947), pp. 49–51, 132–33, 185–94; Erwin Doernberg, *Henry VIII and Luther: An Account of Their Personal Relations* (Stanford: Stanford University Press, 1961), pp. 3–13, 27–35, 109–11; A. G. Dickens, *The English Reformation* (London: Batsford, 1964), pp. 59–82, 179, 328–30; William A. Clebsch, *England's Earliest Protestants, 1520–1535* (New Haven: Yale University Press, 1964), pp. 58–59, 66–72, 137–53, 195–97; Neelak Tjernagel, *Henry VIII and the Lutherans: A Study in Anglo-Lutheran Relations from 1521 to 1547* (St. Louis: Concordia Publishing House, 1965), pp. 153–90, 249–54; and Horton Davies, *Worship and Theology in England: From Cranmer to Hooker, 1534–1603* (Princeton: Princeton University Press, 1970), pp. 169–70, 179–81. For help and encouragement in my investigation of the subject of this paper I am indebted to Professors E. Gordon Rupp, James Cargill Thompson, and Wallace T. MacCaffrey.

theology. Yet as early as King Edward VI's brief reign, the Church of England could be seen to be moving from the orbit of Saxony to that of Protestant Switzerland, and by the first years of Queen Elizabeth's reign there were very few avowed Lutherans in the realm.[2] It is usually reckoned that, on the doctrine of the Lord's Supper, there was only one Lutheran on the episcopal bench in these years, namely, Richard Cheyney, bishop of Gloucester.[3] The firm links which by this time connected England to Geneva and especially to Zurich largely determined the clerical reaction to the Formula of Concord. They are also significant for an understanding of the political reaction in England which resulted in a concerted diplomatic effort to forestall or to delay the Formula's implementation.

Writing to his friend John Parkhurst, bishop of Norwich, in August 1561, Peter Martyr Vermigli said: "I send you a Dialogue which I have written, against the Ubiquity of Brentius." He added that Brentius (Johann Brenz) had published a book some months earlier which Martyr, at this time a professor in Zurich, had been urged by his associates to answer.[4] Parkhurst was a former don at Oxford, where Martyr had taught; after the accession of the Roman Catholic Mary Tudor he had gone to Strasbourg, where Martyr was professor of theology, and he had then settled in Zurich, to which Martyr migrated in 1556.[5] Parkhurst was but one of Martyr's many English friends, and the Italian reformer evidently hoped to have their support in his controversy with Brenz, the Lutheran theologian of Württemberg. The dialogue, in fact, contained a dedication to John Jewel, then bishop of Salisbury, whom Martyr had known at Oxford and with whom he had become well acquainted in Strasbourg and

---

2. For this change in theological orientation, see C. H. Smyth, *Cranmer and the Reformation under Edward VI* (Cambridge: Cambridge University Press, 1926), pp. 16–25, 59; T. M. Parker, *The English Reformation to 1558* (London: Oxford University Press, 1950), pp. 118–52; C. H. Garrett, *The Marian Exiles: A Study in the Origins of Elizabethan Puritanism* (Cambridge: Cambridge University Press, 1938), pp. 1–59; and Charles D. Cremeans, *The Reception of Calvinistic Thought in England* (Urbana: University of Illinois Press, 1949), pp. 24–82.

3. See Carl S. Meyer, *Elizabeth I and the Religious Settlement of 1559* (St. Louis: Concordia Publishing House, 1960), p. 85; and William P. Haugaard, *Elizabeth and the English Reformation: The Struggle for a Stable Settlement of Religion* (Cambridge: Cambridge University Press, 1968), pp. 250–54.

4. *Gleanings of a Few Scattered Ears, during the Period of the Reformation in England and of the Times Immediately Succeeding, A.D. 1533 to A.D. 1588,* ed. George C. Gorham (London: Bell and Daldy, 1857), p. 423.

5. Garrett, *Marian Exiles,* pp. 8–9, 45, 244–45.

Zurich. Jewel is represented in the dialogue as Palaemon, the moderator between Pantachus, or Brenz, a ubiquitarian, and Orothetes, or Martyr himself, an upholder of the view that Christ's body was strictly limited in extent.[6] The ubiquitarian controversy, as Martyr indicated in his dedication to Jewel, grew out of disputes over the Lord's Supper. Reformed theologians, such as Martyr, considered Christ's body to be in heaven, at the right hand of God; he could not, therefore, be bodily present in the eucharist. Lutherans, however, considered Christ to be present in the eucharist in body as well as spirit; Brenz argued that Christ's body was not confined to one place but that he could be, and was, everywhere (*ubique*).[7] Out of the whole range of issues which were discussed in Germany in the 1560s and '70s it was this one which chiefly seemed to concern Anglicans.

Jewel had already written to Martyr, in November 1560, to assure him: "That volatile Ubiquitarian doctrine cannot by any means gain footing among us, though there have not been wanting from the outset those who had the subject much at heart."[8] Edwin Sandys, bishop of Worcester, who had spent several years in Martyr's company at Strasbourg and Zurich during Queen Mary's reign, had also written, in April 1560, to promise Martyr that he and his "episcopal brethren" would maintain the doctrine of the eucharist in its purity as long as they lived.[9] Once Jewel had received and read Martyr's diaglogue he wrote back an appreciative letter, in February 1562, associating himself with Martyr in the controversy which seemed certain to continue:

> Must I tell you that I thank you for your Orothetes? I doubt not but that the individual you mention, if he is wise, will think himself much indebted to you. He will, perhaps, however, summon courage, and defend his Pantachus, and prepare himself for a reply, and make his exceptions both against yourself and your Palaemon.[10]

6. The book was entitled *Dialogus de utraque in Christo natura* (Zurich: Froschover, 1561).

7. The significance of the doctrine in Lutheran thought is discussed in Edmund Schlink, *Theology of the Lutheran Confessions,* trans. Paul F. Koehneke and Herbert J. A. Bouman (Philadelphia: Fortress Press, 1961), pp. 188–93.

8. *The Zurich Letters: Comprising the Correspondence of Several English Bishops and Others, with Some of the Helvetian Reformers, during the Early Part of the Reign of Queen Elizabeth,* ed. Hastings Robinson, 2 vols. (Cambridge: Cambridge University Press, 1842–45), 1:92–93.

9. *Zurich Letters,* 1:73; Garrett, *Marian Exiles,* pp. 283–84.

10. *The Works of John Jewel,* ed. John Ayre, 4 vols. (Cambridge: Cambridge University Press, 1845–50), 4:1247.

Peter Martyr Vermigli, however, died in November of that year, leading Jewel, in a letter of March 1563 to Henry Bullinger, the chief minister of Zurich, to engage in some rather ill-conceived wit at Brenz's expense:

> I do not wonder that your Hercules of Tübingen [Brenz], the forger of monstrosities, is now triumphing at his ease; I wonder whether he is able to confine himself within the ample limits and regions of his Ubiquitarian kingdom.[11]

But Jewel, out of respect and filial piety for his deceased friend, was willing to answer any attack made against Martyr by Brenz, "if for no other reason," he said to Bullinger, "at least to let the world know, that England and Switzerland are both united against these Ubiquitarians."[12] A subsequent letter to Bullinger, in March 1565, revealed that Jewel, despite other concerns demanding his attention, had written "very copiously" on the ubiquitarian question.[13]

Bullinger had meanwhile undertaken to answer Brenz himself, an enterprise in which he received considerable encouragement from his Anglican friends. John Parkhurst, having heard of the work in progress, wrote to Bullinger in September 1561, expressing the hope that he and Martyr would have every success, and that the Palatinate of the Rhine and Hesse, which seemed inclined to the theological viewpoint of the Swiss, would be strengthened and preserved by the divine spirit.[14] By April 1562, Parkhurst had heard from Bullinger that a copy of his book against Brenz was on its way; by the end of the following month it had arrived.[15] Parkhurst expressed his approval of its contents in a letter of August 1562 by relating that an elderly minister in his diocese, formerly addicted to Brentian views, had "embraced the truth" once he had read Bullinger's answer.[16] Robert Horne, bishop of Winchester, once the pastor of the English congregation of exiles in Frankfurt, wrote to Bullinger in December 1563 to report having received three books in refutation of Ubiquitarianism, a

---

11. *Zurich Letters,* 1:123.
12. Ibid.
13. Jewel, *Works,* 4:1264.
14. *Zurich Letters,* 1:98.
15. Ibid., 1:108, 110–11. This work would appear to be Bullinger's *Responsio qua ostenditur sententiam de coelo et dextera Dei libello Bullingeri . . . adversaria D. Joannis Brentii sententia non esse eversam* (Zurich: Froschover, 1562).
16. *Zurich Letters,* 1:121–22.

subject on which a countryman of his was writing a book which would show "that the people of England entertain on these points the same opinions as you do at Zurich."[17] Several years later, Richard Hilles, a merchant in London, Richard Cox, bishop of Ely, Edmund Grindal, archbishop of York, and John Parkhurst all received copies of Bullinger's latest work against Brenz.[18] Grindal commented that he found Bullinger's treatise "moderate and pious."[19]

The community of interest which had been established between Swiss and Anglican divines may be illustrated by the reaction of Grindal and Parkhurst to the Second Helvetic Confession, the lengthy doctrinal statement which Bullinger issued in 1566 on the request of the elector of the Palatinate, and which was subsequently accepted by many of the Calvinistic churches of Europe.[20] Grindal, then bishop of London, wrote that "even to this day (notwithstanding the attempts of many to the contrary) we most fully agree with your churches, and with the confession you have lately set forth."[21] Parkhurst, writing to Bullinger on June 29, 1574, said: "That confession of true religion which you published in 1566, is now read in English, and in the hands of everyone."[22] Grindal's feeling that the English Church was quite distinct theologically from the Lutheran churches is suggested by his remark that his church had flourished under the faith Bullinger had defined, "which under other circumstances would have become a prey to the Ecoebolians, Lutherans, and semi-papists."[23] Thus, when the events began which were to lead directly to the drawing up of the Lutheran Formula of Concord in 1577, the attitude of the Anglican bishops tended to reflect that of their Swiss correspondents. Writing to the Zurich minister Josiah Simler on March 10, 1572, Parkhurst said of the man who was to be a principal author of the Formula:

17. Ibid., 1:135; Garrett, *Marian Exiles,* pp. 188–90. His countryman was presumably Jewel.

18. *Zurich Letters,* 1:241, 243, 258, 266. The letters bear dates from July 1571 to March 1572.

19. Ibid., 1:258. Grindal's personal indebtedness to Bullinger for having led him away from the views of Luther on the subject of the Lord's Supper to "a correct opinion," some twenty years earlier, is expressed in a letter of February 8, 1587. Ibid., 1:182.

20. *The Creeds of Christendom, with a History and Critical Notes,* ed. Philip Schaff, 6th edition, 3 vols. (New York: Harper, 1931), 1:390–426; 3:233–306.

21. *Zurich Letters,* 1:169.

22. Ibid., 1:304.

23. Ibid., 1:169. Ecobolus was an adviser to the apostate Emperor Julian, who attempted to be reconciled to the church after the emperor's death.

I have heard nothing at all about James Andreas, but I am well acquainted with all the parts and arts both of him and of all Lutherans. As it was formerly, so it is now. Let them rage, let them storm, let them roar! Truth will conquer, and their Ubiquity will be found nowhere but in Utopia.[24]

When Jacob Andreae, under the patronage of the elector of Saxony, began work on a statement of doctrine which would resolve the disputes wracking Germany, Parkhurst wrote to Simler, on February 7, 1574: "That ubiquitarian James Andreas, who threatens to write against the divines of Wittenberg and my Zurich friends, will lose his labour and betray his folly to everyone."[25]

The efforts of Andreae and others to resolve the theological issues in dispute by distinguishing clearly between teaching that was authentically Lutheran from that which was not was no doubt widely viewed by Lutherans as a step toward harmony. Inevitably, it seemed just the reverse to many of those outside the Lutheran tradition. Bullinger wrote to Bishop Sandys on March 10, 1574, that unity among brethren was essential for the well being of the church. At that very moment, he observed, "some morose, haughty, and obstinate Lutherans" were tearing themselves away from their fellows and even attempting to force upon others "their own superficial opinions."[26] Writing on the same day to Archbishop Grindal, he complained of the activities of those "who pride themselves upon being Lutherans" but who were in fact "most shameless brawlers, railers, and calumniators." Never ceasing to attack "our churches, ourselves, and our doctrine respecting the Lord's Supper," Bullinger wrote, they had lately launched an assault "against us and our friends at Heidelberg."[27] Bullinger observed that the controversy which had begun between himself and Brenz had now broadened to include such matters as "the doctrine respecting one person and two natures in Christ, the omnipotence and omnipresence (as they say) of the humanity of Christ, his ascension to the heavens, and [his presence] in heaven."[28] A few days later, on March 16,

---

24. *Gleanings*, p. 448.
25. *Zurich Letters*, 1:302. The divines then dominating Wittenberg were those called Philippists or crypto-Calvinists; they were replaced in the same year by Lutherans much more hostile to the Reformed point of view. *Creeds of Christendom*, 1:266–67 *et passim*.
26. *Zurich Letters*, 2:241.
27. Ibid., 2:245.
28. Ibid., 2:246.

Rodolph Gualter commented to Bishop Cox that "the Ubiquitarian divines are grown more furious than ever . . . for, not contented with what Luther long since wrote rather intemperately against our teachers, they now exclaim that we are all Arians, and worse than Mahomet."[29]

The response of the Anglican bishops, informed about the activities of the Lutherans by their friends in Switzerland, was to condemn the party held responsible for such attacks. "May the Lord grant to James Andreas and Andrew Musculus a better mind; or, rather, may He restore to them the mind which they appear to have entirely lost," wrote Bishop Parkhurst to Rodolph Gualter on June 29, 1574.[30] Bishop Cox, writing to Gualter on July 12, and William Cole, president of Corpus Christi College, Oxford, writing to him on July 31, 1574, both expressed satisfaction over the learned treatise by Josiah Simler, which attempted to answer the attacks of the "Brentians."[31] Cole sent special thanks by way of Gualter to Simler, "because you will not allow the enemy to attack the sheepfold at his pleasure."[32] In the following year, Cox expressed to Gualter his hope that "the treatise of that venerable old man, master Henry Bullinger, in which he invites and persuades the ministers of the churches to unity, will be of great benefit to this kingdom: I wish it might be so throughout all Germany."[33] By this time, however, the news of depositions and persecutions in Saxony against those held to be insufficiently orthodox had begun to reach England. Cox, grieved at the news, commented that the "Lutheran party is very cruel."[34] Robert Horne, writing to Gualter on August 10, 1576, found some solace in the fact that the English Church and state had found a large measure of stability under Queen Elizabeth. "As she has always abominated popery from her infancy," he wrote, "so also will she never admit Lutheranism, which is a greater disturber of christianity [sic]."[35] It was in this light that the English tended to see the movement toward "concord" in Lutheran Germany.

29. Ibid., 2:253.
30. *Gleanings*, p. 494.
31. *Zurich Letters*, 1:307; 2:256–57; see also 2:245.
32. Ibid., 2:257. Gualter's son was at that time an undergraduate at Corpus Christi College.
33. Ibid., 1:315. The treatise was presumably Bullinger's *Adhortatio ad omnes in ecclesia Domini Nostri Jesu Christi Verbi Dei ministros, ut contentiones mutuas deponant* (Zurich: Froschover, 1572).
34. *Zurich Letters*, 1:315.
35. Ibid., 1:321.

By 1576, word had reached England of Bullinger's death, prompting Bishop Cox to write to Rodolph Gualter, Bullinger's successor as chief minister of Zurich, that his sorrow was great over the passing away of "so great a man, and excellent a friend." Cox took comfort, however, in that "the most gracious Lord, who never forsakes his flock, has set in the place of Bullinger yourself, who possess no less zeal in feeding the flock, and no less courage in keeping off its enemies."[36] In the same year, on August 24, Gualter took a bold step indeed by writing to his friend Edmund Grindal, now archbishop of Canterbury, the leading ecclesiastical official in England, to ask for his and Queen Elizabeth's help in dealing with the developing crisis in Germany. Gualter informed Grindal that a meeting of German princes had taken place in Saxony at the palace of the Elector Augustus, giving rise to the fear that a political coalition was being organized, with the special intention of bringing the Palatinate back into the Lutheran fold. Even Catholic princes such as the duke of Bavaria and the emperor seemed involved in an intrigue against the present elector of the Palatinate. The elector's son Louis was feared to have come to some understanding with his father's enemies.[37] There could be no doubt of Augustus's hostility: "fresh examples of cruelty are every day exhibited by him against those whom he discovers to be of our sentiments." As for Jacob Andreae, "an ambitious and abusive man," he had apparently ceased trying to counter the arguments of the Heidelberg theologians and was "endeavouring to overwhelm us by the authority and power of princes."[38] Gualter therefore appealed for the intervention of the English queen:

> What therefore I lately recommended for the defence of our common cause, seems not more useful than it is necessary; namely, that her most serene majesty should interpose her authority. For the elector Palatine has long been an object of their [the German princes'] hatred, and they are aware that he is not reverenced and honoured even by all his own subjects as he ought to be. The Swiss possess no influence whatever with the princes. As to Geneva, they [the German princes] not only hate but execrate it. But they cannot thus despise or disregard the most serene queen of England, who possesses weight both on

---

36. Ibid., 1:318.
37. Ibid., 2:273–74. Elector Frederick III had, in 1562, taken steps to establish Calvinism in the Palatinate; his son Louis was to reverse this policy, by restoring Lutheranism to its former position. See Claus-Peter Clasen, *The Palatinate in European History, 1555–1618* (Oxford: Blackwell, 1966), pp. 12–19.
38. *Zurich Letters,* 2:274–75.

the ground of her royal majesty and of her great resources; and who, in fine, is in a position to afford valuable assistance to the whole of Germany against their common enemies the papists.[39]

Not long after Grindal received Gualter's letter he became embroiled in a dispute with the queen over the "prophesyings" among the English clergy, and as a result he was suspended from his functions, beginning in June 1577. His restoration was still not complete at the time of his death in 1583.[40] Meanwhile, however, advice from another quarter led Elizabeth to act in very much the way Gualter had recommended.

On July 15, 1577, some two months after the Formula of Concord had been drawn up by Lutheran divines meeting at Bergen, near Magdeburg, Duke John Casimir, the younger brother of Louis, who was now the elector of the Palatinate,[41] wrote to Queen Elizabeth to inform her about certain disquieting developments in Germany. Unlike his elder brother, John held firmly to the religious faith of his father Frederick—a faith expressed in the Second Helvetic Confession —and he assumed that Elizabeth and the English Church were of the same persuasion as he. Those in the empire who had broken with the papacy but who differed from Elizabeth and himself on the doctrine of the Lord's Supper, he reported to the queen, were planning to hold a solemn assembly at Magdeburg in October. There, it was feared, they would condemn those within the empire who differed from them. John Casimir urged Elizabeth to send a well-informed representative to the assembly to transmit her counsel, in order that "our Confession and the public tranquillity" might be preserved.[42] Essentially the same message had been conveyed a month before in a letter from Hubert Languet, the French Protestant diplomat who served as an adviser to John Casimir, to the young Philip Sidney, then enjoying the favor of the queen and the English court. He asked, "Why should not your most gracious Queen send some active agent to this meeting, to set before them [the Protestant princes] the dangers which threaten

---

39. Ibid., 2:275.

40. See Patrick Collinson, *The Elizabethan Puritan Movement* (London: Jonathan Cape, 1967), pp. 159, 198–201.

41. Louis had become elector of the Palatinate in 1576 in succession to his father Frederick III, and had at once begun to reintroduce Lutheranism as the official faith. See Clasen, *Palatinate*, p. 19.

42. State Papers, German States, 1557–1579, Public Record Office, London, ser. 81, vol. 1, fol. 1.

all who have cast off their allegiance to Rome, if they persist in these contentions?"[43]

Queen Elizabeth was notoriously cautious in her conduct of foreign affairs and she disliked hair-splitting discussions of theological issues, yet she soon acted in accordance with these suggestions. Why? The reason seems to be that she had become, almost despite her intentions, a supporter of both the Dutch rebels against Spain in the Netherlands and of the Huguenot rebels against the monarchy in France, and was looking for support for both these groups from the German Protestant states. Reluctant to involve England directly in these conflicts, she sought German backing for the insurrectionary movements. John Casimir, who was in close contact with the Protestant faction at the English court, acted as one of her agents in this endeavor, recruiting soldiers in Germany to be used in both France and the Netherlands. By 1577 the decline of Spanish power in the Netherlands made it seem possible that these provinces could attain autonomy if they had sufficient diplomatic and military support from the Protestant states. Elizabeth was thus involved in a campaign long favored by certain of her ministers—especially by Sir Francis Walsingham and the earl of Leicester—to encourage the Protestants on the continent to unite in their own defense. Earlier in the year she had sent Sidney across Germany with the duty of expressing her condolences to Emperor Rudolph on the death of his father; his real task, however, was to help organize and encourage the Protestant cause in Europe. The developments reported by John Casimir seemed to threaten the unity of Protestantism and to diminish the prospects for successful Protestant actions in international affairs.[44]

In the autumn of 1577 the queen employed two diplomatic agents to carry her message to the princes of Germany. One was the versatile and gifted Daniel Rogers, who was already engaged in furthering

43. *The Correspondence of Sir Philip Sidney and Hubert Languet,* ed. Steuart A. Pears (London: William Pickering, 1845), pp. 107–8.

44. Elizabeth's foreign policy in the 1570s is discussed in the prefaces to the *Calendar of State Papers, Foreign Series, of the Reign of Elizabeth,* ed. Arthur John Butler, vols. 14–17 (London: H. M. Stationery Office, 1901–1907); R. B. Wernham, *Before the Armada: The Growth of English Foreign Policy, 1485–1588* (London: Jonathan Cape, 1966), pp. 290–336; P. S. Crowson, *Tudor Foreign Policy* (New York: St. Martin's, 1973), 188–202; and Wallace T. MacCaffrey, *The Shaping of the Elizabethan Regime* (Princeton: Princeton University Press, 1968), pp. 268–90, 399–453. For Sidney's mission, see James M. Osborn, *Young Philip Sidney, 1572–1577* (New Haven: Yale University Press, 1972), pp. 448–95.

the queen's policies with the German princes, having been sent with Sidney on his journey to the imperial court in the spring and then, after Sidney's return home, sent again to the continent to consolidate the work which they had begun. Rogers was at home in Germany and in theological discussions. He was the son of John Rogers, a noted preacher and scholar who had been the first Protestant martyr of Queen Mary's reign in England. Daniel Rogers had been born in Wittenberg, while his father served a congregation there, and he returned to his birthplace to study under Melanchthon during the Marian period. Since 1565 he had lived almost continuously on the continent, serving on various diplomatic missions in France, the Netherlands, and Germany.[45] The other was the clerk of the council, Robert Beale, who had served under Walsingham at the embassy in Paris and had, in the two preceding years, undertaken missions to the Netherlands.[46] In his Instructions to Beale on August 22, 1577, Walsingham, then secretary of state, directed the envoy to seek to prevent the holding of an assembly in Magdeburg in October on the grounds that such a step would be divisive. He was to point out that it was rather "high time to thinke uppon some good association and League" by which to withstand the machinations of the enemy. Likewise he was to convey to Duke John Casimir his government's wish that a meeting of those not of the Augsburg Confession planned for Frankfurt at the end of September be deferred, lest it "give some cause of doubt that they make themselves a partie."[47]

By the end of September, Rogers had unfolded the queen's plan for a united Protestant association to John Casimir, who wrote to Walsingham that he wanted nothing more than to see "the establishment of the Churches, an assured peace, and a mutual Union."[48] He had also discussed the matter with the landgrave of Hesse, who feared the proposed league could never go forward while religious dissensions among

45. See John Strype, *Annals of the Reformation and Establishment of Religion and Other Occurrences in the Church of England during Queen Elizabeth's Happy Reign,* 4 vols. (Oxford: Clarendon Press, 1824), 3,1:393–95; J. A. van Dorsten, *Poets, Patrons, and Professors: Sir Philip Sidney, Daniel Rogers, and the Leiden Humanists* (London: Oxford University Press, 1962), pp. 10–12, 19–22, 46–58, 53–55.

46. Strype, *Annals,* 4:115–19; James M. Rigg on Beale in the *Dictionary of National Biography,* 21 vols. (London: Oxford University Press, 1937–38), 2:3–7.

47. State Papers, German States, 1577–1579, P.R.O. ser. 81, vol. 1, fols. 5–7.

48. Ibid., fols 8–10 verso, 13 (verso refers to the reverse side of the folio).

Protestants in Germany continued.[49] Beale had arrived in Frankfurt, where he reported on September 21 that the assembly proposed for Magdeburg had been transferred to Naumburg but that the meeting of Reformed theologians planned for Frankfurt was scheduled to begin in a few days' time.[50] Just what the queen intended these diplomatic agents to convey is suggested by her own memorandum to the elector of the Palatinate carried by Beale. This document is, in effect, her own treatment of the problem of religious division in Germany. She professed entire sympathy with the task of defending the church, a task undertaken in Germany through the writing of a new formula of religion. But she urged that the time was not propitious for condemning other churches for their beliefs, as the document was said to do. The churches which had broken with the authority of Rome were at that moment beset on all sides: by the duke of Guise in Lorraine, by Don John of Austria in the Netherlands, by the king of Poland outside Danzig, and by the Turk in the East. Unity among these churches was essential for their survival. The elector was asked to consider the fact that the pressing of the Formula would not only break the unity of the German churches but would separate those within Germany which adhered to it from those outside Germany which dissented from it and were condemned by it. This last group included all the churches of England, Ireland, Wales, and Scotland, as well as several on the continent. The queen suspected the activities of ambitious divines to be at the bottom of the difficulties. Such divines, ever bringing forth new doctrines, as recent discussions had shown, had to be firmly controlled; otherwise they would have brought into being a new papacy and primacy over the consciences and goods of princes. She argued that if such issues as had been discussed were to be settled, the appropriate means would be a general synod of all the Reformed churches. In the meantime she hoped that condemnations would be avoided; she renewed her proposal for a defensive league put forward by Daniel Rogers.[51]

Beale took the queen's messages deep into Germany, finally reaching Saxony itself. There he apparently found a warmer reception than he had been led to expect, although the elector contented himself, in a letter to Elizabeth of November 8, 1577, with general professions of

49. Ibid., fols. 50 verso–51 verso.
50. Ibid., fols. 45–57 verso.
51. Ibid., fols. 60–63 verso. Another copy, with minor changes, was sent to the duke of Württemberg (fols. 60, 63 verso).

friendship, referring specific matters to a future meeting of all the princes professing the Augsburg Confession.[52]   Many years later, in 1591, Beale remembered his journey as one "making a circuit to and fro of 1400 English miles at the least; repairing personally to nine princes, and sending her majesty's letters to three others."[53]   Languet, writing to Sidney from Frankfurt on January 8, 1578, said of Beale's mission:

> The Sirens of Saxony detained the excellent Master Beale so long, that we were not a little anxious on his account; but he relieved us from our care by returning safe and sound, and made us happy for some days by his agreeable conversation. . . . Master Beale has met with no small difficulties in going through his appointed task, but by his prudence and dexterity he has so surmounted them, that I hope our churches are saved from the perils which threatened them from the movements of Jacobus Andreas and some other Theologians.[54]

Languet himself was not optimistic about the plan for a league which both Rogers and Beale had broached to the German princes.   But he commended the queen in that she was "so anxious for the safety of the Churches and Princes who have thrown off the yoke of Popish tyranny, as to invite them to a union of policy and of power . . . and offer herself as the leader of the undertaking."   If such efforts were continued, "you might gradually arrive at the league which for the present is past hoping for."[55]

Rogers's most conspicuous role in the proceedings seems to have been largely unintended on his part.   After Beale's arrival in Frankfurt on September 17, 1577, he had sent word to Duke John Casimir, by way of Rogers, Languet, and others, that the queen considered that the meeting of Reformed theologians planned for that city in late September could only "breede ialousyes and misliking with the adverse partie" and that it was "more expedient to proceede by way of intercession."[56] But Beale found that it was too late to prevent the divines from gath-

---

52. Ibid., fols. 109–109 verso.   The electress also wrote, expressing her wish for cordial relations between England and Saxony (fols. 105 verso–107).

53. Strype, *Annals,* 4:118.   Papers in the Public Record Office describe Beale's visits to Duke John Casimir and the elector of the Palatinate.   Letters are preserved which he sent to the duke of Württemberg and the marquis of Brandenburg, and in them he states that he is on his way to visit the electors of Saxony and Brandenburg. State Papers, P.R.O. ser. 81, vol. 1, fols. 69, 83, 85–88.

54. *Correspondence of Sidney and Languet,* pp. 132–33.

55. Ibid., pp. 135–36.

56. State Papers, P.R.O. ser. 81, vol. 1, fols. 47–47 verso.

ering. Once they had arrived, from France, Poland, Hungary, the Netherlands, and the Palatinate, John Casimir met with them and then sent them on, without warning, to Rogers. The English envoy protested that he had no commission to meet with them; he advised them, nevertheless, to supplicate the electors of Saxony and Brandenburg to stay the condemnations threatened against the Reformed churches, and to send this supplication to them by way of Beale, the queen's ambassador. If they persevered in their intention to draw up a confession, he advised that it be as close as possible to the Augsburg Confession.[57] The way this appeared to observers in Zurich was indicated in a letter of Gualter to Bishop Cox on March 4, 1578. The Zurichers were eagerly awaiting further news of the drawing up of a common confession, which had been decreed "in the synod of Frankford, the ambassador of the most serene queen being present, and moderating the whole business." The queen, he felt, had, in this matter, "performed an excellent work, and worthy a nursing mother of the church."[58] Cox, for his part, was unsure how to answer his friend, being "altogether ignorant" that such an endeavor was underway. He wrote to Lord Treasurer Burghley, on May 16, to inquire what the queen had done to promote such a "confession and consent of Christian kingdoms in the true religion of Christ." It was, he added, an ardent wish of his, which he had publicly expressed in a sermon before the queen some years before.[59] The common confession, however, did not materialize, for the reason given by Gualter in a letter to Archbishop Grindal on March 8, 1580. Gualter reported that the Lutheran Formula of Concord, or as he called it, the *discordis concordiae formula,* had been subscribed by the three electoral princes of Saxony, the Palatinate, and Brandenburg, but the proposed common confession of the Reformed churches, drawn up by Jerome Zanchius, had been examined by the Genevan and Swiss churches and had been found lacking in brevity and clarity.[60]

The missions undertaken by Rogers and Beale in 1577 were not the only diplomatic initiatives by Queen Elizabeth on behalf of Protestant unity in Germany. By early April 1578, Rogers was in Mainz, appar-

---

57. Ibid., fols. 77–78 verso. Rogers's report to Walsingham is dated October 10, 1577.
58. Strype, *Annals,* 2,2:103–5.
59. Ibid., pp. 105–6.
60. Ibid., pp. 371–72, 679–81.

ently on a new mission to try to solidify German Protestanism and to coordinate German support for the Protestants in the Netherlands.[61] At the end of the same month Duke John Casimir wrote the queen to inform her of a proposed meeting of "the theologians of the princes who claim alone to have the true understanding of the Confession of Augsburg," along with some political leaders, to be held in June in Schmalkalden.[62] Once again the queen responded, this time by naming five delegates, including Rogers, to attend the meeting, and by writing the elector of the Palatinate, the duke of Württemberg, the landgrave of Hesse, the prince of Anhalt, and the duke of Brunswick to urge them to work for the true concord of churches by refusing to condemn those holding a different view of the Lord's Supper from that held by Luther.[63] By early June, however, it was clear that the proposed meeting had been called off and the English delegation was released from its assignment.[64] Even then the dangers which Elizabeth feared did not suddenly dissipate. In September 1580, she ordered Rogers to go to Germany to induce the duke of Saxony to conciliate the differences which threatened to lead to schism among German Protestants. This time, however, he was taken prisoner within the empire by an adventurer in the pay of Spain, and it was to be four years before the English government was able to procure his release.[65] Elizabeth's diplomacy in Germany was dogged by frustration.

Thus, for both religious and political reasons, informed Elizabethans were inclined to look with suspicion upon Lutheranism and the Formula of Concord. This suspicion endured. When the Parliamentary leader Sir Edwin Sandys, the son of Archbishop Sandys, toured the continent of Europe to see for himself the diversity of religion there and to assess the chances for unity and peace, he was particularly struck by the vehemence of Lutheran preachers in their condemnation of the tenets of Calvinism. The Lutheran princes and people, he reported in 1605, have the Calvinists in such great detestation that they "professe openly, they will returne to the Papacy, rather than ever admitte that Sacramentarie and Predestinarie pestilence." He added that "one of

---

61. State Papers, P.R.O. ser. 81, vol. 1, fol. 134 verso.

62. Ibid., fols. 142–142 verso.

63. *Calendar of State Papers, Foreign, 1577–78,* pp. 715–16; State Papers, P.R.O. ser. 81, vol. 1, fols. 152–58 verso; *Zurich Letters,* 2:301.

64. State Papers, P.R.O. ser. 81, vol. 1, fols. 165 verso–167.

65. Dorsten, *Poets, Patrons, and Professors,* pp. 68–75; Sidney Lee on Rogers in the *D.N.B.,* 17:116–17; *Correspondence of Sidney and Languet,* pp. 189–90.

their Princes, namely, the Administratour of Saxonie, is strongly mis-doubted to practise with the Emperour, for the ioyning of the Catholike and Lutherane forces in one, and by war to roote out & extinguish the Calvinists."[66]   In an era in which many Englishmen were Calvinists, this kind of news from Germany was not reassuring.

66. Edwin Sandys, *A Relation of the State of Religion and with What Hopes and Policies It Hath Beene Framed and Is Maintained in the Severall States of These Westerne Parts of the World* (London: Simon Waterson, 1605), fol. Q4 (as emended in the British Museum copy).

10

The Dutch Reformed Response

W. Robert Godfrey

When the Formula of Concord appeared in 1577, the religious and political climate in the Netherlands did not encourage relaxed theological reflection and response. The Reformed Church in the Netherlands enjoyed only a precarious prominence and the state struggled in a bitter revolt against Spain. Yet despite these problems in the Netherlands the Formula of Concord evoked reaction from the Dutch. The Dutch Reformed, like other European Calvinists, believed that the particular sections of the Formula relating to the Lord's Supper and the Person of Christ presented a harsh and unfair condemnation of the Reformed faith. Their own unique and difficult circumstances convinced the Dutch especially that Protestant unity was crucial to Protestant survival not only in the Netherlands, but also in Europe as a whole.

The Reformation in the Netherlands ran a rocky and complex course. The Dutch Reformation followed roughly four stages of development: First came the Lutheran phase (1517–26) followed by the Sacramentarian (1526–31), although it is often difficult to distinguish between the two. Neither the Lutheran nor the Sacramentarian movements attracted wide popular support. The Anabaptists ushered in the third stage of the Reformation in the 1530s and early 1540s, and they represented the first popular expression of Protestantism in the Netherlands. The Anabaptists paid dearly for their faith, and between 1531 and 1574 some fifteen hundred Dutch Anabaptists were martyred.

The Calvinists were the fourth group to enter upon the scene, appearing first in the south in the mid-1540s and later in the north about 1560. Calvinists remained a minority everywhere in the Netherlands in the sixteenth century, but their organization and clearly defined objectives made them both an attractive and influential minority. While the other Protestant groups continued to have followings, the Calvinists clearly dominated national life by the 1560s and became the most powerful mobilizing force in the revolt against Spain.

The further development of the Dutch Reformation occurred against the backdrop of the Dutch revolt against Spanish rule which broke out in earnest in 1572 and was not finally settled until 1648. The initial political objectives of the revolt were limited to the protection of the ancient Dutch liberties from the encroachments of the sovereign of the Low Countries, King Philip II of Spain. The Dutch reacted against Philip's tyrannical attempts to alter the administrative, financial, and religious situation in the seventeen provinces of the Netherlands.

The years between 1577 and 1581 were particularly critical for the course of the revolt. William of Orange, the leader of the revolt, labored diligently to keep the Netherlands united in its opposition to Spain. To maintain Dutch unity, he realized that the goals of the revolt must remain political. He knew he must prevent religious differences from dividing the country and thus weakening the revolt. William's task was far from easy. The great nobility, on whom he relied for troops and financial aid, were largely Roman Catholic. They were jealous of the Protestant William; they resented his popularity and distrusted his ambitions. The core of William's support, however, came from staunch Calvinists who saw in the war an opportunity to advance the cause of the gospel.

The Dutch hoped that the goals of the revolt had been realized when the States-General of the Netherlands issued the Pacification of Ghent in November 1576 and the Spanish governor accepted the Pacification by the Union of Brussels in January 1577. Their agreement demanded the expulsion of the Spanish troops from Dutch soil and religious toleration throughout the Netherlands. The Pacification of Ghent stated that the religious rights of Roman Catholics were to be respected by all. The Reformed faith, however, was to be recognized as the dominant expression of Christianity in Holland and Zeeland and could be practiced privately in the other provinces. The Union of Brussels repeated the demands of Ghent with an added pledge of loyalty to Philip. Hopes were raised that peace was at hand. Unfortunately the duplicity of Don John, Philip's new governor, combined with Calvinist militance to wreck this effort to restore peace and unity to the Netherlands.

The revolt flared again, and in January 1579 the states of the seven northern provinces drafted the Union of Utrecht to strengthen the war effort. The Union was intended to be a defensive alliance and to renew the goals of the Pacification of Ghent. The members of the Union of Utrecht hoped that all the other provinces would join them. Alexander Farnese, duke of Parma and Don John's successor, however, encouraged the Roman Catholic nobles to respond with a union of their own. The Catholic aristocracy, angered by Calvinist encroachments, formed the Union of Arras in May 1579. The duke pressed his advantage by coupling impressive military successes in the south in the early 1580s with flattery and money lavished on the nobility. By courting the great lords who had hitherto supported William, he wooed most of the Roman Catholic nobles back to Philip's cause.

This defection of the nobility forced William to rely more heavily on his Reformed supporters, and the revolt took on an even more decidedly religious cast. On July 26, 1581, the states of the Union of Utrecht formally abjured Philip as their sovereign, and the rift in the Netherlands between north and south, Protestant and Catholic, widened. Historian Charles Wilson summarizes the situation:

> The next three years, between the Pacification and the formation of the Unions of Utrecht and Arras in 1579, between the fragile but genuine unity of the former and final division of the Netherlands by the latter, were a political and military watershed in European history.[1]

Thus the Formula of Concord appeared on the Dutch scene not only against the backdrop of an escalating political and religious crusade against Spain, but also against a complex scenario of internal religious tensions in the Dutch Protestant community. In the Netherlands, as elsewhere, relations between the Reformed and Lutherans were strained.[2] The Lutherans demanded their right to religious self-determination, while the Reformed resented Lutheran independence. In 1580 the states of Holland declared that both the Reformed and Lutheran religions could be exercised "freely and unhindered,"[3] but

---

1. Charles Wilson, *Queen Elizabeth and the Revolt of the Netherlands* (Berkeley: University of California Press, 1970), p. 43.

2. Contact between Reformed and Lutheran congregations in the Netherlands was not extensive because of the limited size of the Lutheran community. For example, there are very few references from the sixteenth century to Lutherans in J. Reitsma and S. D. van Veen, eds., *Acta der Provinciale en Particuliere Synoden,* 8 vols. (Groningen: J. B. Wolters, 1892–99).

3. J. W. Pont, *Geschiedenis van het Lutheranisme in de Nederlanden tot 1618* (Haarlem: E. F. Bohn, 1911), p. 370.

the Reformed were not willing to accept this situation. The situation in the city of Woerden in southern Holland demonstrated typical tensions between the Reformed and Lutheran Protestants. In Woerden the Protestant congregation was initially Lutheran. Reformed antipathy surfaced at a provincial synod in Holland as early as 1574 when the Reformed objected to the "spitefulness" of a letter from the Lutheran congreagtion in Woerden.[4] When the Reformed gained the upper hand in the city, increasing pressure was placed on the Lutheran congregation. In 1582 a Lutheran minister was expelled from the city on political grounds, and in 1583 the city authorities, sympathetic to the Calvinists, tried unsuccessfully to force the Lutherans into union with the Reformed.[5] The history of the Lutheran congregation in Antwerp followed a similar pattern of escalating Reformed opposition to Lutheran Protestants.[6]

The growing Reformed antagonism toward Lutheran independence was expressed in a telling letter of recommendation written by the Consistory of Amsterdam on behalf of Libertus Fraxinus. The letter was addressed to the National Synod meeting at The Hague in 1586. One of Fraxinus's chief commendations for the ministry was that "he is skilled in discouraging such enemies of the truth as Anabaptists, Libertines, and Martinists."[7] Clearly the Lutherans were condemned as sectarians for their refusal to identify with the Reformed Church.

The strained contacts with Lutheran congregations within the Netherlands, however, did not insure that the Dutch Reformed community would be aroused by the Formula of Concord when it appeared. This was especially true because the Dutch Lutherans were themselves very slow to accept the Formula. Dutch Lutherans generally accepted the views of Matthias Flacius Illyricus (1520–1575), who late in his life served as a pastor in Antwerp. The Formula rejected his theology of sin, which made the Formula unpopular with Lutherans in the Netherlands. Only late in the sixteenth century, when Dutch Lutherans turned increasingly toward Germany, particularly Hamburg, for theological leadership, did the Formula begin to gain official adoption. For example, the Lutheran congregation in Amsterdam did not

---

4. F. L. Rutgers, ed., *Acta van de Nederlandsche Synoden der Zestiende Eeuw* (The Hague: Martinus Nijhoff, 1889), p. 134.

5. Pont, *Lutheranisme,* p. 376.

6. Ibid., p. 414.

7. Rutgers, *Acta,* p. 612.

formally accept the Formula until 1597, and the congregations of Woerden and Leiden received it only in the early seventeenth century.[8]

Dutch Reformed response to the Formula of Concord, then, did not come primarily in response to domestic squabbles with Dutch Lutherans. Concern over the Formula reflected rather Reformed zeal to unify the Protestant movement in Europe and dismay at the condemnation of Calvinism contained in the Formula. Many Reformed Protestants throughout Europe, including the Dutch, believed that the Formula of Concord represented the most flagrant expression to date of Lutheran exclusiveness.

The Dutch Reformed particularly had already suffered from Lutheran refusal to cooperate with other Protestants. In 1567, German Lutheran princes refused to aid William of Orange in the incipient revolt against Spain unless William accepted the Augsburg Confession, a step which he never took. Only in 1572 did William finally receive permission even to hire mercenaries in Germany. Again in 1578, when William was in desperate need of troops, he was refused aid by German Lutherans.

The Dutch, therefore, were glad to cooperate in one of the earliest efforts of the Reformed community in Europe to refute the charges of the Formula and forestall its wide acceptance. This effort was the conference at Frankfurt called together in 1577 by John Casimir, younger brother of Count Ludwig VI of the Palatinate (1576–83), to discuss appropriate ways for the Reformed to oppose the Formula.[9] Representatives came to Frankfurt from the churches of France, Navarre, Hungary, Poland, and England. The Netherlands was represented by the statesman Johannes Junius. John Casimir, who was not present, was represented by the distinguished theologians Zanchius, Toussaint, Zuleger, and Petrus Dathenus, a leading figure in the Dutch Church.

The conference decided that the best way to promote Protestant unity was first to draw up a common Reformed confession for all the

---

8. Pont, *Lutheranisme*, pp. 452ff. and W. J. Kooiman, "Philippus Nicolai contra Petrus Plancius in de Strijd om de ubiquitas corporis Christi," *Nederlands Archief voor Kerkgeschiedenis*, n.s. (1967), 48:232–66.

9. James I. Good, *The Origin of the Reformed Church in Germany* (Reading, Pa.: Daniel Miller, 1887), pp. 244ff. and J. N. Bakhuizen van den Brink, "Het Convent te Frankfurt 27–28 September 1577 en de Harmonia Confessionum," *Nederlandsch Archief voor Kerkgeschiedenis* n.s. (1941), 32:235–80.

Reformed churches and secondly to send a delegation to the Lutheran princes and cities in the empire urging them to reject the Formula of Concord.

The conference realized its second goal by appointing a delegation, including Knibbius, a Dutch lawyer, which traveled to various courts in person arguing against the Formula and presenting a forceful letter written by Hubert Languet stressing the pragmatic importance of Protestant unity. The letter urged that in the face of Roman Catholic and imperial opposition the theological differences between the Lutherans and the Reformed were minimal and should not be allowed to destroy Protestant unity. Languet's letter argued that the Formula's magnification of theological differences would endanger the Protestant cause in all of Europe.

On the first point the delegates at Frankfurt hoped that a new confession would increase the sense of unity and promote communication among the Reformed churches. A common confession would also answer the Lutheran charge that the Reformed were sectarian because they could not even agree among themselves on a unified confessional statement. On the basis of a common Reformed confession the delegates hoped to promote discussion with the Lutheran theologians that might result in Protestant unity in Europe.

Zanchius was given the important assignment of writing the new confession. Zanchius completed his task and ultimately published the work in 1585 as *De Religione Christiana Fides*. When Zanchius sent a draft to Beza, however, he was told that rather than adopting a new confession, it seemed more expedient to harmonize the extant confessions of the various Reformed churches. This new approach resulted in the *Harmonia Confessionum* of 1581 which failed ultimately to accomplish the goals of the Frankfurt conference.[10]

Beyond their participation in the Frankfurt conference, the Dutch Reformed responded to the Formula of Concord by synodical action within the Netherlands. At the National Synod of Middelburg in June 1581 the classis of Amsterdam registered concern over the Formula and expressed the need to produce material against it. The classis sought the advice of the Synod on whether it would be better to prepare a Dutch translation of the confrontation between Reformed and Lutheran theologians at Maulbronn in 1564 or to translate the work *Contra Formulam Concordiae ab Ubiquitariis editam* by the Reformed

10. Bakhuizen van den Brink, "Convent te Frankfurt," pp. 273ff.

theologians of Neustadt. The National Synod instructed the classis to prepare the latter work for distribution and ordered the Synod of North Holland to oversee the work and insure its printing.[11]

A more distinctively Dutch and more theologically detailed reaction to the Formula of Concord came from the pen of the Dutch Reformed minister, Pierre Loyseleur de Villiers.[12] Villiers was born about 1530 in the southern part of the Low Countries. His family was probably part of the lower nobility, and he was raised in France where he studied at Orleans and Paris. The origin of his Protestantism is unknown, but he did go to Geneva to study theology under Beza. He was a preacher in France, perhaps in the service of Odet de Châtillon, and in July 1577 he became a court preacher for William of Orange He joined the historic company of such notables as Junius, Saravia, Dathenus, and Taffin.

In 1579, Villiers wrote an open letter to "the honored brothers in Christ" who had authored the Formula of Concord, in which he firmly but irenicly protested the Formula's condemnation of Reformed Protestants.[13] His argument, presented in seven chapters, sought to minimize the issues dividing Lutherans and Calvinists and to stress the theological and practical importance of Protestant unity.

In chapter one he began boldly by asserting that the light of the gospel was revived sixty years earlier through the diligent work of Luther *and* Zwingli. He continued by showing how the gospel was brought to the Netherlands where its fruits had been sealed by the blood of many martyrs, "as you beloved brothers" surely know.[14] Despite past sufferings and the present war, the peace of the gospel had been brought to many souls because William of Orange had won the right "to preach the gospel freely and publicly."[15] Villiers then

11. Rutgers, *Acta,* pp. 371, 439.

12. The only detailed biography of Villiers is C. Boer, *Hofpredikers van Prins Willem Van Oranje: Jean Taffin en Pierre Loyseleur de Villiers, Kerkhistorische Studien,* 5 (The Hague: Martinus Nijhoff, 1952).

13. The letter is printed in David Gerdes, *Scrinium Antiquarium sive Miscellanea Groningana Nova ad Historiam Reformationis Ecclesiasticam Praecipue Spectantia,* book 1, part 1 (Groningen: Corn. Barlinkhof et G. W. Rump, 1749), pp. 121–200. The first edition title of the letter was: "Ministrorum qui verbum Dei in Reformatis in Belgio Ecclesiis concionantur ad authores Libri Bergensis, qui etiam Concordiae dicitur, Epistola." Villiers's work was subsequently translated into Dutch and German.

14. Ibid., p. 136.

15. Ibid., p. 138.

explained that the churches of Christ in the Netherlands were distressed to learn that they had been condemned by a Formula which seemed "to introduce to all under the lovely title of concord odious discord."[16] He argued that to condemn fellow Protestant churches unheard could almost be called a schismatic action. Surely to remedy the discord a synod ought to be held where true peace and concord could be attained for all Protestants.

In chapter two Villiers argued that the only areas of theological disagreement were, first, the Lord's Supper, and second, the Person and two natures of Christ. Villiers first presented the Reformed view on the Lord's Supper in fifteen propositions, each of which was derived from the writings of either Martin Luther or Johann Brenz. From these unimpeachably orthodox Lutheran sources Villiers presented the Reformed view of the Lord's Supper as a sacrament which gives all that it represents to those who receive it by faith. He asserted a distinction between the external and the spiritual elements of the sacrament using words similar to the Heidelberg Catechism: "In the Supper of the Lord the mouth of the body receives bread and wine and the mouth of faith receives body and blood."[17] He argued that the Dutch views were those held in common with the French, English, Scottish, and Swiss churches as well as the presecuted brethren in Italy and Spain. He referred also to the basic agreement between Luther and Bucer on the Supper.

Villiers continued by noting three Reformed positions on the sacrament which were condensed by the Formula: 1) that the sacrament is "a sign or figure of the body," 2) that the "flesh of Christ is not consumed by the impious" and 3) that "the body of Christ is not really, substantially or carnally in, under or with the bread."[18] Villiers first pointed out that Luther was much more open-minded on all three points than was the Formula. On point one he noted that even Brenz and Andreae as well as many of the Fathers referred to the sacrament as a sign of the body of Christ. He noted that point two was taught by Augustine and many of the Fathers whom the Formula would not wish to condemn. On point three he argued the problem resulted from the Formula's doctrine of ubiquity, "a new dogma and unknown

16. Ibid., p. 141.
17. Ibid., p. 148.
18. Ibid., p. 155.

in any time before our own."[19] By insisting on ubiquity the Lutherans were engaged in crass materialism and in repeating the error of Pope Nicholas who condemned Berengarius.

In chapter three Villiers turned to the christological question, offering four propositions which summarized his commitment to Chalcedonian orthodoxy and his explicit rejection of Nestorianism and Eutychianism. He cleverly affirmed the idea of a *communicatio idiomatum,* but defined it not ontologically, but as "a form of expression in which a property appropriate to one nature is said concretely of the person."[20] He maintained that the doctrine of ubiquity stood contrary to orthodox Christianity, citing Augustine, Theodoret, and Gregory of Nazianzus. He claimed that the Reformed teaching "is the catholic faith which the Apostles taught, the martyrs confirmed and the faithful until now have preserved."[21]

Chapter four returned to the Lord's Supper and argued that the Reformed view was not a defection from the Lutheran, but rather predated the Lutheran position, finding its origins in the Albigenses, the Waldenses, the Hussites, and Wyclif as well as more recent theologians such as Cranmer, Ridley, Latimer, and Lefèvre d'Étaples. He noted that many Germans including Melanchthon, Peucer, Capito, Sturm, and others who were expelled from German universities also supported the Reformed position.

The issue of ubiquity surfaced again in chapters five and six. Villiers's critique became stronger by attacking the novelty, absurdities, and arrogance of those teaching ubiquity. The action of six theologians condemning six thousand was reminiscent of the methods of the pope. Moreover, the doctrine of ubiquity undermined the ascension, one of the articles of the faith. He concluded that if the Reformed were given to easy anathemas and condemnations, they might argue that the Lutherans were schismatic.

The seventh chapter returned to the themes introduced in chapter one. Villiers called for a reexamination of the issues that divided the churches. He reminded the authors of the Formula that not only Zwinglians but also some adherents of the Augsburg Confession could not sign the Formula, which threatened the unity and peace of the empire. He noted that Queen Elizabeth and other princes had recom-

19. Ibid., p. 165.
20. Ibid., p. 167.
21. Ibid., p. 169.

mended a colloquy to settle the problems raised by the Formula. Otherwise "like censors and dictators of the universal church you will have condemned churches which have not been heard, defended or convicted."[22] He testified to the desperate condition of the Dutch and French churches who needed the support of a strong, united Protestant church. Villiers issued a forceful call for a synod "where we may peacefully hear one another, where love can reign, where truth can conquer and friendly concord can be established."[23] His closing words were a sober warning against the danger of schism and a charge that if there were indeed schism, the Reformed would not be to blame.

Villiers's treatise offers interesting insights into Dutch Reformed reactions to the Formula not only by the issues he addressed but also by issues he chose to avoid. For example, he said nothing about predestination as an issue between Reformed and Lutheran. The Reformed did not seem to view that doctrinal issue as a basic point of contention with the Lutherans. Further, Villiers did not use the designations "Lutheran" and "Reformed" in his letter.[24] He always used the distinction "our church" and "your churches" to stress the unity and parity of the Lutheran and Reformed churches and to make the differences appear to be more geographical than theological.

Villiers did not avoid the real theological differences, but rather sought to emphasize the areas of common belief. His approach to the areas in controversy was threefold. First, he argues that the catholic consensus of the church and very often the best Lutheran authors themselves did not support the peculiarities of the Formula of Concord. He was eager to demonstrate that the Formula was not a defense of Luther's theology, but a defection from it. Second, he insisted that truth and unity would not be served by unilateral condemnation, but rather by the decisions of a synod. With typical Reformed optimism Villiers assumed that a synod could solve all the problems. Third, combining the themes of catholic consensus and unfair condemnation, he warned the Lutherans against straying into schism. Although the Formula had accused the Reformed of heresy, the sin against the truth, Villiers did not reply that ubiquitarians were the real heretics. Rather he adopted the attitude of the injured, but tolerant brother who was

---

22. Ibid., p. 194.
23. Ibid., p. 200.
24. The phrase "Reformed Churches in the Netherlands" in the title of the treatise is not an exception. "Reformed" was used even by the Lutherans in the Netherlands to distinguish Protestants from Roman Catholics.

worried only that arrogance and intolerance would cause the Lutherans to drift into schism, the sin against love.

In 1570, Villiers also wrote another work on the Formula of Concord entitled *Ratio ineundae Concordiae inter Ecclesias Reformatas*.[25] The basic orientation of this work was the same as the previous one although there were some interesting shifts in emphasis. He did speak of "Calvinists" and "Lutherans" but as factions within the Reformed churches. The major theological differences were still the doctrines of the Lord's Supper and of the Person of Christ, but he added predestination or providence as a third point of contention.

The single page devoted to the subject of predestination began with an assertion of common agreement on three basic points: that God was not the author of sin, that Christians did not believe in "Stoic fate or fatalistic necessity,"[26] and that God's actions did not destroy the reality of secondary causes. Villiers maintained that the one point of controversy was on the interpretation of texts like "God hardened Pharaoh's heart." The question was whether God willed that hardening or permitted it. Villiers claimed that the difference was verbal, not real, and could be easily resolved at a colloquy. He stressed that all who believed and were baptized would be saved. All who received the promises of God and believed them could count themselves among the elect.

On the sacrament and the Person of Christ the theological argument was substantially the same in the second treatise as in the first. There was a slight shift of emphasis in his method of promoting peace. He continued to stress the value of a general synod. He hoped the discussions there could distinguish between doctrines essential to salvation and those not essential. In the meantime he wanted to be considered a brother in Christ since he confessed that in the sacrament he was nourished by the true body and blood of Christ and rejected the blasphemies of "heretics, Sacramentarians and Turks."[27] He emphasized the role of Queen Elizabeth as the leader of Protestantism and lamented that she, too, was condemned by the doctrine of the Formula. He cited at length Luther's letter to Bucer on the Wittenberg Concord seeing that as an instance of Lutheran and Reformed unity.

25. Gerdes, *Scrinium,* book 4, part 1, 1754, pp. 391–429.
26. Ibid., p. 404.
27. Ibid., p. 409.

He did not mention the danger of schism in this treatise, but he did charge that the ubiquitarians were aiding and abetting Rome.

Reformed reaction in the Netherlands to the Formula of Concord, like so much Calvinistic response throughout Europe, reflected a deep conviction that Lutheran and Reformed Christians were theologically united in essentials of the faith. The Reformed community feared that the Formula of Concord represented Lutheran gravitation toward theological exclusiveness and novelty. The spirit of the Formula seemed divisive and arrogant, and the condemnations of the Reformed brethren unjust. With their typical optimism the Reformed were confident that a synod or colloquy could prevent theological polarization and solve the tensions between Reformed and Lutheran Protestants.

The Dutch Reformed adopted the pose of a slighted younger brother whose older brother had begun a great and dangerous work that had not come to its logical and necessary completion. The younger brother admired his sibling's accomplishments and felt one with him in the work. However, he was dismayed by his elder brother's growing tendency to become rigid, reactionary, and excessively critical of those seeking to bring his work to maturity. For the Dutch Reformed, who were struggling for religious and national survival and were in desperate need of allies, the Formula of Concord was an untimely blow struck against Protestant unity. They faulted the Formula of Concord for defecting from historic Lutheranism, a defection which threatened the peace of the church and disrupted the unity of the Body of Christ.

11

The French Reformed
Theological Response

Jill Raitt

To understand the responses of the French Reformed theologians, one must first recognize that Geneva was the center of French Reformed theology. It was Calvin in Geneva who provided the doctrinal foundations for the French Confession of Faith (1559), and it was from Geneva that the French Reformed churches drew their spokesman, Theodore Beza, for the Colloquy of Poissy in 1561. Again, in 1571, it was Beza who was elected to preside over the Synod of French Reformed churches at La Rochelle which ratified the Confession of Faith.

Secondly, the issues clarified for the Lutherans by the Formula of Concord were also used defensively against the doctrines of the Reformed. Although the Philippists of Wittenberg and the Calvinists of the Palatinate were the first targets, Beza and his colleague in Zurich, Henry Bullinger, clearly understood the danger to the Reformed churches elsewhere, particularly in the Lowlands and France.[1]

Although Calvin's doctrine of predestination was hotly contested in the early 1550s and remained simmering, the center of the polemics of the 1560s was the doctrine of the Lord's Supper out of which grew the controversies concerning the two natures of Christ of the 1570s. It was as a result of these controversies that the Lutherans and Reformed began calling one another derogatory names: "Zwinglians," "Calvinists," and "Sacramentarians" for the Reformed, and "Ubiquitarians" and "Capernaites" for the Lutherans.

These polemics led to the Lutheran theologians' calling upon their princes to outlaw Calvinists. The effort at the Diet of Augsburg in

---

1. Theodore Beza, *Correspondance de Théodore de Bèze,* III, 1566, ed. H. Meylan, A. Dufour, C. Chimelli, M. Turchetti (Geneva: Librairie Droz, 1973), 8, 20–21; 34–35; hereafter cited as *Corr.* and volume number.

1556 and later at Erfurt to force Frederick III, count palatine, to moderate his Calvinism or to sign the Augsburg Confession of 1530 failed, but that theological-political attempt led to the Formula of Concord.[2] Nor were the more determined princes and their theologians loath to make Roman Catholics their fellows in the effort against the Reformed. Appeals were made to the Sorbonne and to Lutherans in the Low Countries, and the services of the cardinal of Lorraine were engaged by Christopher, duke of Montbéliard, in an attempt to force French Reformed to sign first the Württemberg Confession and then the Augsburg Confession.[3]

In 1567, however, the princes themselves grew weary of the constant polemics over the Lord's Supper. Christopher, duke of Württemberg, Charles, margrave of Baden, and Frederick, elector of the Palatinate, were led by William IV, landgrave of Hesse, who maintained that the question at stake was not *what* was present, but rather the *mode* of presence, and since that mode was essentially a mystery hidden in God, it did no good to try to define it. The princes therefore imposed silence on their theologians and ordered them no longer to preach or publish on the subject. The silence was observed during most of 1567 except by Flacius Illyricus who tried to stir up the Roman Catholics of the Lowlands against the Reformed there. Due to his continual attacks, the quarrels flamed up again in 1568.[4]

The reaction of the Swiss to political maneuvers in the empire was to solicit confessional statements from the Reformed churches of France, the Lowlands, Poland, England, and Scotland. Beza himself translated the French Confession into Latin and wrote his *De pace ecclesiastica* as a response of the Swiss churches. Bullinger was equally active internationally, and his confession was preferred to Beza's statement and became the Second Helvetic Confession.[5] These efforts bore fruit since it seems likely that the pressure thus brought to bear upon Emperor Maximillian probably averted the dreaded condemnation of Frederick III.

---

2. Walter Holweg, *Der Augsburger Reichstag von 1566 und seine Bedeutung für die Entstehung der Reformierten Kirche und ihres Bekenntnisses* (Neukirch: Neukirchener Verlag des Erziehungsvereins GmbH), 1964.

3. Beza, *Corr.* V, 1564, 40–41. *Registres de la Compagnie des Pasteurs de Genève* III, 1565–74, ed. Fatio and Labarthe, (Geneva: Librairie Droz, 1969), 194–96; hereafter cited as *Reg.* and volume number.

4. *Corr.* VIII, 129–31, 135–37, 194; and *Reg.* III, 227–30.

5. Hollweg, *Augsburger Reichstag,* pp. 148–236.

The collection of confessions thus begun became the basis of the French and Swiss response to the Formula of Concord. After considering the confessions requested of and prepared by Zanchius, the effort to gather all of the Reformed under one confession was scrapped in favor of the *Harmonia confessionum fidei* prepared by François Salvard.[6] The difference between the international community of Reformed churches and the Lutheran churches of the empire is evident in the two documents and their use. The Formula of Concord had two primary goals: the unification of the Lutheran churches, split into three mutually recriminating groups, and the eradication of the "heresy" of the Calvinist "sect." The Formula effected the first goal and then was used to try to bring about the second by compelling Reformed ministers in the empire to sign it.

The goal of the *Harmonia confessionum fidei* was simply to demonstrate the solidarity and orthodoxy of the Reformed churches while allowing minor points of difference to remain unresolved. The opposing attitudes are evident at the Colloquy of Montbéliard in 1586 when Beza insisted that he spoke only as an individual theologian while Jacob Andreae claimed to be the spokesman for all Lutheran churches which were equivalent, in Andreae's mind, to all orthodox churches.

Since Andreae drew heavily on the Formula of Concord in his debates with Beza at Montbéliard, the colloquy provides an excellent locus for examining both the application of the Formula and the response of the acknowledged leader of the French Reformed churches.[7] To express condemnation of the "Zwinglians," "Calvinists," and "Sacramentarians" in the Formula, Chemnitz and Andreae singled out three major areas: the Lord's Supper, the Person of Christ, and eternal election.

To understand the background of the colloquy it is useful to begin with the influx of French Reformed exiles following the St. Bartholomew's Day Massacre in 1572. Having fled from the carnage of France for the sake of their faith, these refugees streamed into Montbéliard, a Reformed area since 1535 when Farel sent Pierre Toussain to take his place there. Toussain had been superintendent of the Montbéliard church until 1571 when Andreae complained of his lack of cooperation in gaining the ministers of Montbéliard to sign the Augsburg Confes-

6. *Reg.* IV, 99–100, 366–71.
7. See my forthcoming book *The Colloquy of Montbéliard, 1586: Paradigm of Late Reformation Patterns and Problems.*

sion and other doctrinal statements, including the Württemberg Church Order and Confession of Faith. Now the refugees were confronted with the choice of giving up their confession and liturgy and conforming to the Lutheran order or of moving on. The "Lutheranizers" and their duke, Ulrich of Württemberg, went so far as to forward Charles IX's demands of extradition to Montbéliard where the sturdy bourgeoisie promptly conferred citizenship on the harried French, placing them beyond Charles IX's power. But the situation was no better in 1577; in fact, the ducal theologians were now armed with cannon of greater caliber. The ministers of Montbéliard were required to sign the Formula of Concord. This raised serious problems for the Reformed who were forbidden to receive the sacraments according to their own liturgy and its language. As had other conclaves of Reformed in Lutheran territories, the Montbéliard refugees wrote to Beza to ask what to do, since, in their opinion, the sacramental and christo-logical doctrine of the Formula was contrary to the Augsburg Confession as they understood it.[8] Nor did they wish their children to be baptized according to a rite which included a "papist" exorcism.

But most critical to the citizens of Montbéliard was their predicament with regard to the Lord's Supper. So acute had this become that they sought a colloquy at which the problem could be resolved. They did not know that this played into the hands of Andreae, who was sure that the young count Frederick, now free of the tutelage of his uncle Christopher, although still a vassal of Christopher's successor Ulrich, could be persuaded to support the Württemberg effort to introduce its variety of Lutheranism.

The colloquy was called for March of 1586 at Frederick's castle. The principal subjects of debate were the Lord's Supper and the Person of Christ, and it was these that Beza and his colleagues had come prepared to discuss. But Andreae and Count Frederick had a broader agenda which included the use of "papist" churches, images, music, and feast days plus the doctrines of baptism and predestination. In reading the protocols published successively in Tübingen and Geneva, one is struck in both by the desire for concilation on the part of Beza and the intransigence of Andreae. Where Beza was willing to agree on the broad lines of evangelical doctrine, leaving the churches free to determine applications and even lesser doctrinal issues, Andreae held out to the end for a complete capitulation on the part of the Reformed to the

8. *Reg.* IV, 101, 110, 309–48.

Württemberg position. He even refused the hand of brotherhood to Beza at the close of the conference.[9] His attitude was even more plainly evident in the last of his résumés of the colloquy, the *Kurzer Begriff* of 1588, while Beza's *De controversiis* of 1593 returned to a pacific, conciliatory tone.[10]

Before we proceed to the theses, the opening remarks require comment. One of the principal problems of this period is the understanding of the declared principle of *sola scriptura.* Both colloquists claim that the Word of God is the sole norm. But by 1586 the major confessions had been promulgated: in 1559, the French Confession, ratified at La Rochelle in 1571, the Second Helvetic Confession in 1566, and the *Book of Concord* in 1580. Each church considered its confession to be drawn from, and to be the correct interpretation of, the Word of God. Both groups of theologians accepted the councils of the first five centuries as true to the Word of God and appealed to them and to their own confessional statements in confirmation of an increasingly important claim: orthodoxy.

The Lord's Supper

The first four theses of the Württembergers present points about which they find no controversy. These are followed by the controversial theses and the Reformed points considered to be contrary to Scripture. The "noncontroversial theses" begin with the declaration that all the faithful, even apart from the liturgy, eat the flesh of the Son of Man spiritually, by faith, unto salvation, as John 6 makes clear. But the eating of the sacrament of the Lord's Supper is another kind of eating and is not always salutary since, when it is taken unworthily, it is judgment. Andreae concludes that, although the two eatings are not the same, spiritual eating is necessary if sacramental eating is to be salutary. Both sides agree that Capernaitic eating of the flesh is a damnable doctrine. Both likewise condemn transubstantiation. Finally the Lutherans, as well as the Reformed, deny that the presence of the body and blood of Christ is physical, local, or inclusive.

The first of the controversial theses deals with the real presence of

9. Probably recalling Luther's attitude toward Zwingli at Marburg.

10. For a bibliography of Beza's works on Montbéliard see Frédéric Gardy, *Bibliographie des oeuvres théologiques, littéraires, historiques et juridiques de Théodore de Bèze* (Geneva: Librairie E. Droz, 1960), pp. 197–99; *De controversiis,* pp. 211–12. Andreae's work is *Kurtzer Bergriff der Mumpelgartischen Colloquii* . . . (Tübingen: Gruppenbach, 1588).

the body and blood of Christ. Supporting this doctrine is a thesis approving the terms "in, with, under the bread" and "substantially, corporally, really, essentially, orally" as descriptive of the mode of presence, and another thesis declaring the literal interpretation of the Words of Institution. The second major concern is with the Person of Christ to whom is ascribed omnipotence so that *quod vellit, possit*: since he wished to give himself to be eaten, he did so. Finally, the Württembergers teach that since the mode of Christ's presence is not expressed in Scripture, it must simply be taken as supernatural and incomprehensible to human reason, and is therefore beyond disputation. But it is clear, they argue, that God can find many ways to make the body and blood of Christ everywhere available other than by the natural and physical mode which is the only mode understood by human reason.

When the Swiss received these written points, they went off to draw up their own theses and to draft replies to the Württembergers. Their theses do not follow the pattern of Andreae's theses, but rather the pattern established in Beza's *Confessio fidei* at Poissy and retained in the 1593 *De controversiis*: 1) the signs, 2) the signified, 3) the conjunction of the signs and the signified, 4) the reception of the signified, 5) the effects of communion, 6) the causes of the salutary effects.[11]

1. *The Signs.* Beza begins by distinguishing two uses of the word sacrament. The narrower meaning refers to those things that our senses perceive, that is, the bread and wine. By virtue of the Lord's institution and commandment they are removed from common and natural use to a spiritual and sacred signification. This signification is not bare and empty, nor is it a mere remembering, but it really attains to God and what is signified is offered to our souls.

2. *The Signified.* The second thesis lists those things that are signified: the body and blood by the bread and wine; the passion by the breaking of bread and the pouring of wine.

3. *The Conjunction of the Signs and the Signified.* This is the heart of Beza's doctrine as he developed it out of Calvin's theology of the Lord's Supper and answered the difficult question of how Christ is present sacramentally. Since the body of Christ must remain circumscribed and localized, it requires a presence by habit or relation rather than by substance.

---

11. Cf. my *Eucharistic Theology of Theodore Beza* (Chambersburg: American Academy of Religion, 1972.)

Since sacraments by their narrower signification are signs, we put the sacramental conjunction in the mutual relation and habit of the signs and the things signified. These things which impinge upon the senses are, by Christ's ordination, taken from their common and natural use and are applied to signifying and offering to us sacred and divine realities.[12]

Beza then argues that the more one insists upon the truth of the body of Christ, the more one must give up the notion of consubstantiation. The rest of Beza's argument on this point deals with the localization of Christ's body in heaven according to the account of the ascension and the return of Christ on the last day.

4. *The Reception of the Signified.* Beza explains the reception of the signs and the signified through the analogy of eating ordinary food. The end of eating is to nourish the body. But the end of sacramental eating is to nourish the soul, to establish a spiritual union between the soul and Christ. Therefore, just as the mouth of the body eats physical food, so the mouth of the soul eats spiritual food. This is the basis of what Beza calls sacramental metonymy whereby earthly elements signify heavenly realities which are offered to the soul and are truly received through the instrument of faith by the power of the Holy Spirit.

5. *The Effects of Communion.* Beza says that the Lord's Supper was not instituted for the sake of bread and wine, but for the salvation of men. The mystery lies in the union of Christ and the faithful, not in the supposed union of the body of Christ with the bread. Through the sacrament, which both requires and confirms penitence and faith, a spiritual conjunction with Christ is deepened and strengthened through which Christ gives all his gifts and benefits to the faithful. The Holy Spirit, the bond of charity, effects this mystical union so that Christ is head of the members of this body united to him and is the source of their increasing unity and spiritual growth into eternal life. The second effect is the condemnation of the unworthy, that is, of those who, through ignorance of this mystery or through unbelief and impenitence, eat condemnation, not from the Supper itself, but from contempt for it.

6. *The Causes of the Salutary Effects.* These are first the Holy Spirit, who effects our union with Christ, a union St. Paul calls a great mystery. All of this comes through the life, suffering, death, resurrection, and ascension of Christ in whom we believe. The instru-

---

12. Jacob Andreae, *Acta Colloquii Montis Belligartensis* . . . (Tübingen: Gruppenbach, 1587), p. 22.

mental causes are the minister doing as Christ commanded, the Words of Institution, the signs themselves, and the sacramental rites. Faith is the principal instrumental cause which is given by God himself. None of these instruments, however, have any intrinsic efficient power apart from the working of the Spirt and the command of Christ.

To the theses of Andreae, Beza poses, among others, the following antitheses. The Lutherans, he claims, destroy the humanity of Christ by insisting on the communication of idioms between the natures of Christ so that his humanity is endowed with the properties of his divinity. The Reformed do not deny, however, that Christ, as Logos, enjoys all the divine properties or that this man who is God may not also be said to be omnipresent and omniscient. But the Reformed assert that the human nature of Christ is bound by the limitations common to all bodily creatures. Since Beza claims that omnipotence is proper to God alone and cannot be given wholly or partially to creatures, it cannot be given to the created humanity of Christ.

The ensuing debate clarifies the positions of the disputants without bringing them closer to one another. At the heart of their differences is the problem of the *communicatio idiomatum,* and so the colloquists turn to the doctrine of the Person of Christ without having agreed upon the Lord's Supper. Neither of the disputants tries to make use of an important area of common ground, that is, the insistence of each upon a "sacramental presence." Beza simply affirms that, given the doctrine of ubiquity, the presence of Christ's body had to be local, while Andreae rejects the category of relation as a viable interpretative tool for understanding the sacramental presence.

The Person of Christ

The same format was followed in this discussion. The number of theses, however, reaches twenty-one. Four of these are considered *extra controversiam* by the Württembergers and assert basic christological doctrine. The controversy is whether there is a *real* communication between the divine and human natures in the Person of Christ on account of the personal union so that one nature communicates its properties to the other, and if so, how far does that communication extend?

The Lutherans extend that communication to omnipotence, omniscience, omnipresence, and the divine power of vivifying. They claim that the humanity is thereby exalted, not abolished. Andreae appeals to the two similies in the Solid Declaration, namely, the union of the body and soul and that of fire and iron. The body lives by virtue of the soul and iron burns by virtue of the fire, but neither body nor iron becomes soul or fire or is destroyed. The properties communicated to Christ's humanity are then explained as mutually inclusive. To be ubiquitous is to be omnipotent. Further, as Chemnitz had explained, Christ's humanity possessed divine majesty and its attributes from the womb. But he did not utilize them except in performing miracles. Rather, Christ emptied himself, taking the form of a servant until this exaltation. Beza, of course, objects to this reading of Philippians 2, asserting that the "form of a servant" refers to the human nature itself, not to the hiding of majesty only, so that Christ will never put aside the form of a servant even in glory.

Because Christ had the power to be ubiquitous from the womb, continue the Lutherans, he was present to the elect and to his church. But the mode of this presence is not expressed in Scripture. It is supernatural and neither local nor physical. More, affirms Andreae, we cannot say. Christ's exinanition, however, did not detract from his majesty since he governed heaven and earth through his assumed humanity which is what it means to be seated at the right hand of the Father. Another point of dispute is the Lutheran thesis that God suffered for us, although the divinity neither suffered nor died. But unless the Son of God poured out his blood for us, we would not be redeemed. Jesus Christ is, therefore, our redeemer and is to be adored. The series of Lutheran theses ends on the reiteration of Christ's presence in the Lord's Supper and indeed to the whole church.

In his response to thesis four, Beza raises a critical question as Andreae recognizes in his *marginalia.* Beza agrees to the thesis which, he claims, proves the Reformed point that the grace of union, by which this man is God, produces "habitual grace" which is a created gift. That, comments Andreae, is just what is being disputed: the nature of the grace of union and the created or uncreated nature of the gifts which accompany it.

The gist of Beza's objection to thesis five is that the *communicatio idiomatum* occurs only through the Person of Christ, that is, *in concreto,* and not from nature to nature or *in abstracto.* One can say that Jesus is God, but one cannot say that the humanity is the divinity. Therefore, the properties of the humanity and the divinity cannot be truly said of each other.

From thesis eight on, Beza simply disagrees. The human nature cannot be said to be ubiquitous, even nominally. The Reformed argument is simply that to attribute divine properties to the human nature which, as bodied, is essentially located and circumscribed, is to destroy that human nature.

Beza attacks the similies of body/soul and iron/fire as containing as many differences as likenesses. For example, Christ has two wills, one divine, one human, while the embodied soul has only one. The only way the divine properties can be said of the humanity is *kat' 'àllo* or with reference to the concrete person Christ, not to his humanity alone. Beza then quotes Cyril, Gregory of Nyssa, and Damascene on the raising of Lazarus: the divinity raised him; the humanity wept.

So Christ's knowledge, both in time and in glory, is a created gift, not the communication of a divine property. Nor did Christ put off the form of a servant, that is, his humanity, in glory. He shed only his humbled state to ascend above the angels.

Beza admits that Christ's flesh vivifies, but he denies that it is by the power of the divinity. Rather his flesh vivifies through his passion and death. We must receive it, therefore, spiritually by faith in order to eat eternal life. So Andreae reports Beza's response in the *Acta*. But to understand this rather enigmatic statement, one must turn to Beza's *Response*. Here he explains not only this thesis, but in doing so, clearly sets forth the Reformed doctrine of the *communicatio idiomatum*.

Beza begins by affirming that only God can give life and that this power is incommunicable. The flesh, as flesh, cannot give life, but the flesh of Christ is called vivifying and is truly so because it is the flesh of Christ who is God and man. It is also appropriately termed vivifying because, in his flesh, Christ abolished our death, having suffered and done in it and through it all that is required to obtain eternal life for us. Nor can we have eternal life in Jesus Christ except through this flesh which is communicated spiritually through faith. The effects of Christ's life and death belong to the person of Christ considered in his unity. Even though the natures and wills and actions of Christ remain distinct, nevertheless, one does not operate separately from the other. This is true as much because of the unity of the person considered in its totality as that this human nature served as the instrument of the Word.

Of course Beza insists that the body of Christ must remain circumscribed to remain truly human, and he specifically denies that "the form of a servant" is equivalent to the state of exinanition so that both were put off when Christ entered into glory. Rather, Christ reigns in heaven in both natures. Finally, Beza denies that Christ is present in the Lord's Supper by reason of the hypostatic union. He is present by sacramental institution. The body of Christ is in heaven as it was on earth, so we must eat by faith. Christ's person and power are present in the church, and in an inscrutable mystery, in word and sacrament, we eat his most true and most efficacious flesh.

Thus both Andreae and Beza end on the mutually agreeable note of an essential mystery at the heart of the Lord's Supper. But this agreement is lost in the argument itself which is not summarized in the *Acta.* Beza, however, does summarize the points of agreement and disagreement. The points of agreement are less interesting than those which Beza finds still controversial. The first of these points deals with the *communicatio idiomatum.* The Württembergers think that, because of the personal union, one can predicate the properties of the two natures of one another *in abstracto* as well as *in concreto.* The Reformed, however, teach that one cannot say that this humanity is divinity although one can say that this man is God. Further, the Württembergers deny that the exchange of properties is fully mutual since the humanity receives all the divinity but bestows nothing upon it. The Reformed affirm that, speaking concretely, the interchange is mutual; thus God died for us, and Jesus Christ is all-powerful, and so forth. But there is no traffic between the natures themselves apart from the reality of this man Christ who is the Son of God. Further, the Württembergers make no distinction between adoration of the divinity and of the humanity. The Reformed adore Christ because he is the Son of God, but they do not adore his humanity *per se.*

The last discussion which can be properly considered a response to the Formula is that on predestination. In the first edition of his *Response,* Beza was content to publish detailed answers regarding the Lord's Supper and the Person of Christ, concluding the book with an "Extract from Martin Luther's Book on Free Choice against Erasmus." Since this did not suffice against Andreae's attack on Beza's *Response,* in 1588 Beza published his *Pars altera . . .* which contains his side of the colloquy concerning the questions of church adornment and music, baptism and predestination.

Baptism

Baptism prepared the way for the discussion on predestination because the Reformed doctrine of baptism really rested on it. In harmony with their doctrine of the Lord's Supper, the Reformed taught that the administration of the sacrament is a sign of Christ's presence and of the operation of the Holy Spirit which may take effect at any time that one hears the Word and heeds it. But the rite has no efficacy *in itself*. The Lutherans objected most to the dependence of the efficacy of the sacrament on the gift of faith which might be given at any time during life. Ultimately, this gift depended upon the election of the baptized. It was, therefore, theoretically possible for a baptized infant to be among the reprobate and never to receive the gift of faith or to enjoy the effects of baptism. Beza objected that this was "probably" never the case. With the Reformed doctrine there was also a peculiar doctrine of sin. Once faith had been given, it became impossible for the faithful one to fall into mortal sin since then the Holy Spirit would be withdrawn. But God's gifts are without repentance, hence the Spirit is given definitively. This doctrine led to a lively interchange on the subject of David's sin. Beza exclaimed that it was blasphemous to assert that the Holy Spirit could be "sent away" by the actions of the elect. Rather, the Holy Spirit remained with David even in his adultery, as is proved by David's repentance. Andreae found the association of the Holy Spirit with adultery to be blasphemous.

The last major dispute on baptism was with regard to emergency baptism by midwives. Since election did not depend upon baptism, Beza denied its absolute necessity and found the usurpation of the minister's office by a woman to be not only abhorrent, but contrary to God's law. Andreae, on the other hand, insisted on the necessity of baptism and therefore of the emergency baptism by midwives. This issue had immediate practical consequences, since the Reformed women of Montbéliard sometimes traveled to Basel for their lying-in to assure that their children would be properly baptized by a Reformed minister in a rite that did not include exorcism, to which they objected as a "papist" ceremony but which the Lutheran ritual included. The basis of the Reformed-Lutheran argument on baptism, however, was the Reformed belief that salvation depended upon election which baptism could neither effect nor assure.

Predestination

Beza was neither prepared nor willing to debate predestination publicly. He believed such a procedure would only confuse the auditors. Besides, he objected, he had understood that the colloquy was to be on the Lord's Supper and the Person of Christ. He had not, therefore, prepared to debate predestination nor had he brought materials from which he might prepare an argument on the subject. But Andreae and Count Frederick won on this point and the discussion now turned to predestination.

The Formula of Concord dealt specifically with the subject of eternal election. In consonance with that article the Württembergers rejected any decree of reprobation; rather they taught that from eternity God loved all and each in Christ and wished everyone to be saved. Those who perished owed their damnation to their own neglect of God's call.

The Reformed also taught that those who perished owed their loss to their own corruption and its fruits. But this does not prevent God, who is free from any human influence, to decree that these same shall be left in their native corruption and be damned for their sins.

This thesis on reprobation and that on baptism told heavily against the Swiss theologians. While the French refugees confessed this doctrine, the Montbéliard ministers and citizens had sided with Basel which had given shelter to Castellio when he challenged Calvin and Beza in the 1550s. Pierre Toussain had never agreed to the Genevan doctrine of predestination but had rather sided with Bern, which had once decreed that the issue should not be publically debated and eventually released Beza and Viret because they continued to defend Calvin's doctrine. It was for that reason that Toussain drew many of his ministers from Neuchâtel rather than from Geneva.[13]

While the Montbéliard citizens and ministers were not happy with the outcome of this colloquy, I think it must be admitted that the "unscheduled" articles hurt the Reformed cause. Frederick was clearly convinced of the Württembergers' theses on baptism and predestination. In harmony now with his duke, Ulrich of Württemberg, Frederick assisted the Lutheran theologians to impose the Württemberg Church Order and its theology on Montbéliard. The French refugees were welcome at the Lutheran communion table, but only on condition that they, in effect, become Lutherans. Or, should they remain obstinate, they might abstain from this sacrament. But then, according to the Peace of Augsburg, they would place themselves outside the protection of the law. This harsh mandate, imposing as it did upon the practical life of the people, eventually gained the territory to the prince's religion. After a long and bitter struggle, the bourgeoisie of Montbéliard were brought into conformity with the dictum of the empire: *cuius regio eius religio.*

13. See John Viénot, *Histoire de la Réforme dans le Pays de Montbéliard depuis les origines jusqu'à la mort de Pierre Toussain, 1524–1573* (Paris: Librairie Fischbacher, 1900).

12

The Catholic Rejoinder

James J. Megivern

The late sixteenth century in Europe was a time of escalating hostility, widespread confusion, and wholesale frustration in things ecclesiastical and political. It was an era of controversy when what Melanchthon called "theological rabies" may well have reached its all-time peak. This may explain in part why it has not been a particularly popular area of research, at least among Catholics. But nonetheless it must be dealt with, and the four hundredth anniversary of the Formula of Concord is a good occasion for attempting a brief overview.

When the Council of Trent closed in 1563, the scene was set for a widespread Catholic revival that was spearheaded by the Jesuits and that profited from the growing squabbles among Lutherans.[1] That council signified the Roman adoption of a basically uniform theology that eliminated the problems inherent in pluralism. In this sense, "the history of the Counter-Reformation is in part the history of the triumph of the conservatives and the militant over the conciliatory and the liberal."[2] This made tactical sense, since a single position is more easily defended than a plurality of alternatives, even though the latter represents the healthier (and more traditional) condition for Christian theology.

This changed situation may well explain why the Formula of Concord did not receive nearly so much attention from Catholic polemicists as had the Augsburg Confession. The battlefield had been narrowed and the earlier insecurity of Roman spokesmen gave way to a new confidence gained from the work of Trent. The disarray in Lutheran ranks was capitalized on and made fun of, and contrasted to the growing cohesion of a Catholic united front.

1. Cf. B. J. Kidd, *The Counter-Reformation* (London: SPCK, 1933), pp. 233–62.
2. Owen Chadwick, *The Reformation* (Baltimore: Penguin Books, 1964), p. 267.

That is not to say, however, that the appearance of the Formula of Concord, as part of the *Book of Concord,* went unnoticed. In fact, it was the bishop of Trent, Louis Cardinal Madruzzo, who wrote to Rome on May 29, 1582, expressing the conviction that the *Book of Concord* ought to be refuted rather than ignored.[3] Ptolemaeus Cardinal Comensis took up the issue directly with Pope Gregory XIII, who was in entire agreement with the suggestion. Strategy, however, was a key concern, and the pope felt it would be better for the refutation to be done by a German in Germany "lest the heretics detract from the work, as is their custom, by saying that it was done in our house and in our style." So Comensis wrote back to Madruzzo on June 16, pondering possible candidates for the job, mentioning three: Peter Canisius, George Eder, and Nicholas Elgard. These were simply suggested, as it were, to get Madruzzo thinking, since he was in a better position than the pope to judge who might be qualified; "perhaps there is some other able man from the German College whom you could call upon." The three suggested were not very likely candidates at that time. As Madruzzo replied in his letter of August 12, "Eder is in Vienna, Elgard in Erfurt, and Canisius in Fribourg in Switzerland." Within a year Elgard was dead, while Eder and Canisius were both well past their prime and already overburdened with other important work. So, Madruzzo's idea of a more or less officially sponsored rebuttal of the Concordia seems to have gone no further, lost perhaps in the face of what were perceived to be more important matters as Rome rallied its forces.

Yet it is interesting to note that well before this exchange of letters an attempted rebuttal of the *Book of Concord* was already in print. It was by a German Catholic who had recently become an auxiliary bishop. Published in Ingolstadt in 1581, this work of the irrepressible Johann Nas bears the title: *Examen Chartaceae Lutheranorum Concordiae, das ist, die Aussmusterung und Widerlegung dess Nagelneugeschmidten Concordibuchs.* Whether Madruzzo ever knew of the existence of this book is uncertain, but it probably would not have made any difference. It is a perfect example of the worst kind of controversialist literature, what might be termed "snake-pit" theology. Yet, such tirades were all too often standard fare on all sides in this period. Where learning left off, invective and abuse began,

---

3. For the following account cf. Otto Braunsberger, ed., *B. Petri Canisii Epistulae et Acta* (Freiburg: Herder, 1923), 8:552.

and in Nas's case that was right at the start. With little theology and less comprehension he had played the game of church politics, capitalizing on his oratorical ability to win him a following. The two special objects of his hatred were Lutherans and Jesuits, and with equal ease he could assign the origin of either group to diabolical sources. His harangue against the *Book of Concord* is thus hardly worthy of notice, except perhaps to show how the dark underside of the religious conflict proceeded at the time. If this were the only record to survive, one would be forced to conclude that Luther and Rome had absolutely nothing in common, differing on the understanding of virtually everything.

A few passages of his attack will be given, if only to show the level of discourse. After referring to the "Augsburg Confusion" as the pestilence of Europe, Nas notes that Luther's followers today want to offer the world a "paper-concordia" because they cannot find any true, living one, "for the world cannot give the peace and concord which God gives, so the authors are working in vain. This *Book of Concord* is nothing but an expressly declared rupture, schism, cleavage, and heresy in the things of faith from all nations, tongues, and lands, a separation from the Roman Empire, from his royal majesty the Catholic king of Spain, from the most Christian king of France, etc."[4]

Nas is especially irked by the reverential tone in which Luther is treated in the *Book,* something that provokes his bitterest sarcasm: "Luther enlightened the Empire the way that Sergius the Apostle enlightened Greece, putting the creed of Mohammed together with the Old and New Testaments in a Book of Concord called the Koran, which all the Turkish rulers, all the Persians and Tartars signed and became one. Ergo."

Moreover, Nas sees the inclusion of the three Creeds "stolen from the Catholics" as a mere ploy to fool the reader into thinking that what follows is of the same worth and authority.

That works like this should appear in the midst of such bitterness and emotion is understandable, even inevitable, but to find them institutionalized by being guaranteed a captive readership is cause for greater grief. For instance, in the Constitutions and Decrees of the diocese of Regensburg for 1558 the list of books which rectors of

---

4. Nas, *Examen*, p. 18. The following two quotations are from pages 33 and 83, respectively.

churches were directed to purchase includes "the homilies of John Nas."[5]

Surely there were better Catholic theologians around than Nas. But, for the most part, they did not seem to share Madruzzo's concern about refuting the *Book of Concord*. Let us explore a few who might have been expected to undertake a refutation. One obvious possibility was Gregory of Valencia.[6]

Although of Spanish origin, this able Jesuit studied in Rome and spent most of his teaching career in Germany. He arrived there in 1575, the same year that the *Summa Theologica* of Thomas Aquinas replaced the *Sentences* of Peter Lombard as the basic text for theology at the University of Ingolstadt. His approach is best seen in his most important work, *Analysis of the Catholic Faith,* of 1585, where the emphasis is on the theme used increasingly by post-Tridentine Catholic polemicists: the absolute necessity of an infallible teaching authority to determine the one truth from among so many conflicting opinions demonstrated by those who had broken from Rome. When the Lutheran theologian James Heerbrand unleashed a particularly vicious attack on his Catholic opponents, whom he declared to be devils who ought to be executed, Valencia responded in kind in 1579. The more levelheaded and kindhearted Peter Canisius expressed his concern in a letter to the Jesuit general, Eberhard Mercurian, observing that in this affair "Gregory the Spaniard exceeds the bounds of discretion which befits our theologians. Soon, I fear, he will be embarking on a third defensive pamphlet in order to refute this abusive and extraordinarily quarrelsome antagonist. What real benefit accrues to our Society or general readers from this kind of word-fighting, I cannot understand."[7]

In this atmosphere, despite the ability of Valencia, he was hardly the man to attempt an objective evaluation of the Formula of Concord. Eucharistic doctrine was an area of special concern to him, and in 1582 he published his *Disputation against the fundamentals of two sects,*

---

5. Cf. Hermann Scholl, S.J., ed., *Concilia Germaniae* (Cologne, 1767), 7:1057, 1071–72.

6. Cf. Johannes Janssen, *History of the German People at the Close of the Middle Ages,* trans. A. M. Christie (New York: AMS Press, 1966), 14:329ff.; A. & A. de Backer and C. Sommervogel, *Bibliothèque de la Compagnie de Jésus* (Brussels: J. Schepens, 1898), 8:388–99.

7. Janssen, *History of the German People,* 10:159–60. Even in his more serious work he cannot refrain from such excess. See, e.g., in *Commentariorum Theologicorum Tomus Quartus* (Venice, 1600), p. 112, where, in his discussion of Jacob Andreae's teaching of the ubiquity of Christ's body, he remarks that Andreae learned the doctrine from his "not so much Doctor as Seductor Luther."

the ubiquitarians and the sacramentarians, on the real presence of Christ. The work provoked a refutation by Andreae within a year.

A likelier candidate, one of the ablest Catholic theologians of the time, was the Englishman Thomas Stapleton. To associate him particularly with the Formula of Concord, however, is difficult. For one thing, he was more concerned with the problem of Calvinism, since this had become much more of a threat in England than Lutheranism.[8] Yet from his vantage point, first at Douai then at Louvain, he was well aware of both movements, and any complete study of the theological issues of this time would certainly have to take into account his four-volume work of 1582 on the doctrine of justification. The third volume of this work is entirely against Martin Chemnitz's evaluation of the teaching of the Council of Trent, but Stapleton does not deal directly with the Formula.[9]

Another prospect who could be looked at is the well-traveled Jesuit diplomat, Antonio Possevino.[10] Pope Gregory XIII had sent him as his personal representative to King John III of Sweden in 1577 after John had expressed a desire to become a Catholic. Subsequently he was papal legate to Russia and then nuncio to Poland. But in 1587 he was assigned to teach theology at the University of Padua, where Francis de Sales was his most famous student. Possevino was well read in the controversialist literature of the day; he concluded his brief *Judgment of the Augsburg Confession* with an interesting list of earlier Catholic works attacking the Confession, extending from Cochlaeus to Bellarmine.[11] Originally published in 1586, this work of Possevino is much indebted to Cochlaeus, endlessly making light of the Augsburg Confession because of all the variations to which Melanchthon had subjected it. Fifty years may have passed meantime, but that was still the level on which Possevino continued the discussion.

In terms of chronology it is interesting to note that the publication of the *Book of Concord* coincided with a new phase in a particularly brilliant Jesuit academic career. In 1580 Francisco Suárez started teaching at the Roman College. He was only there for five years when he returned to his native Spain to spend the next thirty years

8. Cf. Marvin R. O'Connell, *Thomas Stapleton and the Counter Reformation* (New Haven: Yale University Press, 1964), pp. 54–55.

9. Ibid., p. 64.

10. Cf. L. Karttunen, *Antonio Possevino: Un Diplomate pontifical au XVIᵉ siècle* (Lausanne, 1908).

11. A. Possevino, *Judicium de Confessione Augustana* (Lugduni: J. B. Buysson, 1604), pp. 316ff. (in Woodstock Collection, Georgetown University Library).

teaching successively at Alcalá, Salamanca, and Coimbra, augmenting his reputation in each instance. Had he been sent to Ingolstadt instead, the Formula of Concord might have received a noteworthy Catholic response. As it was, his famous tract on *Grace,* published in the year of his death (1617), reveals his wide familiarity with Protestant positions. In chapter seven of the fifth prolegomenon, "On the Error of Luther, Calvin, and their followers concerning the Grace of God and Free Will," he goes after Melanchthon and Chemnitz as well, and in doing so quotes Stapleton several times in support of his contentions.[12]

This does not exhaust the list of Catholic controversialists active in the 1580s who might have responded to the Formula of Concord.[13]

But even if there was no scarcity of literary activity among Catholics, especially Jesuits, in the decade following the appearance of the *Book of Concord,* the theological quality of much of it was debatable, to say the least. Over fifty years of quarreling and frustration in all attempts to come to an understanding of one another had taken its toll, and

12. F. Suárez, *Opera Omnia,* ed. C. Berton (Paris: L. Vives, 1857), 7:267ff.

13. Brief treatments of the men mentioned below may be found in Christian Gottlieb Jöcher, *Allgemeines Gelehrten Lexikon* (Hildesheim: G. Olms, 1961), vols. 1–4, as well as in Janssen and Sommervogel. First there was the Jesuit Francis Coster who published a *Handbook of Controversies* in 1585. Coster was a renowned teacher in Cologne and later wrote a special refutation of Lukas Osiander. Then there was an English Jesuit who studied in Rome and died in Poland in 1591, Laurent Arthur Faunt. He had published a work in 1586 attacking Lutheran and Calvinist eucharistic teachings. Also, William Lindanus (d. 1588) in 1585 published his *Concordia Discors,* which is possibly the next work after Nas's to deal explicitly with the Formula of Concord. (A work published in 1607 by the Swiss Protestant Rudolph Hospinian bears the same title and is an explicit attack on the Formula of Concord.) Other Jesuit writings, probably more in the "snake-pit" tradition, were Sigmund Ernhoffer's *Der evangelische Wetter-Han* of 1587 (first published anonymously as a "corrected" version of Luther's Small Catechism); George Scherer's *Der Lutherische Bettler Mantel* of 1588; and Nicolaus Serarius's *Oratio* against the Lutherans, also of 1588. One might examine the two Thyraeus brothers, Hermann and Peter, both Jesuit controversialists active in Germany at this time, and both responsible for several publications against Lutheranism. Hermann, who died as provincial of Mainz in 1591, is supposed to have compiled "6000 doubts and 2000 irregularities" gleaned from the Augsburg Confession, to which, therefore, he considered all Lutherans implicitly held. Peter, who died in Trier in 1601, published a *Theological Disputation concerning the Antichrist* in 1584, and a work *On the Sacrament of Confession* in 1585. Finally, mention could be made of the Jesuit Caspar Ulenberg. A convert from Lutheranism in 1572, he later wrote a *History of Lutherans* up to 1571. But in 1589 he published "22 Causes" for becoming or remaining Catholic. Cf. also, Bernhard Duhr, S.J., *Geschichte der Jesuiten in den Ländern deutscher Zunge* (Freiburg: Herder, 1907), vols. 1–2.

much of the so-called controversialist theology was little more than name-calling and the perpetuation of rumors and misunderstandings.

As the decade closed, however, the most famous and accomplished Catholic theologian of the day almost accidentally produced a short response. Robert Bellarmine did not write his *Judgment of the Book of Concord* for publication.[14] This outstanding Jesuit theologian was in the midst of producing his famous *Disputations* (1586–93), which provided him with the opportunity of approaching the whole spectrum of Protestant thought on his own grounds, using his own methodology, elaborating at appropriate length. But someone felt obligated to send him a copy of the Latin *Book of Concord* the year after it was published and asked him to evaluate it. Bellarmine was at this time at the height of his teaching career, having spent six years at Louvain (1570–76) before returning to Rome for his most productive period. Owen Chadwick has remarked that "the Counter-Reformation lost the slickness and abusiveness which betrayed a sense of insecurity, and displayed in Bellarmine its recovery of assurance."[15]

When Bellarmine sent his *Judgment of the Book of Concord* to Germany in 1589, it was not long before the book found its way into print in Ingolstadt, but the Jesuit Peter Hanson also put out a German paraphrase of it with the provocative title: *Entdeckung der Thorheit in dem Concordibuch*. The work is really only a pamphlet, but since it apparently was the closest thing to an official Roman response that the *Book of Concord* ever received, it may be worth taking a rather detailed look at it.[16] In the first part Bellarmine dwells briefly upon the lack of significance in the whole business of gathering signatures for the Concordia. What, he asks, was this supposed to prove? Jacob Andreae succeeds in getting some eight thousand Germans to sign it, most of them people with no special credentials in theology. If that were the way to play the game, imagine what the Catholic Church could do, with vastly greater numbers all over the face of the globe, all

---

14. James Brodrick S.J., *The Life & Work of Blessed Robert Francis Cardinal Bellarmine SJ, 1542–1621* (London: Burns Oates & Washbourne, 1928), vols. 1–2. A one-volume abbreviation is called *Robert Bellarmine Saint & Scholar* (Westminster, Md.: Newman, 1961).

15. Owen Chadwick, *The Reformation* (The Pelican History of the Church: 3; Baltimore: Penguin Books, 1964), p. 305.

16. Robert Bellarmine, *Judicium de Libro Concordiae Lutheranorum (Ad Disputationes R. Bellarmini De Controversiis Christianae Fidei Additamenta et Opuscula Varia Polemica Tomi Quarti Pars II;* Naples: J. Giuliano, 1859), pp. 175–201.

nationalities and languages! His point is well made in a few paragraphs, then he drops it to go on to the main business at hand. His summary objection to the *Book of Concord* is that it contains at least "six grave errors and sixty-seven lies." In part two he examines the "errors" one by one, and in part three he takes up the "lies," one by one.

The third part, the "sixty-seven lies," it turns out, are not in the Formula of Concord. They are over half a century old, the first twenty-four occurring in the Augsburg Confession itself, and the other forty-three in Melanchthon's Apology of 1531, both of which are, of course, parts of the *Book of Concord*. So, as far as our present interest is concerned, it is only "the six grave errors" that call for attention, since they are all located in the Formula of Concord. Before examining them, it is interesting to note that all six turn out to be in the realm of Christology. The ablest spokesman for Rome thus takes issue with the Formula of Concord not over church authority, the use of the Bible, the nature of justification, the role of good works, the meaning of the eucharist, the number of the sacraments, or similar concerns that both before and after have usually been looked upon as the core of Lutheran-Catholic disagreement. Rather, he spends all his effort at trying to show that the Formula contains christological errors that are incompatible with the three ancient Christian Creeds included earlier in the very *Book of Concord*. Let us hear his objections:

"The first error is that Christ was obedient to the Father not only as man but also as God."[17] The reference where Bellarmine finds this error is the Epitome, Article III, first affirmative thesis.

> This error destroys completely the true divinity of Christ, which the Nicene Creed asserted against the Arians. For if Christ as God obeyed the Father, then certainly as God he is distinguished from the Father; so the Father is one God and the Son is another God; but there is only one true God. . . . Again, the one obeying is less than the one obeyed, for the superior commands, the inferior obeys; so, if Christ as God obeys the Father, he is as God less than the Father, and the Athanasian Creed is wrong in saying he is equal to the Father according to his divinity, less than the Father according to his humanity.

He goes on to identify the same position in two later passages of the Epitome, and then observes that this is no surprise, since the same error was made by Luther, by the Augsburg Confession, and by

17. Ibid., p. 175. The "errors" run from 175 to 179 in the above edition; the translation is my own, occasionally condensed for purposes of brevity.

Melanchthon, both in his Apology and in his *Loci Communes* of 1558.[18]

"The second error is that Christ performed his function of mediator and high priest not only through his human nature but also through his divine nature." The reference is to Article VIII of the Epitome. The same point is made as in the first, reducing the position to Arianism. "A mediator is necessarily distinguished from what he mediates. So Christ is mediator of God and men. Therefore, if he is mediator as God, he is as God distinguished from God; there will thus be two gods, one greater, the other lesser, as the Arians maintain." He then launches into citations and commentaries on the point drawn from both Augustine and the New Testament.

"The third error is that the human nature of Christ is really and truly present everywhere." The first reference is to Article VII, affirmative thesis five of the Epitome, which quotes directly from Luther. The controversy was an old one by this time, and its importance in part seems to have been (as is evidenced in the Antitheses that follow in the Epitome) that it provided an alternative explanation of Real Presence in the Lord's Supper without recourse to the excessively scholastic theory of transubstantiation. In any event, Bellarmine spends more time on this than on any of the other five "errors," and in fact proposes six arguments against it. First, the doctrine contradicts Scripture which clearly asserts that Christ by reason of his humanity was not everywhere. Secondly, it contradicts the articles of the Creed concerning his conception, birth, passion, death, descent to hell, resurrection from the dead, ascent to heaven, and descent for judgment. For, if he were everywhere, he would have been "not just in Mary's womb but in that of all women, indeed also in all men," etc. Thirdly, it destroys the truth of the Lord's Supper and, "which is remarkable, confirms the opinion of Zwingli, for the destruction of which it was concocted. For if the body of Christ is everywhere from its very conception, we have no need of the sacrament of his presence." Fourthly, it contradicts the Dresden decree of 1571 to which these same theologians had agreed. With more sarcasm than he usually allows himself, Bellarmine thereupon remarks, "Such is the constancy of the Saxon theologians." Fifthly, the doctrine contradicts the opinion of the principal author of the Augsburg Confession and its Apology, which are both part of this *Book of Concord*. And

18. Ibid., p. 176.

sixthly, it contradicts "Augustine and all the fathers." Bellarmine selects as an example letter 57 to Dardanus where

> he not only teaches that Christ's humanity is not everywhere, but also destroys the basic argument of the adversaries. For they think that it necessarily follows that Christ's humanity is everywhere, if it is joined personally to the Word which is undoubtedly everywhere. But Augustine says that the man Christ was on that day in the tomb according to the flesh, in hell according to the soul, but as God the same Christ was everywhere.

If that is not enough, "besides the example adduced by him, we have the famous example of the rational soul. For the head is united to the soul but certainly is not every place the soul is; for the soul is also in the feet, where the head definitely is not." It is curious how this argument over Christ's ubiquity so exercised the theologians of the day and then receded so completely into the background. We will make a few observations about this shortly.

"The fourth error is that many divine attributes, such as omnipotence, omniscience, omnipresence, and the divine majesty itself, have really and truly been conferred on the humanity of Christ." The reference here is to Article VIII of the Epitome, the eleventh affirmative thesis. "This error destroys the truth of Christ's humanity, renews the heresy of Eutyches, and contradicts the Creed. . . . An infinite attribute requires an infinite essence. Therefore, Christ's humanity is an infinite essence; and thus it is either transformed into divinity or there are two infinite beings." Nor will Bellarmine allow the claim that this is the patristic doctrine of the *"communicatio idiomatum."* For this doctrine "does not give to one nature what belongs to the other, but gives to the one person (*suppositum*) the attributes of each nature." References to Augustine, Ambrose, Cyril, and John Damascene follow; then he adds, "Moreover, the [patristic doctrine of] communication of attributes is mutual, applying no less to divinity than to humanity. But the adversaries attribute real communication of human properties to the divine nature." And once more appeal is made to the Dresden decree of the same Saxon theologians as rejecting the position maintained in the Epitome of the Formula.

"The fifth error is that the hypostatic union consists in the communication of divine attributes." After making the statement, Bellarmine softens it, saying that the authors of the Formula "seem" to be inconsistent in their language, sometimes committing the alleged error, other times not. Here he is clearly into the Solid Declaration, Article

VIII, quoting from paragraph twenty-two: "For this reason the ancient teachers of the church have combined both words, 'communion' and 'union,' in expounding this mystery and have explained the one through the other."[19] To which he exclaims:

> See how clearly they make the hypostatic union the same as the communion of properties. So when they say elsewhere that one follows from the other, they are either contradicting themselves openly or they understand the sequence to be merely logical, not real (*physica*), as we do. . . . But such an opinion entirely destroys the mystery of the incarnation. [For,] since the divine attributes are common to the entire Trinity . . . if the hypostatic union consists in their communication, it follows that all three persons are incarnate. . . . But according to the Catholic faith set forth by the ancient Councils, only the person of the Son is incarnate because the union took place through the communication of the proper subsistence of the Son himself. . . . So if the hypostatic union consists in the communication of attributes, it follows that Father, Son, and Holy Spirit are united hypostatically and are thus only one person. For the Father by generating the Son has communicated to him all his own attributes, and likewise the Father and the Son by producing the Holy Spirit have communicated to him all their attributes. Furthermore they [the Lutherans] would make the hypostatic union consist in the communication either of all the attributes or of only some of them. But if (it consists) of all, the hypostatic union would be impossible. For among the attributes of God, true eternity is included, the absence of beginning or end; but it is impossible for something created to lack a beginning, and it is at least certain that the humanity of Christ did not exist from eternity. By the same token it is proper to God to lack any beginning, but this can in no way be communicated to a creature. But if (it consists) of only some attributes, who can say which those are, since the reason for all is the same? For if you can have the hypostatic union without the communication of eternity, why can't you have it without the communication of omnipresence, or omnipotence? And finally, these attributes, since they cannot be essential to human nature, must be accidental; which is what the *Book of Concord* seems to assert when it explains this communication by the operation of the divinity through the humanity. . . . But that is the heresy of Nestorius, who united the Word to the humanity through operation, and this heresy was explicitly condemned by the fifth General Council.

Thus, Bellarmine found the errors of Arius, Eutyches, and Nestorius recurring in the Formula.

"The sixth error is that the whole Christ, God and man, descended

19. The translation is that of Theodore G. Tappert, *The Book of Concord* (Philadelphia: Fortress Press, 1959), p. 595.

into hell. This follows clearly from the third error and is, moreover, expressly asserted in the Concordia itself." He then quotes from Article IX of the Solid Declaration: "We simply believe that after the burial the entire person, God and man, descended into hell."[20] "But," says Bellarmine,

> this error conflicts with two or even three articles of the Creed, for it denies the death, burial, and resurrection of Christ. For if Christ as man descended to hell, one living, not dead, descended; for one who is dead is not a man, since by death every man ceases to be a man. But if Christ living descended from the cross and living arrived in hell, not only his soul descended but also his flesh: for the soul alone cannot be called a man. But if body and soul descended, what, I ask, rested in the tomb? And finally, if Christ was always man, and was never truly dead or buried, it is certainly also true that he never rose from the dead. For a man does not rise except when by new life he begins again to be a man, who through death ceased to be a man. And so, let these few things about the errors against the Creed suffice.

So ends the little work of Bellarmine in evaluation of the Book of Concord. Once it was published in Germany, it in turn became the chief object of attack by Lutheran theologians, and some ten years later, in 1599, the year he was created cardinal, Bellarmine wrote a *Brief Apologia,* replying especially to the refutation which "the entire Academy of Württemberg theologians" leveled against him.[21] Despite the all-out attack, he notes, "this booklet is, as I hear, still alive, indeed has not lost a single drop of blood," and if its author wanted "to waste his time on such nonsense, he could in ten days write ten other similar pamphlets on the vanity, errors, and lies of this refutation." He chooses, however, to write only a few pages to offset what he sees as the more outrageous points. It is interesting to see how often the accusation of novelty recurs in his attack. His opponents are "the new Arians"; they set forth "a new theology, a new philosophy, a new use of terms"; they embrace "a new definition of obedience"; they issue a challenge to all Jesuits to dispute on one condition: that Scripture alone be the judge, yet "I beseech them to cite one text from the entire Old or New Testament where Mary is designated the Mother of Christ *as God,* or where Christ *as God* obeyed the Father."[22] So their entire case collapses when Scripture is allowed to be the judge. As for the rest of their errors, "since they are similar to the above, I had no

---

20. Ibid., p. 610.
21. Printed immediately after his *Judicium,* it runs from pp. 202 to 207.
22. *Brevis Apologia,* p. 205.

intention of responding to the refutation, but only of showing that it is unworthy of a response."

There are obviously many observations that could be made about Bellarmine's work, but we will restrict ourselves to two. 1) What a far cry his work is from the snake-pit theology of the day! He elevates the discussion to a level of discourse that is much more in keeping with the dignity of what is under consideration, and refuses to stoop to the scurrilous name-calling that afflicted so many of his contemporaries, both Catholic and Protestant. 2) Yet, something is clearly wrong here. The arguments are serious, careful elaborations of christological points, made in line with the best scholastic tradition. And yet, certainly from a modern perspective, they prove too much, putting the worst possible interpretation on every turn of phrase, accusing Lutheranism of maintaining positions that were not really held, which in fact are often explicitly repudiated elsewhere in the same Formula. Perhaps such is the inevitable consequence of controversy, in which truth is the first casualty, and loss of sympathy guarantees misunderstandings. But four centuries later it is worth asking what really happened and how the balance sheet reads today.

Contemporary reappraisals stop short of Bellarmine's indictments. It must be kept in mind that he is the foremost representative of the post-Tridentine Roman theological stance, identifying a single tradition as the only valid one and thereby repudiating any kind of pluralism. Tactically that was a strong move, but, as Vatican II demonstrated, it did less than justice to the Catholic heritage. It excluded on principle any possibility that any other style of theologizing might actually be compatible with Christian faith, yet Luther certainly represented the advent of something new, something that caused difficulties in evaluation for many others besides Roman theologians.[23]

23. Cf., e.g., Paul Althaus, *The Theology of Martin Luther,* trans. Robert C. Schultz (Philadelphia: Fortress Press, 1966), pp. 191, 198: "Luther involved the deity in the humanity with a boldness previously unheard of in theology. . . . His dogmatic theory . . . is not unified within itself but displays contradictions. Theology had to go beyond it." See also, I. D. K. Siggins, *Martin Luther's Doctrine of Christ* (New Haven: Yale University Press, 1970), pp. 215, 216, 227. Sometimes Luther's language "is notoriously prone to Monophysite distortion," sometimes "the specter of Docetism raises its hoary head," "there is a constant risk of misinterpretation, because Luther does not argue in the traditional categories or in the traditional order. Taken out of context there are illustrations that suggest that Luther avoids neither Scylla nor Charybdis, but both separates the natures and confuses them. In context, however, it is possible to say that Luther's doctrine is quite orthodox. He is guilty not of heterodoxy but of failure to eliminate the anomalies which arise when old expressions are used within a new logical schema. . . . Luther's story here parallels that of the early Church."

The whole debate here between Bellarmine and the Formula of Concord, it has been noted, represents "a revival of the antithesis between Alexandrian and Antiochene Christology. . . ." The authors of the Formula "removed themselves from the Latin tradition and moved closer to the Alexandrian-inspired thinking of Greek orthodoxy."[24]

In the atmosphere of the day such a departure from the Antiochene-style scholastic Christology, which had become synonymous with orthodoxy in Rome, could only be perceived as heretical by one in Bellarmine's position. The very possibility of acknowledging the validity and respective merits of different kinds of Christology was precluded as long as polemics prevailed. It is only after the war that one can admit or even see that the enemy was not all wrong.

As we pass into the decade of the 1590s, Lutheran-Catholic hostility escalates. A sad series of events brought to the fore the most dreaded Catholic controversialist yet to appear, Johann Pistorius.[25] A Lutheran physician who had read deeply in theology and law as well as medicine, Pistorius in 1588, when he was in his early forties, had become a Catholic, asserting that the exhaustive study of Luther's works had led him to see Luther as a disturber rather than a reformer of the Christian church. In the following year he joined with the Jesuit Theodore Busaeus in a debate with the Württemberg theologians Jacob Andreae and Jacob Heerbrand at Baden at the request of Margrave James III of Baden-Hochberg, and it did not go well for the Lutherans. The influence of Pistorius was thus a large factor in Margrave James's embracing Catholicism the next year, shortly before his death. Thereupon his brother, Margrave Ernest Frederick, acted in a most unscrupulous manner, refusing to respect his dead brother's will. The subsequent bitterness of Pistorius toward his former coreligionists knew no bounds. In 1591 he published a pamphlet on the motives behind Margrave James's acceptance of the Catholic faith, and if this were taken as accurate, one would have to conclude that the Formula of Concord had failed totally. Pistorius paints a picture of a Lutheranism that "day by day splits up into more and more new sects . . . whole countries, towns, and villages have repeatedly changed their beliefs;

---

24. Wolfhart Pannenberg, *Jesus God and Man,* trans. L. L. Wilkins and D. Priebe (Philadelphia: Westminster Press, 1968), pp. 298 and 301. Cf. also, Wilhelm Maurer, *Von der Freiheit eines Christenmenschen* (Göttingen, 1949), chap. 1.
25. Janssen, *History of the German People,* 10:116ff.

none of the new churches agree entirely with Luther, and he himself altered his meaning continually."[26]

But this was only a first taste of what was yet to come. In 1595 his *Anatomy of Luther* appeared, and Catholic-Lutheran relations would never again be the same. It was one thing for an Italian Jesuit off in distant Rome to nitpick at the Formula of Concord, but it was an entirely different story for a German ex-Lutheran who knew Luther's works inside out to unleash a merciless attack that would make earlier insults pale by comparison. It is true that Pistorius was provoked by the 1593 work of Wilhelm Holder, *The Disembowelled Mouse,* which taunted Pistorius to look at the beam in the eye of Rome rather than the mote in Luther's eye. Up to then he had scruples, he says, about publicizing what he knew about Luther because he was "ashamed to write down things so disreputable, so indecent, and so distressing to many pious hearts." Lutherans Samuel Huber and Cyriacus Spangenberg both brought out replies in 1596, but neither was equal to the task; they flailed in all directions because of the total outrage provoked by Pistorius. The same year the Württemberg theologians decided to respond by trying another route, lowering their voices and admitting that Luther should perhaps be transferred from the realm of the major prophets to that of the minor prophets, since in some points, like polygamy and divorce, he had gone too far.[27]

The uproar was not yet over, for in 1598 Pistorius brought out the second part of his *Anatomy of Luther,* in which he claimed to extract no less than 103 heresies against the Holy Trinity from Luther's works. The next year he brought out the final volume and also published his *Wegweiser* treating the fourteen most important questions in dispute between Catholics and the Reformers. That Pistorius was talented and well-intentioned is true enough, but there is also no denying that he single-handedly drove the wedge between Lutheran and Catholic far deeper than it had been before. In that sense he virtually nullified the possibility of any further concern among Catholics for evaluating the Formula of Concord or anything else of Lutheran origin. Subsequent controversialists such as Konrad Vetter, with his

26. Ibid., p. 131.
27. Ibid., pp. 137 and 144.

abusive pamphlets of personal vilification of Luther, make that clear.[28] It is true that Jesuits James Gretser and Adam Tanner did not sink to such depths.[29] But, as Florimond Rémond, a Calvinist turned Catholic, demonstrates in his history of heresy at the turn of the century, the Formula of Concord was discussed by Catholics only as a subject of mockery and amusement.[30] The conditions for anything more serious had been annihilated.

The final figure in our survey foreshadows what would prevail for the future. Peter Pázmány is a most impressive leader on the early seventeeth century scene.[31] We simply note that in his most famous work (*Kalauz,* or *Hodegus,* 1613) his criticism of the Formula of Concord is similar in approach to Bellarmine's in that he finds it full of "contradictions and falsehoods." But the area of such objections shifts markedly from Christology into ecclesiology. This was Pázmány's trademark; the overwhelming concern was how to identify the one true church of Christ in the midst of the welter of conflicting claims, the path on which most would follow for the next three centuries.

The only warranted conclusion of our survey is to say that the Formula of Concord never did get a very serious Catholic review. If today enough has changed that the question can reasonably be entertained whether the Catholic Church might not recognize the Augsburg Confession,[32] would it be out of place to suggest that it might also be an appropriate time for a more serious, if belated, Catholic evaluation of the Formula of Concord on its four hundredth anniversary? Surely if Alexandria and Antioch can both be listened to by Rome for com-

28. Between 1594 and 1599 he published ten brief attacks on Luther and finally gathered all his insults together in *200 Luthers* of 1607. Cf. Janssen, *History of the German People,* 10:151.

29. Gretser, perhaps the most learned Jesuit of his day, mocks the *Book of Concord* in his *Labyrinths* of 1602; it is in his *Opera Omnia* (Regensburg: Lang, 1739), 13:435. Tanner with his *Anatomy of the Augsburg Confession* of 1613 became the foremost Catholic controversialist in Germany in that later decade.

30. F. Rémond, *L'Histoîre de la Naissance, Progrez et Decadence de l'heresie de ce siècle, divisée en huit livres* (Paris: C. Chastellain, 1610), p. 577.

31. Cf. Nicolaus Öry, S.J., *Doctrina Petri Cardinalis Pázmány de Notis Ecclesiae* (Cherii: Editrice "Fiamma del S. Cuore," 1952). The chief influences on his theology were Bellarmine, Suárez, Valencia, and Stapleton. His 1627 reply to Frederick Balduin's attack on him entitled *Dux Lutheristarum Errantium* is considered by Öry to be Pázmány's profoundest work.

32. Cf. Vinzenz Pfnür, "Anerkennung der Confessio Augustana durch die katholische Kirche?" *Internationale katholische Zeitschrift: "Communio,"* 4:4 (1975): 298–307. There is an English summary of Pfnür's article in *Theology Digest,* 24:1 (Spring 1976): 65–70.

plementary Christologies, might not Wittenberg as well as Trent have insight to offer in ecclesiology?[33]

33. Space does not allow for treatment of other minor figures, but mention could be made of George Amende, who wrote *Funiculus Triplex* in 1616; Martin Becanus, *Compendium Manualis Controversiarum huius temporis de Fide et Religione* (Duaci: B. Belleri, 1625); Adam Contzen and Peter Röstius, who both wrote in reaction against the celebrations of the centennial of Luther's Ninety-five Theses (1617), called by the latter *"Pseudo-Jubiläum."* Also Laurent Forer, a Swiss Jesuit, published a work in 1613 called *Quaestio Vexata*, asking, "Where was the Protestant Church before the Reformers?" And in 1618 Simon Felix, a German Jesuit, published a *Disputatio* on the question "Whether Saint Paul was a Lutheran?" As yet, no one has undertaken to gather these and others of a similar kind into any collective work, but it is an enterprise that could be pursued with profit.

My thanks to library personnel at Concordia Seminary and St. Louis University, as well as at the Folger Shakespeare and Georgetown University libraries, Washington, D.C. A special word of thanks to Dr. Robert Kolb of the Center for Reformation Research in St. Louis, who arranged access for me to the papers of the late Dr. Arthur Carl Piepkorn.